T0168024

CHASING GOOD SENSE

CHASING GOOD SENSE

A BOY'S LIFE
ON THE FRONTIER

HOMER MCCARTY

EDITED BY *CORALIE MCCARTY BEYERS*

THE UNIVERSITY OF UTAH PRESS

Salt Lake City

The Defiance House Man colophon is a registered trademark of the University of Utah Press. It is based on a four-foot-tall Ancient Puebloan pictograph (late PIII) near Glen Canyon, Utah.

LIBRARY OF CONGRESS CATALOGING-IN-PUBLICATION DATA
Names: McCarty, Homer, 1868-1952, author. | Beyers, Coralie, editor.
Title: Chasing good sense : a boy's life on the frontier / Homer McCarty ; edited by Coralie McCarty Beyers.
Description: Salt Lake City : The University of Utah Press, [2018] | Identifiers: LCCN 2018024163 (print) | LCCN 2018029397 (ebook) | ISBN 9781607816560 | ISBN 9781607816553 (pbk. : alk. paper)
Subjects: LCSH: McCarty, Homer, 1868-1952—Childhood and youth. | Frontier and pioneer life—Utah—Anecdotes. | Boys—Utah—Biography. | Utah—Social life and customs—19th century. | Utah—Biography.
Classification: LCC F826.6 (ebook) | LCC F826.6 .M35 2018 (print) | DDC 979.2/02092 [B] —dc23
LC record available at https://lccn.loc.gov/2018024163

Printed and bound in the United States of America.

This book is dedicated to
the memory of Earl,
my barefoot chum in Summit, over whose grave
already have fallen the snows of many winters.

H. M. 1948

To the memory of the guardian aunts,
intrepid typists who preserved it.

And most especially to the memory of my sister,
Nancy Ann McCarty Sumsion,
who rescued it and gave it to me.

C. M. B. 2014

CONTENTS

BEGINNINGS

Way it was, close to 1850 James Hardwick McCarty was a young man all by hisself teaching school in Kentucky. He hadn't a lick of family there. Cuzzins in Indiana had raised him after his mother died when he was just a very small tad and his father moved on alone. They took care of him and schooled him. When he got growed, he taught in Kentucky, right on the Ohio River. Jim was his own man then and always would be. He didn't know it, but he was to become the Father of our family.

In that Kentucky town was a newspaper which printed letters folks sent in, specially ones shouting tarnation to people which thought if you give your dollars to buy a black man, then he is your own property, just like that, and he can't do nothin' about it. It's the law. Stands to reason, he belongs to you same as a horse. Jim choked on that and wrote letters which popped like firecrackers. The newspaper printed every one of them. He kind of warmed to the job.

One day a man came up to him on the street and whispered in his ear that it would be a good thing for him to get out of town quick as he could on account of mobbers was going to burn down the newspaper place and go after that scurrilous Jim McCarty who would soon find hisself floating in the river. He did not waste a minnit throwing his few things and books into his old carpetbag, leaving town just a hop and a jump ahead of the mobbers, his back between his shoulders prickling for that 'spected shot every skip of the way. He did not stop running till he was 'cross the river, 'cross Illinois, 'cross another big river and a little more west in Missouri. There he hooked up with a good-size wagon train heading for Californy to find gold and everyone get rich. He just wanted to go where there wouldn't be people for sale. I wisht I could of gone with him, but it was years before anyone was borned yet or Jim even had a wife.

Jim McCarty was glad to sign on with the wagon train to work his way west, and things started out friendly. But by the time they got onto the prairies he found he had jumped from the frying pan into the fire. Every man Jack of them was a southener which couldn't stand the word 'bolishon. In those days he never thought to keep his mouth shut when things were said that made his Irish flare. No, not a bit. Wrangling turned into blows, not one man on his side. They sent him to the rear of the train to herd livestock, eat dust, and look after the herd at night. On horseback all day every day, with no saddle, his hindquarters was soon very sore on account of he had always been too poor to have a horse and was only used to walking everywhere he went. Now, though he longed to stretch his backside and legs at night, he had to keep moving. He was mighty sorry he had come with this bunch.

The train leader took an awful mean dislike to Jim and wanted to cut him loose to leave him fend for hisself without provisions or gun. Well, Jim carried no gun then and still doesn't 'cause if he did he might shoot a man. "Wolves will soon find him," the train leader said, "and that would be good riddance." Some of the other wagon leaders were not so hasty, and Jim just kept on with his job. But when they were finally into the mountains, Jim took sick with fever in a bad way. Now was the time to dump and be done with him, the boss said. One wagoneer said he would not allow them to do that to another human bean, and lifted Jim into his wagon and took him the rest of the ways to Salt Lake City. There they left him at the side of a road to die or have some kind person come along to give a helping hand.

It turned out the kind person who stopped to help knew about a family which might take him in. That family was Mother's, Lydia Margaret Cragun. Her parents, James and Eleanor Lane Cragun, had joined the Mormon church quite a while back, had lived in Nauvoo, Illinois, and were driven from their home, along with hunnerts of other church members 'cross the Mississippi River into Iowa, 'cross Iowa to the end of Iowa where they stopped at the Missouri River at Winter Quarters to make ready for the long journey to the Utah Territory which they called Zion. They were with a large wagon train of Mormon pioneers to the Salt Lake Valley arriving in 1849, when Lydia was still a young girl. She walked nearly all of that long trail barefoot on account of there wasn't enuff room in the wagon for her. Lots of children came that way. Her feet near froze in a suprise October storm when they were almost at the Valley. Anyways, that's how Father met Mother in 1852, when he was rescued, and married her in 1855. He taught school nearby and farmed, and they started our family with the boys James Cragun, William Murdock, and Samuel Houston McCarty. Mother has told me about those times and so has my brother Jim.

Many people sickened and died on the way to Zion. There were lots of women with children which did not have a husband to take care of them by the time they got to Zion. Church leaders asked some men to marry another wife or two to provide a family. Father was asked if he could step up and make a home for this widow, Mary Ann Matilda Newland, and her surviving daughter Sarah. He said he thought he could, and he did. And that's how we got Aunt Mary and Sarah. In 1861 Brigham Young sent Father and a lot of other families far away in the south to settle the Dixie Mission, the southenest part of the Utah Territory, hunnerts of miles from Salt Lake City. Father was called to teach school.

On account of Mother had Jim just in pants, and Bill still wore dresses and long hair, and Sam, the baby in her arms, not yet a year old, Father thought it best for her to stay with her parents in the Salt Lake Valley. He took Aunt Mary and Sarah, who was already a good-size girl, to get started in that Dixie country which was almost too dry even for a lizard. He would come for the rest of the family when Mother was ready. That was soon. In 1863 in St. George, my big brother Jim says we had double helpings of babies, both girls, one for Aunt Mary, Laura; and one for Mother, Ellie. Two years later, in 1865, it happened again; Eliza for Aunt Mary and Emily for us. Father said he was lucky to of got a head start on boys when he did.

It wasn't called Dixie for nothing. Everything was red rock, red dust, and hardly any water. It would take a heap of getting used to. Worser, nearly everyone which Father met turned out to be from places like Tennessee and Kentucky, where most folks kept slaves if they could and had no mind to change, and if they were too poor to have their own slaves, they were glad for those who could. No one in Dixie ackcherly had a slave of his own, but had plenty of angry things to say about President Linkum and his crazy notion of turning all those black slaves free, and why we had to go to war with the north part of the whole country, and to keep things as they already were. Probly Father let rip some ideas of his own, which again got him into trouble, this time with the school where he was teaching. Someone 'portant told him that he was a fine man in many ways, but he had just "too much dam' republicanism" in him to be a 'propriate teacher for their children. So they sent him from St. George out to the far red hills of Santa Clara where there were mostly Swiss and Injuns. Almost nobody talked Hinglish, and he would not do damage while there.

We were a big bunch then, getting bigger. Father tried farming but could not feed his families with it, no matter how hard he tried. Just not enuff water. Lots of other folks had it hard as us. They called it the Starving Time. If it hadn't of been for pigweed and rapeseed one winter, that's what would of happened to us.

I was borned in 1868 in a wagon box with a little grape arbor to keep the sun shuttered, and didn't hardly get to know a thing about Santa Clara on account of right away Father decided to pick us up and move to Summit, about eighty or so miles north and east of us in a valley which had fields for farming, water, and mountains. Aunt Mary and her girls would stay behind with friends for a while and come later. Father did not ask church leaders if it was all right to leave the Dixie Mission where his families had lived for seven years. He made up his own mind hisself.

❄

As our two wagons made their slow way up the grade out of Dixie, a carriage with a couple of oldish men wearing suits and with white whiskers was coming nicely down the road. They looked to be probly church 'thorities on their way for a visit. Father pulled to the side to let them pass, and they stopped to say "Howd'do," as folks genny do. The older man with longer whiskers leaned over. "Where are you from and where might you be heading, brother?" Father answered, "Up to Summit from Santa Clara." "Have you been released from your mission to do this?" asked the man. Father said, "No. It's just time for me to leave. We have starved long enough." The old man looked sorry at him for a long minnit. "Brother, if you go without the Lord's permission, unhappiness will follow you all the days of your life."

Father picked up the reins again to move on. "Then we will just have to make the most of it we can."

PART ONE

FIGGERING THINGS OUT

SUMMIT

When the family moved to Summit, Father drove the big wagon with the girls and Mother. I was the baby in Mother's arms. Jim, my oldest brother, handled the smaller wagon with Bill and Sam squoze in next to him. Jim and Bill were just a tad bigger than the size of me now when they walked over the Black Ridge in their bare feet on the way down to St. George to begin with in 1862.

In Summit, Father built a house for Mother and all of us belonging to her at the west end of town near the main road, and a smaller one for Aunt Mary and her girls at the east end of town near the track to Parowan. Our house is bigger on account of we are a big bunch.

Now Jim has got a mustash, sort of thin but getting thicker. He says he is training it by smoothing the hairs down with his fingers and a bit of grease which will make the hair lay flat. Jim don't like whiskers such as Father has and will have none of them. He cuts them off fast as they grow out. Bill has got only fuzz. Sam wants some, but Father says he talks too much and too fast for any hair ever to stick on his face. Sam says Father's long black whiskers and black hair make him look like a highway robber, but he dasn't say it to him.

We have a loft in our house where the big boys sleep in winter. They get to it on a ladder which is outside the house. It wouldn't do for us to have a ladder inside the house. No one does that. Mother wouldn't stand for the stuff they would bring in on their shoes. They just scrape them off onto the ladder rungs when climbing up to the loft.

After the boys come Ellie Margaret, Emily Tyresha, and me, Homer; then Martha Evaline and baby Horace Linkum. The girls all sleep in a lean-to room. There is a little straw tick and a quilt for me on the floor by Mother and Father's bed, next to the cradle. That is for when it is cold. When it is warm, I sleep outside with my brothers on the shed roof where it is cool. I can look at the stars. I don't pay as much mind to moon shadows when Sam is next to me, and I know our dog, Herk, is sleeping right in front of the shed. If Sam or Bill is not there, I pull the blanket over my head to hide on account of I know those shadows are full of things that crawl in the night, slithering their way across the yard to climb up onto the shed to grab me. With Sam at my side, I can hear the chickens stirring down below. And if I listen hard I can even catch our ox, Old Buck, chewing on his cud in the corral like a comfit.

Everyone in my family has got two names, starting with Mother and Father, and going right down to baby Horace. Everyone has but me. I'm just Homer. Mother didn't take to having her boys' names nicked, so when I came along she named me without help from Father. It was Homer on account of you can't nick that name down to anything. But Father didn't mind. He said two of his best books was wrote by someone named Homer and nothing else. He calls me Buck and always has. The boys and my best pal Earl call me Buck, even my sisters. But not Mother, no never. I got only one name wrote in the Bible, but I wished it was Buck 'stead of Homer.

I like Aunt Mary a lot. She has yellow curls, talks Hinglish like the Bishop does, and carries a smile. Other folks in Summit are from Hingland, too. I plan to go there someday just to hear that talk. It is mighty sweet. Us children which belong to Mother call her Aunt Mary, but course she's not a reggler aunt like Mother's sisters in St. George. Her girls call Mother Aunt Lydia Margaret. None of us has figgered out, if Aunt Mary's girls are our half-sisters, why isn't she our half-mother? Father never mixes the families up. He spends one week with Mother and the next with Aunt Mary and never forgets which house he is going to spend the week at.

My sister Ellie is like Sarah, both oldest girls which help their mothers, who could not get along without them. Sarah doesn't have any babies to look after, but Ellie keeps an eye on whoever is baby at our house. She just finished up with Martha when Horace came along. Ellie was good to me when I was wearing dresses on account of she is a born mother. She feels she is too old to play now and likes to go to school with Emily, Sam, Laura, and Eliza.

School is not too far from our house. On Sunday, we have Sunday School in it and other church meetings. Benches get moved around from school to church. No matter which, there isn't much space for so many of us, and we do not have room to fidget. Folks talk about building a church house or a school-house, mebbee not soon but sometime.

Horace is the baby now. He can't hardly go anyplace, he is so little. He wears my old baby dresses and don't know a thing yet, no, not a thing. He even pukes right in front of company when Mother is holding him on her lap. Mother makes dresses for the girls or pants for the boys as they need them, if the old ones have wore out. I probly got mine from Sam, and Martha is wearing what Emily, even Ellie, has gone through. That is the way it is with clothes in our house. Us boys finally get into pants, but my sisters just go on wearing dresses. In Summit, nobody throws clothes away. When they get worn to rags, mothers make carpets out of them.

When I was going on five, Mother cut my black curls and took my dress off for the last time. I was now old enuff to be a real boy with two legs reaching down from me that I could see all the time. She made a waist from one of Sam's shirts and a pair of pants from old ones she had saved. She took everything off down to my nekked skin, then slipped on the waist and helped my legs go inside the pants. On my shoulders she fastened cut-down galluses to hold them up. "There," she said, standing me up in front of her and straightening her back in the chair with a happy sigh. "Why, Homer, if you don't look handsomer than you did in dresses!" The pants felt kind of strange, having my legs hanging down in their own scratchy sleeves. But I got used to it.

My half-sister Eliza had come down to our house to play with Emily. Mother told the girls to take me out to the field so Father could see what a fine little man he had. Off we went, each of them holding one of my hands. I had to trot in the middle where wire grass, dead brush, and sharp stones got in the way of my bare feet. That's what I remember, paddling and hopping as best I could while my sisters tripped handily in the narrow paths made by horses' hoofs and wagon wheels.

Nine fathers and a pair of batchlers live in Summit, but there is more families than that as anyone can easy tell just walking around town looking at the houses. The nine men have got theirselfs fourteen wives, which makes the differnce. Counting houses 'stead of men, Summit has got just a dozen families, figgering each batchler a family, which he ain't, least not a reggler family. A reggler family has got to have a mother, else a wife, which the batchlers don't have either of. One lives in a little dugout house with room only just for him. The other lives with his sister. Two other men have second wives, same as Father, and one man has three wives. He had to build four houses on account of he has dozens of children. Aunt Mary's family is only four and a half, counting Father the half one. We got nine and a half, counting the other half of Father.

Aunt Mary has chickens, same as us, but not so many. She keeps a cow and a calf in her corral so she can have milk and butter. When her cow goes dry, Father takes it away and brings a fresh one. Sometimes neither Mother nor Aunt Mary has a cow giving milk at the same time, and then we all have to go without it, but not for long. Father scouts one up soon as he can. She also has a few pigs in her pigpen which she feeds up. When they get to be fat hogs, Father butchers them same as ours and brings the pieces down to our smoke shed. Then both families have ham and bacon to eat. Sometimes Aunt Mary sends a ham over to the co-op store in Parowan to sell for cash.

All of the wives in Summit keep bizy winter and summer. Hardly anyone has any money, so folks have to make things for their families to use and some left over to sell or trade. Some make enuff butter and cheese to sell at the store in Parowan. Some have eggs or chickens enuff to sell, or hams. They are so bizy spinning and weaving that they make everything we wear but shoes. One wife makes cloth enuff all year to take to sell to the big co-op store in Salt Lake City. She says all that work gives her a long hard drive up there and back, with the sun in her eyes both ways, but at least she gets a change of scene once a year. Everyone waits for the freighting man from Salt Lake City to bring shoes to the Parowan store. Some mothers try making moccasins when they get some buckskin, but theirs don't hold a patch on the ones Injuns make.

Each house has at least a loom and a spinning wheel. A wife couldn't keep house without those. Some have a quilting frame, too. Mother weaves carpets for our house on her loom. She sews all our clothes and resews them to fit the next of us coming up the line. It is do and redo and make do. Sometimes she makes hats for us with wheat straw, but it has to be just the right kind. The one she made for me I've wore so much it is raggedy now, so mostly I just go bareheaded even when the sun is hot. She knits for us, too, all the time. Sometimes she knits me a pair of socks from yarn she has unraveled from the top ends of Father's old socks which she has cut off and saved. With socks on, I can wear shoes for a little while at a time without they hurtin' my feet. She ties the shoes with buckskin strings and makes bow knots I can easy untie. I can't stand them on my feet more than just a few minnits. Myself, I don't think feet were made for shoes.

Mother says for a small boy I am a pretty good candlemaker, which I think I am. She can always count on me to help her. If we kill a cow or sheep, we don't eat the fat, not much of it, anyways. We call that kind of fat tallow. Mother melts it in a big iron pot which she borrows from one of the wives. We have to be careful to return it clean so someone else can borrow it for soap or applesauce. We make candles which I help her with, twisting the string to make wicks and putting the strings in the molds so they will be right in the middles of the candles when they are made. Each mold has three holes on each side. She pours the melted tallow into the holes, then carries the hot molds outside and stands them on a bench in the shade of the house. When they cool off, I carry them back inside so she can take the candles out of the molds. We need plenty of candles, and they are always good for Father to take peddling, sometimes when he crosses the desert to the mining towns, like Pioche, or when he goes through the long canyon to the ranchers and townfolk in the Pangwitch neighborhood.

Mothers are so bizy in Summit they need all the children they can muster to look after each other while they are bizy making clothes and cheese and butter and baking. Girls do most of the looking after. Ellie likes me to go with her looking for eggs. Boys genny go out to the fields with their fathers where there is plenty of work waiting for them, or tend stock and muck out sheds and corrals and pens. Father counts on me to pull every weed. Jim and Bill and Sam help mend harnesses and wagon wheels, get wood, replace or repair fencing, keep thatch on the shed so the rain won't get into the chickens or pigs. There isn't much time left for anyone rampaging.

In the house, Mother uses me to pull threads on her loom. I have to be careful to catch them all. While we work she might tell me stories about what she did as a little girl in Iowa getting ready for the move west, with a big wagon train, with her family crossing the wide prairies and hauling through the mountains to Salt Lake Valley. I like to hear about the Injuns they met; about how the children played and had to stay within shouting distance of the wagons on account of the prairies were huge and empty and you could easy get lost; or about the big campfires and singing in the evening when people could stretch their bones and everyone was tuckered out and ready to sleep after all the chores were done and the stock taken care of. She told me about her walking a big part of the way in her bare feet which mostly hurt from rocks and roots, same as mine, and about the early October blizzard in the mountains just before they came down into the Valley when her feet were awful sore with chillblains and just missed being froze. Mother knows just how I feel when I bang my toes.

Best of all, I like it when she tells me about her special friend then which was also named Margaret (Mother was Lydia Margaret). The whole way they played together so much, people called that friend the Other Margaret. The girls were told to be careful and keep a lookout for Injuns when they were playing on account of sometimes Injuns were friendly-like and sometimes not. The two Margarets loved to play Injuns. One time they made headbands out of chicken feathers and rags, smeared charcoal on their faces, and made little bows and arrows out of whatever pickings they could find. And they filled the air with so much noise, whooping, and ki-yi-ing that their mothers were glad when they ran somewhere else to play 'stead of by their wagons.

Out in the tall brush they played hard shooting arrows at what might be a wolf or a deer, and stomping and singing. They did not see the wagon company grow smaller and smaller down the trail. Other Margaret finally grew tired being a Injun and turned back to run to catch up. But not Lydia Margaret. She was still creeping around Injun-style looking for arrows she had shot and did not see her friend leave. When she did stand up to look around her, she found she could not see her friend or, worse, wagons in any direction. Alone in the prairie, she was plum scairt and sorry. Worst of all, she remembered her mother telling her, when children get theirselfs lost in the prairie, they genny stay lost.

The afternoon about over, she was still wandering wherever, when a couple of Injuns on horseback loomed up above the brush and looked suprised at what they found, a makeshift Injun by its lonesome looking back at them, too scairt to make a peep. One slid off his horse, laffed at the limp feathers in her headband, and sort of waved at her to come to his horse. He lifted her up and jumped on hisself. He didn't have a saddle, so he had her in his lap and she could hold to the horse's mane. They trailed straight through the brush and found the wagons, which had all stopped so men could go looking for her. The Other Margaret was already with her family and mighty glad of it. Seeing the Injuns made the men ankshus till they saw Lydia Margaret smiling at them from her perch. The Injun handed her to her pa and said in a sort of Hinglish, "We got plenty Injuns. No need more." Her mother told her she was one lucky girl to bump into Injuns which would do a good thing. I wish I could of been in that wagon train with her.

Sometimes people traveling through on the main road will stop off to camp. If they are new to the Territory, they might look at Summit and think it is too differnt from what they are used to and say a few snippy things about us having more women than men. Boys like Bill and Sam and their friends will sometimes get off a smart joke, specially if they got their hands on a Salt Lake City newspaper which comes to the co-op in Parowan where anyone can read it. Sam says it is full of digs at Brigham Young. He and Bill and their pals might go up on the shed roof to snigger but never say a word about it to Mother and Father. Oh no, they dasn't. They only do it to feel big.

Myself, I think puligemy is good for families. I already know from Father about the time in Santa Clara when Father didn't have so much as a pinch of flour left, his families barely getting by on pigweed and rapeseed. Other families were hungry, too. That was the Starving Time. Brigham Young sent down a wagonload with sacks of flour for the hungry folks, but they cost twenty-five dollars each. Father had spent all of his money. He wasn't teaching anymore and his crops died, so there was not going to be any more money for food or anything. That flour would keep his family alive. Lucky for us, Aunt Mary found twenty-five dollars sewed into her petticoat, and she bought the flour which kept them from starving. If he hadn't of had another wife, they would of all been goners. Good thing I wasn't borned yet and been worried, too.

What's more, puligemy saved my life the time I fell into the ditch running past our house when I was about three years old and still wearing a dress. Well, I went headfirst into the ditch and was floating away with my skirts behind me when Eliza saw me and came running to help. She shouted at the top of her lungs, "Liddy Maggit! Liddy Maggit! Homey's drownding!" She grabbed ahold of my skirt with one hand and a willow bush on the bank with her other hand and held on for my dear life until Mother came pounding down the path, jumped in the ditch, and hauled me out of the water. After that, she took the water out of me. I had sucked in a pile of it.

If Father hadn't of married Aunt Mary so Eliza could of been borned and growed enuff so she could get strong enuff to hold only my dress long enuff so Mother could get there to take me out of the water in time, why, for more than three years I would already be a small boy angel up in heaven missing all the fun I been having in Summit. That is what puligemy done for our family, I know for sure.

EARL AND ME

I'm not five anymore. I can go all around Summit myself or with Earl. In Summit boys play with boys. That's the rule. Earl and me been friends far back as I can go. We just seem to fit. When his mother sees us out in their yard, she says it is like two little birds hopping around, one with a black head, one with a yellow. We go just about everywheres. We know if it's corn or potatoes, if it's carrots or onions growing inside people's fences. Most everyone has squash vines. I like baked squash, but squash pie even better. Everybody has currants. Hinglish currants are red, and wild currants are blue and sweeter than the red ones. Earl likes ripe currants 'bout as much as me. Old Brother Fellowes has more of them than anybody in town. Lots of times I think he wants Earl and me to pick and eat all the currants we can hold, and tells us, or means to tell us, to fill our hat with them to take away and eat later. We have only just one hat between us, and that is mine, the one which Mother made out of wheat straw and is old now. It's got a hole in the top. I have to keep my thumb in the hole so currants don't spill out.

We know the names of every dog in town and all them knows us. We know which bite and which only bark. Folks don't give names to cats so much as to dogs. Seems they are just called

Kitty, which is not a name. It only means cat. We know where each Kitty's house is at and which don't like anybody but their own folks. We know who has got red chickens and who has gray ones. We know who has got the fightenest rooster in their sheds. We know who keep sheep, who has got the fattest hogs, and whose cows have the biggest tits. Father says if anybody wants to know anything about Summit he should ask Earl and me.

He likes to come with me to the field when I pull weeds for Father. He pulls weeds for his pa, too, and knows how sweaty it is, so when I am helping mine, Earl just sits and watches, and that is all right. He's already finished his chores. After I am done, we might take a bucket to drownd gofers out of their holes and bust them with a stick when they pop their heads out. If we don't smack them first, away they scoot fast as they can. We run after them, but the field is full of slivers and stones that hurt our feet, and we don't run fast as gofers, which dive into dry holes. Mostly we get just two or three. They are awful pests, so every dead gofer is one the less, Father says. They build little hills of dirt around their holes which turn the water to one side and make it hard for Father to get water to his corn. They steal what we grow. Gofers ain't good for a single thing, if you don't count that crows and buzzards eat them. Those big birds don't care a whit who kills the gofers or how long they been dead. If they are still a bit juicy or only just got stink left, those birds will eat. That is all a gofer is good for.

After Earl and me have popped some and are tired, we watch Father work. He might be plowing one piece and watering another at the same time and will stop the oxen while he takes his spade and changes water into other furrows, then go back to plowing some more. We don't see how any man with long legs like him can walk slow enuff behind the plow the oxen are pulling. Father says he just starts thinking about something he been reading that makes him forget he is plowing. Earl and me think he should fix a couple plows together which Buck and Blue could easy pull. It just looks kind of queer to see two big oxen pulling one little plow with a long-legged man marching behind it.

When Earl and me are not doing chores, we like to wander around the big rocks near the canyon mouth by Snake Hill. We know it is not a hill, only some piles of rocks where somebody probly kilt a den of snakes one time and bragged about it. There are still plenty snakes, but we don't see them too often. Blow snakes blow their breath on you, which is why they are called blow snakes. They give me the fantods. The breath they blow stinks from the rotting stuff they have in their stummicks, and if you breathe it, your stummick turns over and can make you puke. Rattlers like to hide in the rocks, so you have to watch where you put your foot or hand. Bull snakes are longer than rattlers, bigger round, too. In the brush are plenty of gofers and voles for snakes to eat. They don't ackcherly eat things, just swallow them down sort of slow-like.

Earl's pa told us how bull snakes and rattlers want to kill each other soon as they meet up. Bull snake won't wait for the rattler to kill him first. Each swishes his head around, front-wards and backwards, looking to grab the other without being grabbed hisself. They rear up from the ground a foot or more, swinging their heads so fast you can't hardly see them. All of a sudden bull snake has got rattler by the throat and cuts off his wind. They roll and flop on the ground, twisting around each other. Bull snake hangs on rattler's neck for dear life, squeezing the windpipe tighter and tighter and squeezing rattler's whole body with his bigger one. After a while rattler gives up the ghost. He's dead, all right. Bull snake unwraps hisself and lets loose of the neck. He won't swallow rattler, just glides away to look for something what tastes better. When Earl and me are up there scouting for cottontails, we keep our eyes out for them snakes, you bet, specially rattlers. We know they will be looking, too, and might get their rattles up if two barefoot boys step in their way.

INJUNS

When Injuns first show up, they head for our houses to go begging. Mother genny does not like to see them come. I can tell by the frown between her eyes and the tiny smile she gets when she is not really smiling. Squaws walk right into our house without knocking, and if chairs are handy they sit right down without being asked to. Soon as they get theirselfs fixed they look around the room a minnit or two, not saying a word. They just gawp. Their papooses genny come, too, but they stick mighty close to their mothers, not looking at me or anybody. They only stand still and roll their eyes around at things in the house. Sometimes they don't even do that. They just stare. Mebbee they are scairter of us than we be of them. But I got to hand it to them, Injun papooses got good manners. That is why they are so quiet. Sometimes I have the fidgets when Mother and I are visiting over to a Relief Society Sister's house, and she will say she wishes I could be still as a little Injun child.

When the squaws has finally made up their minds, they bust out talking. But they can't talk plain. They have to throw their arms about and wiggle their hands and fingers. I like to watch their faces when they talk with their frowns and scowls and mad looks. Mother has learned what some of the finger-wiggles and

arm-throwing is all about. If she watches closely she can tell
what they are asking for. Earl's pa is good at Injun talk. Earl
and me laff when he talks to them. The men will nod and look
at him mad and frowny, but he can look plum mad, too. Guess
that is how they do bizness.

Squaws will come right out and tell you what they want.
Mother says she don't egzackly call it begging. If she shakes her
head and says she don't have what they ask for, they act like they
think she is lying to them. But Mother just stands and lets them
talk. Sometimes they want clothes. Mostly that is when she gives
her head a hard shake. Or she says "No!" plenty loud. She tells
them we got use for all our clothes, but then in a minnit or two
it seems she can most times dig up a little dress no baby is using
or a waist to go with the food she puts in the sack they bring.
They never go away from our house empty-handed.

From our house to the foot of the mountains is only 'bout
half a mile or a little bit more. Nothing grows there, only sagebrush, stickery bushes, and prickly pears. It is a place tuff on
bare feet. In the summer and fall, Injuns come to Summit in
big gangs and camp out there close to the mountains and the
water. Only there's no brush where they stick up their little tents
or where they keep their horses. My brother Sam says Injuns
have used that spot so many times they have tramped down
every growing thing. Now it is just a big clearing which could
easy hold our lot and probly Earl's too.

Father says they are called Pieds. They move from camp to
camp for the food they can find, and when the food runs out in
one spot they move on to the next for the nuts, berries, roots, or
rabbits they eat. Sometimes they eat deer meat when they camp
by us. We have plenty deer in our mountains, but we have lots

more rabbits. Injuns eat them more on account of rabbits are easier to hunt. Father says that is probly why they come to our place in the fall when the rabbits are growing thick fur. They don't just roast them on a stick, no sir. They dry dead rabbits and roll them up with their bones into little bundles to save for winter cooking. They make dresses and robes from the fur. Father says they do not waste a thing.

In the summer Injuns come every few weeks. They might be moving up from Santa Clara or the Muddy River where they raise corn and squash on little farms. After they pack up and leave, when they are through with things here, they mosey through our mountains over to the Sevier valley, stopping in meadows along the way. They fish streams and lakes. Sometimes they come just before winter on their way back down to the desert beyond the Black Ridge. I would hate to be an Injun in winter around here. They do not have very good tents, or even what you would call a tent, just mostly bunched-up sagebrush on a few skinny poles. Earl says they are called wickyups. Him and me know we would freeze plum to death if we had to live in one. The Injuns don't freeze. They are tuffer than white folks, we think. I can see that they have to be.

In the winter, squaws come to beg for wood to keep warm and cook with. They go around town and get a few sticks from as many families as will give them some. They know how to beg just right. They want their wood chopped and not in big pieces, either. They won't take it if it is not chopped. Sam says they are too lazy to chop their own wood, but how can they haul wood down from the mountain if they got no wagons, or only very little ones, and no oxen to pull them? Sam ain't so smart. Father says we can easy give them wood once in a while.

Folks have forgot that all the wood and grass and all the land and water belonged to them in the first place. When Brigham Young sent folks out from Salt Lake City to settle towns all over the Territory, like ours at Summit, and Parowan and Cedar City and St. George, the land they settled on was Injuns'. On account of the white folks did not see any towns, they thought nobody owned or used the land. Earl's pa thinks like Father. He says everything us white folks have was took from Injuns without even a howd'do. Folks should not be stingy giving back a little bit of it. Not everybody in Summit thinks that way, but Father says he cannot forget when he and the family lived in Santa Clara in the Starving Time. He will not let another human bean go hungry if he can do something about it.

No matter when they come to the clearing, even before they get their tents set up, squaws start right out begging. Guess they don't have much in the way of food or other stuff with them. If they want supper they have to get out and rustle up something for it. They head straight for our house on account of we live on the outside corner of town. Some keep going through the brush to other houses. Mostly two come together with empty sacks to put their begged things in. But you should see those sacks when the squaws turn back to camp, so full they can't hardly carry them. I bet everybody gathers round to see what is in them. Full sacks are only for the first time or two. After that, the bags are not so heavy.

The chief of the Pieds is Old Wibe. Least, he is the one I hear about. I never have seen him, but I am plenty scairt of him anyways. When thunder bangs off the mountains and black clouds tumble over them, people says it is Old Wibe on the warpath. That is what I been told. We cannot see him on account of the black clouds, but he can easy see us. He roars at us in Injun talk, same as thunder. You can tell he is mad enuff to kill us. Most always, though, he sends rain on us instead. Folks say once in a while he might come along with a band of his Injuns, but mostly he stays back on the mountain. Father is not scairt of him. He says Old Wibe is a good Indian, and he is not dead, either. He says it that way 'cause some folks say dead Injuns are the only good ones.

In summer they don't stick around long, mebbee a week. If they make buckskin, then it is sure at least a week. Takes time to make buckskin. The squaws make it by scraping and scraping the hair off a deerskin and soaking the hide to make it soft and then scraping some more. The men take the buckskin into Summit or Parowan to sell. They won't take flour or ham or potatoes or bread for buckskin. Nope. They got to have cash money. And everybody in town has got to have buckskin in the house, couldn't get along without it. Folks make whips out of it, cut strings to sew harnesses with. They make shoestring and whip-poppers. Everyone likes to have buckskin gloves, pants and shirts, or dresses. They try to make moccasins, too, but theirs are not near as good as the ones Injuns make.

When the tents are out there in the clearing and we can hear their dogs barking, Mother will not let me out the front gate. She says the Pieds sometimes steal little boys and make Injuns of them. After they are stole they never see their mothers or fathers again. And I am the right size to be stole. If I was, she would cry every day. Not wanting to be an Injun boy, I climb on top of our chicken coop where I can easy see the camp and the Injuns doing things there. They have horses and dogs, papooses, too, but not so many as dogs. Squaws look bizy doing things and running after the children. Can't see men being bizy in camp. Seems they sit a lot. Sam and his friends are too big to be stole, so they have been out to the camp to watch them making buckskin. One time, from the top of the shed where I was standing, I could only see women working on something that looked like blankets on some poles. I had to have a real look, right up close.

When everybody at my house was bizy someplace else, I sneaked out of the yard and lit into the brush and layed down flat. Didn't want anyone to see my head sticking above the sage. Then I began wiggling and crawling and sort of duck-walking towards the tents in the clearing. I could easy cut through the brush without anyone seeing me. When I got pretty close I did not have a good place to see things from or even hide, on account of the brush there was too short. Some bushes looked higher just on the other side, so I crawled careful-like and slow over there. I wasn't scairt a bit. But my knees got kind of sore, and I had to watch not to get any stickers from prickly pears in me. They are bad for bare feet. You got to pull them out soon as they stick in your foot. If a sticker gets into the meat under your foot, it starts going upwards in your leg. Mebbee it will come out your shoulder or neck. If your heart gets in the way of it, into the heart it goes. And just like that, you are a dead boy, dead as nits and no one can tell what kilt you. That is why I genny keep clear of prickly pears.

Soon as I got to that big bush I kind of half-layed on the ground and rested my knees and looked at the camp. I saw two dogs fighting, which made an awful racket. A couple of squaws came running out of their little tents. Each one grabbed the hind legs of a dog and began pulling and shouting. They pulled so hard the dogs had to let go or get pulled to pieces. Then the women gave them a drubbing with sticks till those dogs yelped like sixty and ran off. I saw a couple of old squaws sitting outside their tents with a big mess of whip-long willows or grass they were working with their hands into baskets. A few more were squatting beside a flat stone pounding something, mebbee seeds or nuts, or even wheat. Other squaws were scraping away at what was hanging on the poles. They were not blankets at all, but deer hides. There was a squaw for each hide which was being scraped. One hide already had most of its hair off and was white. Now and then a scraper would stop to wiggle her shoulders and rest a minnit. Buckskin-making looked plenty hard.

A boy littler than me by a long shot went over to the hides and started kicking the loose hair that had fallen on the ground. He had on a little waist, but it was too short, and below he was plum nekked. One of the squaws must of been his mother, on account of she turned and scolded him in a loud voice. I could tell it was scolding, it sounded mad like Mother when she is onto one of us boys. He kicked the hair another time and laffed. She yelled at him louder and shook her scraping stick at him. He ran off a ways and stopped, turned around, and stood still for a minnit or two.

I had to keep watching on account of I wished he wasn't so close to where I was. I didn't dast take my eyes off him. Sure enuff, he came sneaking back to the hides and quick grabbed a handful of hair in each hand, and away he went on the run, laffing and shaking the hair at his mother. She dropped her stick and took off after him, hollering like anything. He ran right toward my bush. Quick I crawled a little to the other side of it and layed flat as I could. He kept on running, but his mother was catching up behind him, even if she was near as wide as she was high and wearing a dress that flapped in the wind. She caught him just before he ran into my bush. I tell you she yanked that little boy around and spanked his bare behind awful hard. It sounded like his skin might pop. But that was not good enuff. She layed on more spanking, and he kept jumping and hollering till she drug him back to her deer hide.

I had seen enuff, and right straight I started crawling away, through sage, brush, rocks, and around prickly pears. I was sure I was in the way of becoming an Injun boy, and I did not dast show any of myself to those Injuns. They would grab me, and I would be stole. That boy's mother might take up her stick and pound on me. I did not look back, did not look anywhere but where my hands and knees were moving. Then I heard a dog bark loud and mean and close. I knew I was a goner, and nothing for it but to jump up and run fast as I could. I could not see our house, only more bush and some trees farther off, so I aimed for those. When I saw a horseman riding toward me I knowed it was one of Old Wibe's warriors come to kill or steal me.

"Whoa there, young fella! Where you headin' in such a con-sarned hurry?" The horse stopped. "Well I'll be danged if it isn't little Buck McCarty! What brings you way out here?" I looked up. It wasn't no Injun, only old Brother Sherburne, one of our batchlers, on his rangy roan. I looked around and saw I was not near our house. I had been running the wrong way, out towards Ray Linn's ranch. The horse stopped. Brother Sherburne reached down and gave me an arm up behind his saddle. "What say I just give you a lift home? You look right tuckered and kind of scratched up." My knees felt so good to be off that ruff ground.

After my heart stopped knocking under my waist I felt pretty smart to be riding behind him. We went past the Injun camp. Only a couple of children gave us a look. Soon he dropped me off at my front gate. "You be careful where you wander around here, Buck," he said with a smile. "Don't want none of these Pieds gettin' ideers."

I did not hardly have time to sneak in the door when Mother stepped up and took ahold of my arm like Father's vise. "Just where in tarnation have you been so long!" she demanded. "The girls and I looked all over for you, and I was getting mighty worried. The Indians might have taken you after all."

That did it. I began blubbering, I was so downright glad I hadn't been stole. She saw holes in my pants and my knees showing through, skinned and a little bleedy. "Wherever have you been crawling?" Then she saw the prickly pear stickers in my pants. "Homer! Have you been out to that camp!" Mother can always tell what I been up to. No use fibbing. I told her what I done and what I saw. "Well, I ought to whip you good for being a disobedient boy," she said with a frowny face that made me sorry for what I done and for what she was going to do. "Only this time I won't because I'm so glad they didn't steal you while they had the chance." She smiled and hugged me. Then she took a wet cloth and wiped my knees and put salve on the sore places. "But don't ever do such a stunt like that again. You hear?" Just then it was an easy promise. I seen all the buckskin-making I cared for.

Sometimes after the Injuns have picked up and gone away, it is all right with Mother if Sam takes me out to see if they left anything we would want. Could be an arrow or a bow, or a couple of arrowheads, or just something like a leftover bit of buckskin. He took me out to look soon after this, but the Injuns had not left a thing we would have. There was only stink and lots of deer hair on the ground. Sam says anything they would of left probly wouldn't be worth picking up anyways. Myself, I think they do not have anything to leave behind.

RIDING THE RED BULL CALF

Mostly in Summit I play only with my friend Earl. I can't play with girls. In Summit girls play with girls, boys with boys. That is the rule. There used to be one or two boys about my size I played with besides Earl, but they moved on. He has got a brother bigger than us. I would have to call him a reggler bully, on account of he picks on me, gets mad over I genny do not know what, and has to jump on me when he does. My big brothers Jim and Bill never do that, not even Sam. Guess they are so bizy helping Father they can't take much notice of me. And Sam just mostly teases without being mean. When Ray pushes me around for nothing I feel like fighting, and what I do is to jump Earl to get even with his brother. I would jump Earl and get even on him if I could find him quick enuff after my licking while I am still steamed up. Earl is a good fighter his own self, so we go the rounds, but he can nearly always tell I am just sore about one of Ray's drubbings and does not hold the punching against me. That is the way Earl is.

One day after Ray was snooping around, he chased me out of Brother Sherburne's berry patch. Earl came looking for me before I came looking for him and found me hiding in the brush. He said he sure felt sorry for me, but he did not want me to sail into him again because of Ray. Right then we made a bargain that if his brother ever jumped on me again, Earl would jump on him, and both of us could easy knock him down and beat the stuffing out of him. We bargained that Earl wouldn't ever get mad at me and I would never get mad at him, and we would be friends forever, all the way to Judgement Day. Then we spit and shook hands on it. That means we will really do what we say.

A good thing we had that bargain in our pockets because pretty soon after that Earl and me and Ray were in their corral having a grasshopper jumping game. Each of us had caught a couple of hoppers so if one didn't jump like it oughter, we could use the other one. That is the rule of the game. They were the small kind which don't fly so much but jump all the time. Earl used only one of his, which easy out-jumped both of Ray's, and we laffed. Ray couldn't pick a good jumper when he saw one. He didn't say anything, only looked sour, but we could tell he was mad as heck and we were probly to blame.

Then Earl tried his other hopper just for fun. It jumped clear over to the calf pen. When we ran over to pick it up we saw there were calves in the pen. They were laying down kind of half-sleeping while their mothers were out in the brush of the pasture munching away. We looked at the calves a minnit or two without saying nothing. We hadn't any of us rode a calf for quite a while. It had been longer for me on account of we don't have as many calves as Earl's pa. He has cattle in the mountains in the summer. Father doesn't. Right straight we made up our minds to ride one, mebbee more. We forgot all about the grasshoppers.

Only the day before, their pa had brought home from the mountains a little red bull calf, along with its ma and some other cattle. Soon as we saw him laying there, we knowed he was the one we wanted to ride before any of the others. We all wanted to ride him first. But Ray chimed in right off with his gruff bully voice. "Huh, you ain't either one gonna ride that bull first 'cause I'm the one who's gonna do it."

"If we all want to ride first, then let's draw cuts," Earl said. "Then it's fair."

"I ain't gonna draw cuts with punky little kids like you," his brother said. "I'm bigger'n both of you put together. That gives me the right to ride first if I want to, and I want to."

Earl growled in a low voice only I could hear, "All right, then. I hope he bucks you off first jump."

In the stable we found a rope about as long as a lasso but more limber. We took it and climbed into the pen. Right quick those calves bunched together at the end of the pen, and that little red bull faced frontwards towards us just like a big bull ready for a fight. We could tell he was excited, mad, or even awful scairt, anyways like he wanted to bunt us out the gate. We stood still and looked at him. He looked at us, then ducked his head and pawed dirt a couple of times. We didn't like that dirt-pawing. He looked too much like a reggler big bull. Sam says that pawing means, in bull talk, "Don't come any closer or I'll hook the living daylights out of you." That little calf already knowed how to do it. I could unerstand that. He had been borned in the mountains where there are bears and wolves and lions. Probly he had seen his pa or ma scare off varmints like that, pawing the way he was doing now. And probly he hadn't seen boys before and thought we were varmints same as bears or wolves, come to eat him up. Whatever he thought, he was ready to fight the three of us.

Earl's brother was going to show us how to do things and sneaked up on one side of the calf and throwed his arms around its neck. Right off that little bull went plum wild. Quick I grabbed his tail to help Ray hold him. That calf kicked and bucked and knocked us sideways against the other calves and against the fence, but we held on for dear life. All the other calves got wild, too. A good thing the gate was fastened tight, else all of them would of got away and run out to where the cows were browsing. Then Earl's folks wouldn't of had any milk for supper, and those boys would of got a good licking.

Just when Earl's brother was about to let go his grip on the calf's neck, Earl looped the rope around the little bull's neck and fixed it so it wouldn't draw tight and choke. We all three held on to him till we got him out of the pen and into the corral where he would have lots of room to buck in. We couldn't hardly hold on to him while Earl put a loop around his nose so Ray could hang on to the rope. If you don't have a rope to hold on to you get bucked off in less than a second.

Ray was looking sorry he had bullied his way to ride first. But he didn't dast back out after all he had said about not drawing cuts. Me and Earl held the bull best we could till he got up on its back, kind of trembly like. Earl quick handed the rope to his brother, and then we each let go at the same time and give that bull a good punch in the ribs to get him started.

Away went the red calf, bucking and bellering. Earl and me laffed and hollered loud as Injuns. Earl's brother gripped his long legs tight around the calf and was sticking with him pretty good. But it didn't last more than a breath or two. Less than half way 'cross the corral, Ray flew into the air and hit the ground all doubled up and rolling, and then got all spraddled out on account of the rope had got caught around his foot, and the calf dragged him around in the dust till he pulled his foot loose. That little bull was so worked up he went on bucking and bellering and running around the corral dragging the rope behind him. He didn't know he had bucked his rider off the first four or five bucks. We laffed so hard we had to sit down.

Ray got up on his legs kind of staggery and looked about for a stick or something to throw at that calf, which was still bucking around the corral close to the fence, not out of steam yet by a long shot. Ray looked mad enuff to fight him with his bare fists. If the calf's pa had come over, he was ready to fight him, too. Instead, he came running towards me with his fists doubled up. I could tell he was going to bust me one on the nose. So I jumped to my feet and moved away quick, only just in time. Earl couldn't quit laffing. I hopped around, dodging Ray best I could. Earl was laffing too hard to come help. Ray ought to of had more sense, but he didn't. Folks who get mad don't have much sense. That is what Father says.

Then Earl's brother hit me on the cheek and I stopped laffing. It stung hard, and my Irish started in. Father says we have too much of it and should leave it home if we can, but right then I did not care to be good and started in jabbing at him. Earl could now see a reggler fight was going on. He jumped up and came running to help, like he bargained he would. And a good thing on account of his brother had grabbed my hair and was yanking so hard I thought I was being scalped and was about to cry, but I didn't want to be a sissy. Earl grabbed his brother's hind legs. Down we all went together, Earl on top, his brother in the middle, and me on the bottom, not hardly getting any breath. Earl started on his brother's hair, then took ahold of him by the ears. His brother yelled and told Earl to quit 'cause it was hurting him. But Earl kept on jerking those ears. I wiggled out and got on top with Earl. We hammered his brother on the face. It was a wild free-for-all for a minnit. Then Ray's nose started to bleed. Some of the blood was going down his throat sort of choking him. He started to sniffle and cry.

Soon as we got off, his brother scrambled to his feet, rubbing the blood out of his mouth with his hands and spitting. All that blood made it look like we had almost kilt him. He ran back to their house, bellering loud as the calf. Earl and me looked at each other and grinned a little. But we didn't laff anymore. We didn't know what was going to happen now.

The calf had quit bucking around the corral and stood by the calf pen, daring us to come ride him if we thought we could. But Earl and me wouldn't of even tried. We wouldn't of rode that little bull for a whole hat full of store candy. We would just as soon of rode his pa if he'd a been there. We sneaked up to him soft and careful and took ahold of the rope. The calf didn't move. He just stood there looking at us. All of a sudden he had changed his mind and wouldn't lead, wouldn't run. He wouldn't do a thing. Earl and me had to push him back into the pen. Calves get that way sometimes.

"What you mean jumping onto your brother like you and Buck been doing!" Earl's pa had come into the corral, madder than a bull with horns. Earl's brother trailed right behind him holding a bloody towel up to his face. He glared at Earl and then at me. His pa glared too. I thought Earl was sure going to get a lickin' then and there. I was wishing I was home.

But Earl took that old bull of a pa by the horns and told him how it all had come to be and how his brother had jumped me and was pulling my hair. His pa "humphed" a couple of times. "Well, Ray, it appears this fuss serves you right for picking on boys littler than yourself." That was one time Earl's brother had enuff sense to learn more sense. Anyways he hasn't jumped me anymore. Sometimes we even play together without piling onto each other. But Earl and me have the most fun playing only with ourselfs. Seems two of us can have more fun than three on account of we promised with spit and a handshake not never to fight with each other, no siree.

SALT

Mother has been after Father to get some more salt on account of we are about out, and soon she will be needing it to salt the meat for winter. It is quite a trip to go for salt. We have to head our wagon towards Parowan a ways and then drive out across the valley to red hills at the edge where you can see a strip of blue. That is what folks call the Little Salt Lake, which is just a pond if you was to put it side by side of Great Salt Lake, but plenty big enuff for us here in Summit and Parowan and Paragonah. Everybody goes there to shovel salt.

Mostly this is done after the wheat is cradled and shocked. Then the men go out to Little Salt Lake and shovel salt into piles that look like a big field of shocked-up wheat when you are not too close, only bigger and whiter. I can't see how each man can tell which are his piles of salt on account of they all look alike to me, and there's piles and piles of them scattered over the ground. Father says each man goes to the same place where he got his salt last year. That's the rule with salt-getters. That way it is fair. These piles are let stand in the sun for quite a while, several weeks or even more. The water has to soak out and the salt get dried up. Then the men come back, shovel their piles into their wheelbarrows, a load at a time, and push them

over to the wagons on planks which they have layed over puddles and the softest ground, and shovel the salt some more into
barrels or bags, and then haul the salt home. They have to do
this before the rains come and squash out the piles.

Father always figgers on two big piles to sell or trade and one
half-pile for us, which makes three wagonloads. We put the salt
into a bin where rain or snow can't get to it. Dust can't blow
down on it, either, and make it dirty. We sell to folks passing
through or to some which haven't been able to get out to the
lake their ownselfs to dig their own. Father takes salt when he
freights to Pioche or goes peddling over to Pangwitch or even
Orderville. He genny don't charge much, mebbee a little bit
more for the miners on account of they seem to have more cash
than folks over here. He even gives it to folks which don't have
money or anything to trade us. It don't cost us much to take
the wagon out to get it, he says. All we do is pile it up and haul
it. He would not sleep good if he charged much for things like
salt which he gets for nothing. Earl's pa says a man oughter
count the use of his wagon and team and his back which did
all the shoveling, lifting, and moving. But Father says everybody has to have salt.

One man told Father, when he was buying a sack of it, that
he thought it was mighty decent of God to put that lake so
close and handy. "I think so, too," Father said back to him.
"Don't know what this end of the Territory would do without
that lake of salt."

"Guess God knowed the Saints were coming into these valleys someday," the man said, tying his sack with buckskin string.
"When they got here, He knowed they'd need a heap of salt."

We need a lot of salt ourselfs. Over to Aunt Mary's we butcher
a couple of fat hogs every year, sometimes more if Father plans to

take some when he goes peddling. We like ham and the bacon. Father cuts up the hogs, then puts the pieces in barrels with salt, which after a while turns to water. Later on we smoke the hams. We have a special place for doing that; most all Summit families do. Smoked ham and bacon are just about the tastiest food you can have. It smells so good when the smoking is going on, my mouth fairly waters.

Father says the family should eat plenty these days just to catch up with what they hadn't got to eat in Dixie. Mother said she went weeks without tasting a piece of bread or smelling a slice of meat. The whole family lived on pigweed greens and cane seed, and each time she put those greens on the plates, they looked worse and tasted worse than they did the day before. When Father thinks of those days he wants to salt down another fat hog, just in case. Here in Summit we are still poor, he says, and it's taken every cent he can make to pay for our land and home, but we never would of had decent land and a home at all if we had stayed in Dixie. So he is mighty happy to have the hogs and the salt to keep their meat in.

The first time I went with Father to get salt I was littler than I am now. I heard Mother say that if he did not take me, I would be wading in the ditch making my chapped feet worse. When the skin on your feet gets too dry, or if they are in the water too long, they turn red and make little splits in the skin that itch if the chapping is not too bad and hurt if it is. Playing in the ditch, which I did most every day spite of Mother's scoldings, I had chapped both feet about as much as my ankuls and toes could hold. Mother tried rubbing them with tallow before I went out to play, but the grease did not last long. If I stayed home and went wading again, she told Father, I would be fussing all night. Father gave me one of his looks from under his hat and

said gruffly that if I went he would not put up with any tom-
foolery. I promised to stay in the wagon.

Mostly Father takes the oxen for work like this. He likes
to make a day of it, which is what Buck and Blue are good
at doing. We have horses, too, but Father likes the oxen for
going to the lake. He is not in a hurry. This time we didn't
have a reggler springseat on account of Jim and Bill had broke
it when they were driving with horses somewheres in a hurry,
and it wasn't fixed yet. He had layed a board across the top of
the wagon box with a quilt on it. It was hard to hang on to.
There weren't any good handholds on the quilt. We bounced
along while Buck and Blue took their time getting to the lake.
I was glad the oxen went slow, else I might of been shook off.
I didn't mind that it would take more than twice as long to get
to the lake as it would with horses. When it is just the two of
us on the wagon, Father and I sing songs, look for interesting
things to look at, and he tells me about what he did before he
came to Summit. He isn't much of a talker in our house. There
must be too many of us already talking for him to get a word
in sledgewise. Sometimes he says that in our tribe we don't have
any Injuns, everyone is Chief.

When we got to the lake Father stopped at the end of a long
trail. Here the ground was level and I could tell other wagons
had stopped there, too. We went down the trail a ways. I could
see the salt was out past us towards the water, where I could
see salt piles standing to dry. There were some good-size puddles along the trail, and planks had been layed across them, one
plank to a puddle. Father jumped off and turned the oxen loose
to eat among the scanty brush. He spread some fodder he had
brought along so they would have plenty. They stick around

and don't run off. Well, not run egzackly, but mosey. He took his shovel and wheelbarrow and told me again to stay put on the wagon and wait for him. He said if I walked around, the salt would get in my chaps and hurt awful bad, because even if I didn't see any salt in the dirt, it was there.

It was warm and quiet out at the lake, and the board seat made me tired sitting on it for so long and being so still. Buck and Blue did not pay me any mind. They had their own bizness. Pretty soon they layed down to chew their cuds and look sleepy. I didn't dast lie down on account of I might roll off. The trail looked dry, the planks looked dry and clean, too, and I sort of slid down from the seat and onto the trail just to walk around a little where the ground was soft and felt good to my toes. I thought it would not hurt to walk along the trail a little. Father was already a ways out to the salt piles with the wheelbarrow, and he would not see me. If he did, then he would scold. I just went to where the first plank crossed one of those puddles. I could easy see into the clear water, and not any wigglers or bugs in it. I reached down and swished my fingers in it, then squatted down to look at something shiny on the bottom, mebbee a piece of glass. I reached for it, but the water was deeper than it looked. I kept reaching farther until kerplunk! Down I went with both hands and feet into the puddle. Oh Lordy! Out of that puddle I jumped, screaming and yelling. Father could of heard me a mile away. "Oh Lordy! Oh Lordy!"

Over and over I tumbled and rolled, kicking and yelling. That water was hotter than boiling. My feet were cooked, all of a sudden, like pig's feet. I hollered and yelled and rolled on the ground. Father came running fast, sweating and breathing hard. He could hardly get ahold of me I was tumbling about so fast.

Both feet had been roasted and fried all at once. He grabbed me up and carried me back to the wagon. Shaking out the lunch Mother had wrapped for us, he used the cloth to wipe my feet and ankuls dry, and rubbed my feet with his big red hankerchiff. He did not scold me, even about shouting "Lordy" all over the Territory, only breathed on my feet soft and warm. After a while the hurt felt better. But when the hurt went away, my feet didn't have any feeling. Seemed they were dead. I couldn't move my toes, or walk, or even stand up. I just felt sleepy. All that yelling and cussing had wore me out.

Father wrapped one of my feet in his red hankerchiff and took off his old hat and put it over the other foot. He tied them on with buckskin string he had in his pocket and layed me on the quilt on the ground, then covered me with the big coat he always takes along in the wagon, and turned to get back to work. Pretty soon I must of snoozed.

"Hey, Buck!" I heard Father saying to me. He was shaking me a little. "Got to wake up now. The salt is all loaded, and it is past time we started home." He lifted the wheelbarrow up on the salt that filled the box, put the quilt on the springseat board, and lifted me up on it. Buck and Blue were still laying down, working on their cuds, watching Father. He called them. "Come, Buck! Come, Blue!" They got up slowly, not being in any hurry to get home. Father called again, "Time to go home." They always wait for his second call. Then they came up to the wagon, each to his own side of the tongue, and stood still. Before we started he took his hankerchiff off my foot and gave it to me to hold and his hat off the other and put it on his head. Then he swung his long whip gently over the oxen's backs, and we turned for home.

The hurt had gone from my feet, but they were numb and dead. The skin felt awful tight, like something stuck on the lower end of my legs which didn't belong there. With one arm Father held me close to him so I wouldn't fall off. He used the other hand to swing the long ox-whip. I couldn't shake my sleepiness.

When we got home it was way after dark. Father lifted me onto the ground, and I fell over and couldn't get up. So he carried me into the house. Mother put me in a chair, washed my feet with clear water, and spread some greasy stuff all over my feet. She said it was made of sheep tallow and gum from pine trees, all melted together. She wrapped my feet in nice soft rags and put the foot of an old sock belonging to one of the boys over each foot so the quilts wouldn't rub my feet. Then she carried me to bed.

Next morning my feet were almost well. They still felt funny, but I could walk, sort of. And I didn't have chaps anymore! That hot water had cooked them plum to death. I couldn't get through my head why that water was so cool to my hands and so awful hot to my feet. Mother said the water wasn't hot; it was only full of salt. It was the same as rubbing salt into bloody chaps. And she hoped that I would remember that. It would save me a heap of misery if I did. Well, I did, you can bet, as best I could.

CAMPERS

Our house is handy to the road which goes one way to Salt Lake City and the other way to St. George. Earl and me like to hang over the fence to watch wagons roll by with their teams and wave to the traveling people. Sometimes a wagon will stop at our house for the night. If the camper is a Mormon like us, he calls Father "Brother McCarty," and we can easy talk with him. If he calls Father "Mister McCarty," we keep the talk on road problems, weather, crops, and water, and stuff which won't raise dander. We got a big table to eat on; have to on account of we are a pretty good crowd by ourselfs. Mother thinks ten people, which is all of us, is a good crowd to sit down to a table, but says she can always handle a few more if need be.

Once in a while the gang which stops is so big I have to sit on the floor where I have a little box for a table all by myself. Martha is too little to sit on the floor by a box, but I am just the right size. I sit a little ways from Mother's chair, where she can see what I am eating and keep an eye on my manners. I used to sit closer to her, but if someone turned around to cough he might cough into my plate. And you can't tell when someone will whirl his head around quick and start choking. A man did that not so long ago, and my box was in the way of it.

His wife had to beat him on the back and hold up his arms. He got red in the face. Mother and Father and some others stepped over quick to help thump him on the back. Looked like he was going to die. Mother yanked me and my box to one side, then went back to helping. In a minnit or two he started getting his breath back in gurgles and loud belches. Most men carry red hankerchiffs in their hip pockets. But they are hard to get at if you are in a hurry and sitting on a chair with a back to it, like this man was. He didn't have time to even think about getting his out, it happened so sudden. After he had got his breath and everybody was sitting in their place again, he felt awfully shamed. He couldn't unerstand how it happened. He said the coffee tasted so good he guessed mebbee he was pouring it down his neck faster than he could swallow, and some of it went into his Sunday pipe. Which I think that's what it did. Mother took my plate outside and emptied it into the pig's barrel, then brought me another from the kitchen with more food on it. The man's wife got a cloth and wiped the floor while Mother cleaned out my ear and wiped my neck. She wiped the box, too. That is when she moved it over to the corner.

Mostly campers only eat supper and a breakfast with us. They all have a bed of their own out in their wagons. If they are in a hurry, I don't see them in the mornings, but most of them like to tuck into a good breakfast before heading out again, so I can eat with them and then wave goodbye from the fence.

Sometimes campers bring stuff in from their wagons to help out with the meals. Once a woman had a loaf of bread she could spare, but when she brought it in she began making excuses for it. Said it wasn't so good as it oughter be on account of she probly didn't use enuff Salt Rising, so then the dough didn't come up as it should of. Mother told her she musn't 'pologize for bread good as that. And Father said it was fine, about as good as he ever tasted. Myself, I didn't think it was a patch on what Mother bakes. The crust was too hard. "Uh-huh," Father said as he chunked his teeth into that crust, "You don't need to feel sorry for this bread." The woman told Mother how she made it and said Mother oughter try her recipe, but when Mother baked next I could tell she made hers same as before and as good.

Some campers say they hate to sponge on folks and are glad to help out in any little way they can. Even though Mother puts up pickles herself out of our garden, we get lots of jars of pickles from folks traveling with a five-gallon keg of them and wanting to share. Mother tells them right quick they are not sponging at all. She is glad to have them stay and visit a while. I like having them come, too. Sometimes after supper in the summer, we can all sit out in front of the house and talk, and if it's winter we sit around the fireplace. Course I don't talk any, just sit close to the fire and listen. I find out a lot of things.

Mostly everybody talks about other people who ain't there, sometimes about Gentiles and the things that will happen to them 'cause they ain't Mormons like us. One of these days they will find theirselfs dead. They would know they was dead when they waked up on account of they would see all the Judgements had been poured out upon them and be mighty sorry for it. But mostly men like to talk about the differnt valleys between here and Salt Lake—which has the water, which has the soil a man can get a plow into, which will grow enuff food to keep a family, which hasn't filled up with Gentiles yet, which is still not too comfortable with the Injuns. Quite a few of the men seem to be looking for a better one.

One night a St. George man stopped at our house, traveling all alone. After supper we sat around talking in the candlelight. It wasn't cold enuff to have a fire. "Do you know, Brother McCarty, there's only four men here in Summit what are living their religion?" He had a voice like he knew people had to pay him mind when he talked.

"When that many are living their religion, as you say, I think that is doing well for Summit," Father told him.

"Oh sure, that's not doin' so bad," the man owned up, "but if ony one more man hussled hisself another wife that'd make more'n half the town. Then Summit would set a fine sample for all the other towns down here in Dixie."

"Well, why don't you just hussle yourself another one?" Father smiled through his whiskers. "Seems to me, St. George is the town to set the example."

"You know, I been ponderin' on that very question you ask, yup, ponderin' a lot. But the wife I got now keeps tellin' me if I marry another one, she'll make it so hot for me long as I live that when I do get to hell, the climate will seem downright chilly."

Father smiled a little smile again. "You shouldn't let a thing like that scare you."

"Say," the man roared," I know my wife better'n you do. Lived with her comin' now a dozen years, which you ain't. And I can tell you she's a man of her word. No siree, Brother, I just dasn't tackle it."

Mother breathed a deep breath, doubled up her knitting, and went into the kitchen where she lit another candle and shut the door. She won't listen to the men when they talk about having new wives. The man cleared his throat and began again. "You know, I been wonderin' how a man can keep a couple of wives or more in the same house, like some of 'em do. You got any notions on that?"

"It must work or they wouldn't do it," Father said. He had stopped smiling.

"Well, my neighbor was tellin' of a man up north some place, mebbee Manti, has thirteen wives and keeps every one of them in the same house. Sure, it's a big house, a mighty big house, mebbee three stories tall. He useter be an officer in the Danish Army. Handles his wives and children just like he did his soljers. One wife looks after the kitchen, another takes care of the eatin' room and dish washin'. One weaves the cloth on the loom, another looks after sewin' the clothes and patchin'. One looks after the milkin', churnin', feedin' the hogs and chickens. And so forth. They all got jobs to do. Ever' month they change shifts, as the miners say. Then nobody has the easy jobs more'n a month at a time. It takes a year and 'nother month to go the rounds. And he says it is a sight to see 'em all marchin' off to Sunday meetin' like a parade goin' down the walk, first the wives, then big girls, big boys, little girls, little boys all in Sunday best, and their pa at the lead lookin' straight ahead and mighty proud."

Father didn't seem to be listening anymore. The man kept on talking. "Seems you got the right idea here, with one wife on this corner of town and the second on the other side. That's as far apart as you can get and still keep both of 'em in town, ain't it!" He laffed a snorty laff and slapped his knee.

"So, when you been over on the Sevier last?" Father asked him with a frown between his black brows.

"Quite a while now," the man said. "Mebbee I'll stop over there on this trip. I'm in no hurry to get back to St. George."

Father looked interested again. "I hear it is a very good valley. I may go over myself next spring to look around." He stood up and put his chair back to the table. "How's the dam on the Virgin River holding?"

"Have to say, ever since you pulled out, that dam's still been big trouble. But we got her fixed up now so she oughter hold." The man could tell the talking was done. He got hisself up, stretched, and said, "Must be gettin' late. See you in the mornin'."

He went out to his wagon. Father put the other chair back to the table. I could tell he didn't care for that kind of talk. We knew he already had his hands full with two families to take care of. He didn't like throwing words around about wives with a man he knowed just a little and probly that was more than enuff.

Nobody pays for what they eat when they stop over. Lots of them couldn't go anywheres if they had to pay for every meal they eat on the way. Some folks brag they can travel all the way from Salt Lake City to St. George without it costing them a cent. They get food for theirselfs and feed for their animals, all for nothing. Father doesn't think that is such a bad thing. It is what he likes about this part of the country. "I hope I never live to see the day out here when people have to be paid for every kind act they do for someone else."

But one time a man and his wife pulled up to our gate who Mother and Father hoped would never come back. He was tall and slim and had a long, skinny neck with an Adam's apple that bobbed up and down when he talked. He had a loud voice for such a thin neck. His wife could of been skinny or fat; I couldn't tell, on account of she was bundled up in shawls. She had a little face under her big poke bonnet.

That evening we had only bread, fried pork, and potatoes and gravy for supper. Mother thought it would help some if she put a pie on the table. She had made one of cooked dried apples and sprinkled a bit of sugar on it. We don't have much sugar, never use it on mush. Nobody puts it in tea or coffee. Mother keeps it for special things like pies and when we are sick. Sometimes she puts a little in water to drip over our bread when we got nothing else to go with it. She makes good pies. I know she and Earl's mother are the two best pie makers in Summit.

When Long Neck tasted the pie he smacked his lips out loud and puckered them. "Mother," he said, looking sideways at his wife, "ain't we got a good pie out there in the wagon?"

"Uh-huh, you bet!" she said. "We got a couple at least."

"Go fetch one in," he said in his loud voice. "I can't go this one. Never did like dried apple pie, nohow."

Out went his wife to fetch her pie. Mother looked at Father. He looked right back at her. Our Jim got up and said, "Come on, Sam, Bill. We got chores to do." Bill left without a grumble. Ellie and Emily sashayed into the kitchen giggling. Long Neck didn't notice and kept right on talking. "This'll give my wife a chance to show off her pies," he said, winking his eyes across the table at Mother. "She brings 'em along just for times like this."

His wife got back with the pie. It was made of dried cooked peaches, same as Mother's was made of apples. "Now folks, here's a pie for you," he said and cut the pie with his knife and passed a piece to Father, who shook his head, saying, "I've had all I can eat. You and your wife have at it." Long Neck went right on talking and cutting.

"Here, boy, guess you might still have room for a piece." He stood up, reached over the table, and put one on my plate. "I'll bet you'll be askin' your ma to make a pie like this." I went to the task. It was good pie, all right, only the peaches were kind of soggy and squished around between my teeth.

Mother went to work clearing the table, and soon the campers were out in their wagon for the night with the rest of their pie. They left in the morning without coming in for breakfast or to say a goodbye on their way out. I heard Mother go "humph" a couple of times. "I never till now saw a man looking just like that Itchabody Crane I read about. Someone ought to give that rude fellow a fright of his own." She looked at Father and laffed. "I hope we don't see his hide here again." Father smiled with his eyes and nodded.

Sometimes the folks stopping at our house chew tobacco. Genny they tell stories while they chew and spit into the fire when they stop for a minnit. Once they get wound up, that leads to a lot of spitting. It's sort of like they need to see who can spit the most or the fartherest. Mother shuts down the fire if anyone's spit lands outside the hearth. She won't stand for having her floor stained and smelly. My Sunday School teacher told us boys and girls we should never, never use tobacco. If we did it would scatter our brains. He said while we're at it we should never drink tea or coffee, either. If we did it would stunt us. We learned a verse about tobacco. It's a long one, and we used to say it together. Here are the two verses I learned:

Oh, no, I'll never use tobacco,
Says little Tommy Reed.
I'll never put it in my mouth,
It is a nasty weed.

Now there is little Bobby Jones,
He's filthy as a pig.
He smokes and chews tobacco
'Cause he thinks it makes him big.

St. George folks are likely to bring with them things we don't get at all in Summit or Parowan, like molasses, grapes, and peaches. Some bring Dixie wine. They peddle these along the way. Mostly they are out of wine when they get this far. Seems Cedar City men don't take to the notion of any of it getting past their town. Dixie is all red desert, down below the Black Ridge, an awful hot place in summer. They grow cotton, grapes, apples, peaches, figs, and sugarcane for molasses. Those grapes make good wine, they say. One man bragged to us that men like that wine on account of they can get drunker on it than from anything else. But they don't drink it at our house. Father wouldn't stand for that. He trades cured hams for molasses in a five-gallon keg and for some dried apples and peaches, too. Sometimes we make candy out of the molasses, the kind you get to pull.

Our campers only come some of the time, but the Bishop's house has lots more. Seems anyone traveling who is poor and don't know anyone in town stops there. I heard one of the Bishop's wives tell Mother it was no easy matter to be a Bishop's wife. "You're cooking and doing for people all the time. It's all right to have company once in a while, like what stops at your place. They're mostly friends. I think it's right nice having them call on you. But we have to cook and care for everybody, friends, strangers, and church 'thorities, and I tell you, church 'thorities always got to have the best of everything."

One night two families going differnt directions, north and south, stopped at our house and turned out to be old friends of each other in St. George. Each family had six boys and girls with them, and they all looked like they wanted to stretch their legs and play. That's what we did, in the yard and out to the shed and over to the corral. We had a good time. That was more boys and girls than I ever played with before. Mother and the women worked at supper. Then another wagon drove up and stopped. It was a man and wife that didn't have any children with them. The woman told Mother that the grandma was staying with their youngsters in St. George while she and her man went on this trip to Salt Lake City. They smiled and joined right in. This time at supper the boys and girls sat on the floor with their plates of food on their laps, there were so many of them. I sat at my box. One of the little girls was sat by me at the box. We could hear everything talked about at the table. Everyone had a good time. That little girl said soon as she got home she was going to have her pa fix a box like this for her. It would be easier than sitting on her knees at the table and asking folks to pass things.

After our meal everybody sat around the fireplace easy and friendly. No one chewed tobacco. It wasn't very cold, but Father said we would probly feel better looking into a cheerful blaze. Soon as we all got squared away, they started telling stories about people and other towns. They talked a lot about the hard times the Saints were still having in Zion even though Zion was promised us. All of them, same as us, had kept on doing the best they could and figgered God was trying his people to find out which could stand the heat or the cold or being wet or parched, or hungry. We knowed enuff about pigweed and cane seed. Mother said those were terrible hard times for them in Santa Clara, but folks there hadn't died so much from sickness that followed the first bunches of early pioneers, like her mother and father, crossing the plains all the way from the Mississippi River to Salt Lake Valley. She told me graves were numbered like flowers on those prairies. She gives me a little hug when she thinks of those times.

"But even if we do have our share of troubles," one of the men said, "we should be thankful God has called us out of Babble on and brought us to Zion."

"I'll say Amen to that," a mother chimed in. "I'd a darn sight ruther be here wearing rags and going hungry than living back there partaking of the sins of the world."

Then the man traveling with just his wife told us he was a singer and the leader of the singing in his church. He said he always carried his little songbook with him so that if he found himself with a party of wonderful people like this bunch, who would enjoy those songs, everyone could sing together, and he would lead us. "Let's sing the songs of Zion," he said. "They will help us forget our trials. Then when we go to bed tonight we will lay our heads on happy pillows."

The very first song he picked out was the Babble on song, which talks about Elders of Zion going out to rescue the weary and hungry and cold people everywhere who would be better off in Zion. I already knowed and could sing some of it, specially the part that slipped in between each verse:

Oh Babble on! Oh Babble on!
We bid thee farewell;
We go to the Mountains
Of Ephryum to dwell.

We sang all the verses, and after each of them this part I knew, which I sang as loud as them. I think that song is about me and my family living by our mountains, a long ways from places Mother and Father have lived before, and long times ago. We sang more songs, with the leader waving his arms at us so we'd sing together, mostly ones I never heard before. It didn't matter. I just opened my mouth and let sounds come out. No one noticed, they were all so bizy. We sang "Hard Times" and "A Poor Wayfaring Man," which everyone liked so much they dabbed their eyes with their aprons or hankerchiffs. At Sunday School we sing one song more than all the others, "Come, Come Ye Saints." We sang that, too. It makes me feel sad and glad all at the same time.

Before they went to their wagons to go to bed, everyone kneeled down by the chairs. The little girl and me kneeled by the little box. And we had prayers. That was a special crowd. We all had a good time and remembered it. The songs hummed in my head for a long time.

REBECCA

Every once in a while Summit has a dance for folks to stretch their legs, put their feet to work, and stir up a lot of laffter. Sometimes it will be a dance just for boys and girls, like the one last summer. Sam says they are more fun than a rabbit drive. Dances are always in the schoolhouse on account of it is the only place big enuff to hold us. I never been to one before that time, or Earl either. Mother told me I could go if I wanted to. Earl's mother told him the same thing. So we did. Only I got there before he did and felt lonesome as a leftover egg in the nest.

Mother had made me a new waist with blue stripes and galluses with red spots on them, and even new pants which had belonged to Sam and Mother had saved. They are kind of big around the top and are kind of heavy. If I didn't wear galluses, then a button might break off my waist and show a piece of my skin. The girls would giggle and the boys would laff. With galluses you can forget about your pants.

I was fixed up extra clean. When Earl did come in and saw me, he said I wasn't looking like me. I could easy see his ma had cleaned him up better than he ever looked before, too. Funny how differnt we look when we been scrubbed and brushed and combed. If I'd knowed everybody had to be so clean to get in, I wouldn't of been keen to come. When we are out in the brush and in the fields, we don't even think about keeping clean. What kind of fun would that be?

Benches with ends together made a row all around the room close to the walls. Boys who got there early sat on benches by the door, I guess so they could leave in a hurry. Girls were 'cross the room, all in their best dresses. Right straight I tried to hide in a corner closest to the door. I didn't feel so good with new clothes on. I feel best when they are soft and kind of wrap around and fit just me. I felt better seeing Earl. We were all waiting for dancing to begin and wondering what it would be like.

I went to the dance barefoot, which I did not mind. Besides, I didn't have any shoes just then. But what was bad, Mother had washed my feet so clean they looked like a girl's. I didn't have any chaps on my feet or a stubbed toe. Gosh! You would not catch me at a dance with chaps on my feet or a toe with a rag on it. Quite a few boys had bare feet same as me. I could see their necks been washed same as mine. When I saw that I felt even more better. Some girls had come barefoot, too.

Right at that time, another woman stood in the middle of the floor and started praying. Always at the beginning of any time folks in Summit get together, a man else a woman prays the Lord to give us a good time and asks him to keep us from getting hurt. Then after the good time, some other man or woman prays to thank the Lord for the good time we've just had and because nobody got hurt. Soon as she was through, the woman in charge stood up and told all them with shoes to be careful not to step on bare toes. Then a man stepped out from the place where the fiddle man was standing and yelled way up loud: "Boys choose partners for the first set. Get going right now!"

Away went boys in every direction 'cross the room on a fast trot to where the girls sat to get their partners. Everybody is a partner to the one they dance with. It wasn't long before boy and girl partners were standing out on the floor ready to start. And just then—Oh, oh! a woman came steaming right towards me. "Buck!" she called. "Come dance with Rebecca!" Oh m'gosh! I hadn't seen her 'cross the room. I was scairt plum stiff and acted like I had not heard her. I never even ackcherly met Rebecca, much less danced with her. We've never said a word together. I only know where she lives and that she is Emily's friend.

"Come on!" the woman ordered, standing in front of me. I let on I didn't hear her, same as before. She reached out to grab ahold of my arm and yanked me on my feet. Down to the other end of the room she took me on the run, almost dragging me every step. I tried to hang back, but couldn't. My bare heels would not hold on to the floor. Soon's we got there she whirled me around and stood me up like I was a fence post right at the side of Rebecca. I almost fell over and shut my eyes so I could fall.

All of a sudden the fiddler started fiddling, the caller started calling. Everyone began stomping their feet, laffing and talking. All over the room the dance had started. Rebecca didn't say anything to me, probly not wanting to dance with me either, but she grabbed my hands like a good sport, and just like that we were swinging around and around same as everybody else. In a swing and a half I had come back to myself and opened my eyes and saw Rebecca laffing. I was laffing, too, couldn't help it. All of us were laffing out loud and jumping around like we do when we play Injun war dance. That woman, standing close to the caller, was saying and showing us how to do it. This dancing fun had got all through me. I was hopping and swinging same as if I had been doing it all along. But it was differnt from anything I done before. It was differnt from sitting

in Sunday School in this same room, where you have to be still
every minnit and you wish it was time to let out and everyone
go home to dinner. It was differnt from sitting behind Father's
oxen on the way to Parowan and thinking. The world had got
plum new. Something had got into me that filled my whole
insides. I said to myself, I bet this is the way angels feel.

That is the first time I met Rebecca. I liked her right from the
start of that dance. I knowed I would. Her hair looks like wheat
when it's getting ripe. My sister Ellie says it is blond. I think it
is ripe wheat. Her fingers are soft and smooth, smooth as my
little sister Martha's fingers. It was the first time I ever had hold
of a girl's fingers, a girl the size of Rebecca. Sisters' fingers are
not the same. When she laffed, her eyes sparkled like pieces of
blue glass in the sunshine. She had shoes on. But I only laffed
when she stepped on my toes. I can't remember that she said
anything to me, we were so bizy dancing, and my tongue was
stuck behind my teeth.

Right then I knowed how sweet little girls are. I was awful
glad Mother had fixed me up, so I was combed and smelled
good. I danced with Rebecca every dance I could, which was just
a few on account of other boys wanted to dance with her same
as me. When the caller shouted for us to choose partners for
another dance, away went the boys after Rebecca and the other
girls, some going straight ahead, some going kitty-korner both
ways. They bumped into each other. They made a jam. Too bad
for bare feet, the shoes came in handy and mostly got the girls.
When I wasn't the one, I had to choose someone else I didn't
want so much, but I did not mind dancing a bit with Emily.

After the dance, I still did not dast say a word to Rebecca,
or get close to her if she should see me on the sidewalk on her
way to school or back. Seems I just can't unstick my tongue.

And that is the way it stays. I don't get close to her, only stand off a ways and look. Rebecca is more than a year older than me, but I don't care about that. I like her. She goes to school. I will go this winter and will see her with my sisters at school. But now I can watch her come home from school. Mebbee that is better than if I went to school, too. I would not dast speak to her there. Someone would snigger.

Along the way from school to her house is a corral with a high pole fence which runs along the sidewalk. It is across the street from her house. Between the poles are peepholes, high enuff for me to stand up in the corral and look through easy. They are just little enuff so no one can see me peeping through them. I sort of squint sideways so I can see her coming before she gets to that part of the fence. Mostly she comes by herself. That is when my heart beats fastest. I feel so good when I see her.

Next to Rebecca's yard a reggler pole fence runs along the sidewalk from the corral to the street where her house is. One day the folks who live inside that fence hung a big carpet over it, reaching clear to the ground on both sides of the fence. I figgered it would make a better place to hide and look at Rebecca when she passed. She wouldn't see me, but I would see her through the peepholes. I was careful that nobody was coming down the sidewalk when I stepped inside the carpet fold and sat down a little ways back from its front. It was dark and musty.

After a while I saw Rebecca coming, almost a block away. Soon she was so close I could see her hair had a blue ribbon in it. I could see her pretty face. She was sort of smiling. I wished she was thinking of me. Right then my whole world went pretty. Soon as she passed my end of the carpet, I dropped on my knees and hands and crawled fast as I could to the other end and stood up and peeked through that opening. I was feeling so good I was shaky. I watched her till she had gone across the street and into her house. When the door shut, I crawled back to the other end and came out from the carpet fold and stood up, just looking at her house. I breathed big long breaths and coughed a little. If she looked through the window she would of seen me standing there 'cross the street. Oh how I wished she was thinking of me.

I wanted to sing. When boys feel good as I was feeling, they got to sing something or bust. But I did not know any song just that minnit. Then one jumped into my head, one Earl and me sing lots of times when we play in the fields:

> *This old man, he plays one,*
> *He plays knick-knack on a gold gun.*
> *Knick-knack, crack-a-jack, sing a man a song,*
> *This old man goes joggling along.*

> *This old man, he plays two,*
> *He plays knick-knack on a old shoe.*
> *Knick-knack, crack-a-jack, sing a man a song,*
> *This old man goes joggling on.*
> *This old man goes joggling on.*

That is the way I joggled home. Each verse is the same; only two words are differnt, which sound the same. It kept my happiness going. A flock of blackbirds must of heard me singing. They darted and lit on our fence and busted out with a song of their own. All that day everything stayed pretty. When supper was ready I washed my face and hands better than ever before.

I used soap. I combed my hair so my curls layed flat. I bet that is the way Rebecca likes to see Buck's hair. It was still combed when we sat down to eat. "Look, everyone! Buck has got his hair combed! Is the world comin' to an end?" That was Sam being smart again.

"It surely would be the end, Sam, if you were to put a comb in your hair once in a while," Ellie said to him in her soft voice. She always sticks up for me. Mother chimed in with her you-better-watch-out voice. "Samuel Houston, I think you should be 'shamed letting your little brother set you a good example. The least you can do is to pull a comb through your hair, keep your mouth shut if you can't say something nice, and not cause an uproar."

"I was only joking," Sam told us, with red cheeks, but he did not say another word after that, only gave me a friendly look 'cross the table. I could see a little smile cracking behind Father's black whiskers. Then everybody talked about something else, and soon we were all laffing.

I just kept on looking for Rebecca whenever I was out and about. I could easy see her at Sunday School, but she was always with other girls or her parents. I went more often, kind of hoping to see her by herself. But I know myself if I did and she spoke to me, probly I would drop dead.

WHAT I LEARNT FROM
OLD DOG TRAY

We didn't have more dances on account of measles, and Mother says there is no point in asking it to come right on in the house. Everyone knows all children have to catch measles, and we did. I don't hardly remember mine 'cept for itching. Emily, Ellie, and Martha caught theirs together. Ellie's measles were the sickest and lasted longest, but everyone is better now.

Christmas came. Mother made nut and apple cake and new socks for all of us. Earl and me had our birthdays, and in January we went to school. We were now seven. It is a good thing I am on account of we got a new baby in our house, another boy. He has got two names, same as all my brothers, wrote in the Bible, Norman Franklin. Sister Persis brought him over after harvest. It was her brought Horace to us about a couple of years ago. Mother says she brought Martha, too. Seems in Summit the Lord has her do all the baby bizness for him. The new baby is husky, besides being extra good looking. I heard Sister Persis tell the family about him. She says he is lots better looking than most babies she takes to people, which I think myself he must be, on account of Mother says he looks a lot like me. She is plenty bizy with the baby and Horace and Martha and says it is a blessing most of us bigger ones can go to school for a spell and clear the house.

Earl and me sit on the first bench, which is for boys and girls getting started with school. Emily sits back a row or two with Laura, Eliza, and Rebecca. I can easy snitch a look at Rebecca's yellow curls when I come in to take my seat. Going to school is fun. We do not learn much, I think. I can't learn fast enuff and do not know a thing before we start. Teacher said so. He thinks Earl and me will have to go to school till we are growed up men before we will have good sense, which I think myself is probly right. But who cares for that? We can easy wait for our good sense to come.

I only have one book. It belonged to Emily before it belonged to me. Before that, it was Ellie's, Sam's, and mebbee Bill's, too, for all I know. Father brought it from Salt Lake City a long time ago, when him and Mother moved to St. George, for him to teach school with and for us to use later. Mother said I should take good care of that book, on account of Martha will need it after me. It is shabby from all this handing down. Each of us has to be careful with it when it is our turn. Books are hard to get, and they cost money.

It is a spelling book. If you go to school without a spelling book then you got to sit by someone who has one. That is why Earl sits with me. If you do not sit by someone with a spelling book, you have to be still and only look around at other children learning their lessons. First thing you know, you might go to sleep. Teacher gets awful mad if you go to sleep. He says only children sleep who do not know better.

Some of the leaves in my book are tore a little. Couldn't help but be, so many of us already gone through it. It has blue backs.

One of them is broke a bit. Mother mended it with a stout piece of cloth which she sewed inside of the broke place. That book mending is hard work for her. She has had to do it quite a few times. When the needle pricks her finger she pops it into her mouth for a minnit and frowns, then grumbles about her and Father having to sell their nice farm near Salt Lake City when they moved down to St. George, while Brigham Young and his best friends stay right there living in nice houses, wearing decent clothes, and specially getting to send their children to a fine school built just for them where they can learn some sense and have all the books they need to do it.

When Mother is feeling this way, Father sits very quiet for a bit, then reaches for his hat and steps outside to chop wood. When he comes back, the book is mended and Mother is bizy spinning or knitting and humming a bit of song. Father has some books of his own, but not for us to use. He likes to sit when he gets a chance, stretch his legs out, and bury his whiskers in one. Could be one wrote by that other Homer.

Earl and me sit together so we can both look in the book at the same time when we study our lesson which we never know much about. Teacher says we don't know how to study on account of we are always thinking too much of what we will do when school is out, which is the very truth, all right. We wish teacher could not tell so easy what we are thinking about. We dasn't think at all when he steps close to us on our bench. Emily says it takes a while to get used to him.

The book has got spelling words all through it and quite a lot of reading, too, with some pitchers. The pitchers are of the stories. I like it when teacher reads stories to us. He shows us how we can learn something from them, on account of they all have an ending which is like a little message to make us better boys and girls.

One of the stories is about a good dog name of Tray, which lived all alone with his folks close to the road which went in front of his gate, same as it does in front of our gate. Seems he must of lived on a ranch which is quite a ways from any town. Living that far off makes it kind of lonesome for a dog, even if his folks love him and take care of him. One day Tray was on his front doorstep feeling lonesome. While he layed there thinking about how lonesome he was, he saw a big fine-looking dog coming along the road in front of his house, all alone, too. Tray got up kind of slow-like, his eyes bunged out. He never seen such a big fine-looking dog before.

Big Dog was joggling right along like he knowed just where he was going, and probly thinking of what he was going to do when he got there and how he was going to do it. Without asking his folks if he could go, Tray ran out through the gate and waited by the road for the big dog to come up alongside. Soon as he got close, Tray asked if he could go along with him to wherever he was going. Tray could see it would be lots of fun to trot along with a big fine dog like that. He knowed if any other dogs saw him joggling along with him, they would think Tray was some special dog his ownself.

"Come along if you want to," growled the big fine dog, which was a mean dog, only Tray didn't know it. He looked kind of sideways when he spoke, which was in a rough voice, more like a growl. His tongue was hanging out a little. Tray wasn't as smart as he was good. Teacher says lots of folks are the same way. Smartness and goodness don't seem to go together often as they should. Good dogs have to learn and find things out for theirselfs, same as good little boys and girls have to. But just now Tray was happy, his lonesomeness all gone.

So away they went along the road, each almost beside the other. They did not talk. Big Dog was thinking about what he was going to do when he got to where he was going. Tray was feeling the best he ever could feel, happy sparkles in his eyes as he looked up at that big fine dog he was trotting along with. Big Dog acted like he did not know Tray was anywhere in his world. If Tray could of seen that dog's eyes he would of seen the meanness there and turned right around.

By and by they came to a good-size town, could of been the very place Big Dog was headed for. Now Tray's home was a long, long way from here. Soon as they got in the middle of the place, the town dogs gathered around to look at the two strange dogs. They were friendly and asked the two dogs to stop a while and rest theirselfs. They specially wanted to get to know Big Dog. They did not know, either, that he was mean. All they cared about was how fine and big he was.

One of the town dogs remembered where he had hid a bone. Away he went and brought it and layed it on the ground in front of Big Dog, then looked up smiling with his teeth. Another said he could get a piece of fresh beef if the big dog wanted some. Another said he knowed where a chicken was hanging in the shade behind a house and would run and get it if Big Dog wanted chicken for dinner. Still another said he could come and sleep at his house tonight if he wanted to. The town dogs did not pay any attention to Tray.

By that time all the town dogs were close around the two vis-iting dogs, wagging their tails and letting their tongues hang out. Then before he even growled a single word, Big Dog jumped up with a great growl and began biting and chewing up every town dog he could get his teeth into something awful, shaking the stuffing out of them and throwing them rolling and whimpering on the ground. The poor friendly dogs were too suprised even to bark. Quick he grabbed more, biting, chewing, and shaking them like sixty, and they let loose with terrible yelps and howls you could of heard clear up to the hills. When the people of the town heard that noise going on, they looked out of their windows and doors and saw their dogs being bit, chewed, and murdered.

Tray didn't bite any dog. He was just standing by, looking on, hoping not to get bit or have his stuffing shaken, and wishing awful bad to be home where he belonged. When the people came running out of their houses they grabbed up clubs and heavy sticks and began beating up Big Dog and any dog which got in the way of their clubs, hard as they could. They didn't know Tray was a good dog and beat him the same way. They meant to break their backs and bones. Poor old Tray did not know if Big Dog was murdered or not and could not look for him; he was nearly murdered his ownself.

He was so sore all over he couldn't hardly crawl back home. He couldn't even limp but had to waddle, slow and careful-like, with his head hanging down and his tail dragging the ground. It took a long time for him to creep all those miles, and all the way he was thinking to hisself that if his life could only be spared this time, he would never ever take up with any more dogs which he didn't know. With every sore step he felt like his heart would break. Poor old dog Tray. All us boys and girls felt sorry for him, so sorry we almost cried. His folks were so glad to see him, least what was left of him, that they didn't scold or tie him up. They bathed his hurt places and made a soft bed of hay for him in the shed where he could lay down and get better. They brought him water and marrow bones. They loved him. Don't know what happened to fine Big Dog. He didn't have anyone to feel sorry for him or love him, but Tray lived with his folks so long they made a song about him:

Old dog Tray's ever faithful,
Grief cannot drive him away,
He's gentle, he is kind;
I'll never, never find
A better friend than old dog Tray.

Teacher sang this last bit. He said all that trouble was what Tray got for being found in bad company. Little boys and girls, he said, should stay away from bad company if they did not want to get in trouble. He told us bad company most always comes along looking fine and pretty, else big and stout like the big mean dog. But Earl and me do not know anyone like that, well, mebbee a couple of bully boys, but mostly folks in Summit would not allow it. When each of us is with the other, then we both got the best company there is in Summit.

SCHOOL IN WINTER

We have learnt our ABCs, which teacher says is only the start of reading. We got to go way past them before we get a little good sense and can read. Earl knows a growed-up woman with quite a few children. He can't figger why the Lord sends her so many babies when she has not got the sense to know her ABCs. I can rattle mine off like sixty, same as I say the blessing on the food.

We also learn about figgers. Mostly we learn those from the blackboard which the teacher uses to put the figgers on, then tells us what they mean, but it is lots harder than ABCs to get the figgers into our heads to stay. Earl and me have to use our fingers. There's only ten figgers to learn, same as we got ten fingers and ten toes. Teacher says that makes it easy to remember how many figgers there be, which I can see myself they are a big help. Teacher taught us about odd and even figgers. It is funny how we have so many even things which belong to us, ten toes and ten fingers, two thumbs, two eyes, and two nose holes, but only one mouth, which teacher says is half a mouth too much. Mother says a closed mouth is a proper mouth. I can write all the figgers in a straight line on my slate, which is not really mine but Emily's which she lets me use. Next year she will have a double slate, and this one will be mine then.

She says I am good at learning things by heart, which I think myself I must be.

Earl can make better-looking figgers on his slate than me. And he can draw pitchers on it, too. He drawed the teacher with a nose, mouth, hair and whiskers, and big ears just like him. One day teacher came by just as Earl had made a pitcher of our Herk, salty muzzle, flopping ears, and all. Quick he grabbed that slate out of Earl's hand, looked at what was on it, and smiled a big smile. "Only one thing wrong with it," he told Earl. "If Buck whistled, I'm sure that dog would run right off the slate and into our schoolroom. Then I would have to put him out in the yard. This isn't any dog school, even if we do have a couple of frisky puppies sitting here together." We grinned right back when he handed the slate to Earl. He said it was almost too good a pitcher to rub out, but Earl would have to do it. Just now him and me had better get at our spelling lesson. Earl rubbed his pitcher out and said he does not plan to be a man who figgers all the time or a pitcher-maker. He wants to be a freighter, else a carpenter.

Even in winter I sometimes go to school barefoot. So do lots of other boys. But school is not a good place if you have stubbed a toe. Then you have to stand by yourself and not play when we are let out for playing on account of boys, specially big ones, get rough as Injuns, and you dasn't get among them with a stubbed toe. It would be worser than being barefoot at a dance. This winter genny hasn't had much snow in it, and folks has started to be ankshus about next summer. And just then there was a big storm came, kind of late for a reggler one. When I went to bed that night the wind had started to blow, but not a cold wind, and in the morning the sky was full of sunshine, but the ground was drownded in snow all over the mountains, in the valley, and on all the houses and sheds in Summit. Emily said it looked like she wouldn't be able to get to school, and so she wasn't going to try. She would stay home with Ellie and help with the baby. Sam and Bill were not even thinking of their school in Parowan. Father was not at home on account of it being Aunt Mary's week and would not be back till Monday. Mother was bizy with Norman and Horace and Martha and needed Ellie to help, and this day she would have Emily's help also. I hankered to be out in that white deep snow, but on account of I had a stubbed toe I couldn't get my shoe on over it, I thought it would be fun to get out there in my bare feet. Jim had already cleared the snow off the path from our door to the front gate and had cleared the walk as far as the end of the fence. That left only two long blocks or more. Jim said the snow was at least ten inches deep. He had measured with his steel square he measures boards with. When it is Aunt Mary's week, Jim takes charge of things like that at our house. He sees the animals get fed their fodder, the pigs their bran slop and swill, and gets Sam out to feed the chickens. He sees to it the cows are milked and the wood is chopped and brought into the house at night. Jim knows just what to do when Father is gone. He wants to be a farmer. Course Bill and Sam have to help, too, but Jim is the one Mother counts on. He laffed when I told him I was going to school anyhows. "Careful you don't get chaps," was all he said.

There wasn't a single track of anything in that snow from the end of where Jim had swept clear up to where we turn to get to the schoolhouse. In the house I rolled my pants up to my knees. It took four rolls. If you do not roll them up, snow gets under the pants and freezes on your skin, and my pants would feel snowy and cold and wet and stick to my legs. I could even get chaps.

I was wearing a hand-me-down jacket of Sam's. I took the spelling book in my hand. Mother opened the door and shook her head at what I was about to do, and I skittered to the gate, then down the walk, dog-trotting far as Jim had cleared. After that I gritted my teeth and took a running shoot into the deep white snow. Away I went like a jackrabbit, hopping step after step from the hole of one footprint to make the next. Still, I was so fast I left a little cloud of snow dust behind me. Mother watched at the gate until I turned up at the corner. When I came home that afternoon she told me tears came to her eyes to see me running to school barefoot and bare-legged in the snow.

Twice I had to stop running and push the snow down off my calves to my ankuls so it wouldn't stick and start freezing me. The third time I ran straight to the schoolhouse. Good thing there was fire in the fireplace. I ran up to it to warm my legs, then rolled my pants down. Others were warming their legs, too, some barefoot same as me. They all laffed when I came hopping through the door, and we laffed at each other, but there was not a one which had to run so far as me without any tracks to step in, not even Earl. He made it easy as nothing.

At playtime most barefoot ones stayed in the schoolhouse, but a few of us tuffer ones rolled up our pants again and ran out to take turns seeing which of us could run furtherest out in the snow and back again fastest. Earl and me were good at it. If there had of been ice, we would of gone sliding on it, which is a favrit treat, but we have to hurry with our turns before big boys come with their heavy boots and make ruts in the ice which we cannot slide on. The sun was shining hard and warm. When school was out in the afternoon and time to go home, a lot of that pretty snow had already been melting. Water was running everywhere. I had to wade through mud and puddles to get home. Each time my feet got all muddy I found little cold pools to wash the thicker mud off. I splashed all the way home. Mother kept me at the door till she had taken off my cold wet pants and dried off my muddy legs.

Next day, Earl said his Uncle Gideon told his pa that this snowstorm was a godsend to our dry land. It had wetted up the ground so wheat would grow good and all the crops. Earl asked his pa what a godsend was. We never heard of a thing like that. His pa said it was something which people have needed awful bad, hoping and praying for it, but which they now have even quit thinking about on account of it probly would never happen. Then all of a sudden God sends it, mebbee late, but he sends it like he did that snowstorm. I can easy see Earl and me have got to learn a lot to have as much sense as his pa or mine.

BITTEN BY A VALENTINE

Winter is rushing past us, and we haven't had much snow since
the big storm. Valentine Day will be next week. Ellie has told
me boys send valentines to girls they like best. That is what
Valentine Day is for, so I said I sort of wanted to give a valentine to Rebecca but didn't know how. Ellie did not laff at me
like she could of. She is almost a big girl and knows all about
valentines and has had some her ownself. She would help me
with mine. There wasn't much in the house in the way of paper,
but she found a scrap of red paper we could use. The first one
we made had to be the one I would give. She cut little fingers
around the outside edges, then drawed a heart with a arrow
going through it like a pin. I did not want any arrow going
through Rebecca's heart. It was arrows Injuns kilt people with,
and what would Rebecca think if I gave her something like that?

"But on a valentine the arrow only means you love her," she
said. "The heart and the arrow are valentine langwige you don't
have to say. Everybody knows what they mean."

"Then put two arrows in it." I spoke up kind of sudden,
which made Ellie laff at me, but only a little. I was glad Sam was
with pals somewheres else and not around to hear me say that.
Nobody but Ellie knows how much I like Rebecca. "Someday

when you get to be a big boy you will want to put another arrow in some other girl's heart." She said it with her sweet smile. But I didn't believe her. She told me, too, she thought I was starting out sort of early shooting arrows into a girl's heart and probly would look better if I started with only one arrow.

Valentines have to have something to read on them which make the heart and the arrow make more sense. Ellie remembered something she thought Rebecca might like:

> *Roses are red*
> *Violets are blue*
> *Sugar is sweet*
> *And so are you*

I could feel my cheeks burning. I didn't think I could say something like that even to Rebecca. Mebbee my valentine could say:

> *Valentines are pretty*
> *You are pretty*
> *Be my valentine*

Ellie laffed and said she would write what I wanted, which would make a fine valentine. I could tell boys like me need to know a lot of things we don't know now when we start to like a girl. I was only just getting started.

After supper, when it was getting dark, Mother said I could slip over to Rebecca's house to leave my valentine and come right back. Good thing there was no snow. Hers is a big stone house only a block and a piece uptown with a big yard and a gate. Her father is brother to the Bishop. Still as a mouse I layed the valentine on her doorstep and gave the door a loud bang with my fist. Then I beat it for the front gate in the dark and ran headfirst into a big somebody by the gate, almost knocking him over. Oh m'gosh! It was Rebecca's brother Jed. "Hey there!" he shouted, grabbing for me. "What are you doing sneaking in my yard, Buck McCarty?" We had a scuffle. He grabbed the valentine off the step. I tried to get away but he was hanging on like a bear trap.

He must of guessed what I been up to. Probly he been doing the same with his girl. Quick he slung me up like a sack of potatoes over his shoulder and ran inside shouting, "Look what I just found sneaking around our house!" He pushed my valentine at Rebecca's mother who was sitting in the room with a basket of darning. Upside down, I could see her looking at my valentine, for Rebecca only, with a little smile, then setting the valentine on the table next to her. Couldn't see sign of Rebecca. Straight off, so mad and scairt I didn't know what I was doing, I lost all manners Mother has drummed into me and began kicking, biting, and scratching on Jed wherever I could reach, and it was hard to find something to hit on when I was dangling like a bag of squirming cats about to be drownded. "Jedediah, you put that boy down!" his mother lit on him. She is friendly with Mother and always nice to me when I see her on the sidewalk or going to Sunday School. She got up and came towards us. "I say put him down right now! For shame, a great boy like you picking on a tad the size of Buck!"

"Buck knocked the wind out of me there by the gate," he said, letting me down feet first on the carpet and laffing. "I just thought to give him a little suprise, too." Quick I snatched the valentine from the table and scrambled for the door, lit out and ran all the way home. I did not think his joke funny at all, and I will beat the stuffing out of him soon as I get big enuff. Earl will probly help with it like he did when his own big brother was on me about the red calf. I felt better just thinking about it.

That stunt did not make me quit liking Rebecca, but I knowed I would never ever try another valentine, no matter how much I like her. Course she can't help having a big brother which thinks he is awful smart. I have a couple of those my ownself, and all big brothers I know seem like that, too. Things don't mean the same to them the way they do to me. Guess I'll stick with looking for glimpses of her, mebbee getting a real long look that makes me feel good inside. That has happened at school when I have turned in my seat when teacher isn't looking and rested my eyes for a little minnit on Rebecca, without her seeing me do it. You can bet I keep a lookout for Jed. But I have to say, sometimes it seems best of all to be hiding and hoping to see her. I can easy think about her all I want then, and not have some bully of a brother laffing at me. Probly Rebecca doesn't care if she sees me or not, after my wild stunt at her house. Even if she wasn't ackcherly there to see it herself, you can bet Jed told her plenty about it, and she is glad she didn't. I didn't know valentines could be such trouble. It was like I just stabbed myself with Rebecca's arrow.

HORSES AND OXEN

Once when Father and me went to Parowan, the dust was awful bad. Hadn't rained in a long time, so the wheels went wobbling along in deep tracks which made lots of new dust when the wheels slammed into chuckholes and brought up a bucketful to throw into a reggler cloud. I tried to hold my breath. Fooey, couldn't do it long enuff. My eyes got almost blinded. My nose filled up. Father's whiskers got so full of dust he looked like a wild old man same color as the road. The oxen blowed their noses again and again. Father shook his head like them and blowed his. "Confound this dust!"

When we got off that part of the road, he stopped the wagon, and we hopped down to shake our clothes, rub our eyes, and blow our noses some more. Bally is the hardest and loudest sneezer of all. He about busts hisself open. Father told me I must not get in front of old Bally when he is working up a sneeze, else the blow of it would knock me down and roll me on the ground like a whirlwind. He laffed out loud when I told him that even so I would ruther be in front than behind old Bally when he lets go.

Father does bizness in Parowan quite a bit, and sometimes he takes me along on account of I am pretty good company, he says. The dust ain't always bad. But it is a good half-day if we take the oxen and start early and don't stop to chin with someone we meet on the road. And if we want to get home in daylight we better not stop long in Parowan. Father mostly likes to settle into serious talking with the men he knows there about what the *Salt Lake Tribune* has to say genny about the world, but mostly about what's going on in Salt Lake City. Just Passing the Time of Day, he says. Mother calls it just wasting time. He reads that paper when he can in the Parowan Co-op and once in a while brings one home. He says he could easy walk to Parowan and back in a day and do his bizness, but he likes to rest his legs and feet behind the oxen bringing home a load of stuff from the co-op, which he couldn't do if he walked.

Besides oxen, we have horses, too. Mostly Father uses oxen to go out to Little Salt Lake to get salt. That isn't very far. He takes horse teams when he goes freighting out to Pioche and other Nevada mining towns, or through our mountains peddling in the Sevier valley. Horses just nacherly go faster. He doesn't mind driving horses, but he has never been seen to of rode one. It would take a month to drive oxen out to Pioche and back on account of it is a hunnert miles across the desert. Just around Summit, Jim and Bill always choose to work with horses when they can. Oxen go so slow it gives them the eppyzootics. If it wasn't for meeting someone on the Parowan road who they have to turn out for, they would get out of their wagon and walk to the place where they are going, then lay down and sleep till the oxen get there with it.

There are things about oxen Father specially likes. They would ruther travel than stand still. I would, too, if I was a ox on account of flies gather round them when they stop and suck up their blood. They don't have big enuff tails to swish them off their backs and legs. Another thing, oxen don't get scairt of something and run away, like horses. Oxen would never do a stunt like that. An old weed or anything else that could get in their way don't bother them. They keep going right along, mebbee give the upper ends of their tails a few quick jiggles as if they liked having their bellies scratched by passing tumbleweeds. They don't get mad at things. You can't never call a ox skittery.

Even better, Father's oxen know him. When he turns them loose to eat in the brush after we get someplace, they stick around and don't run off, like horses will. If they feel like it, and they mostly do, they lay down and chew their cuds. When he wants to hitch up to leave, he calls, "Come Red! Come Bally!" They stop chewing their cuds, get up kind of slow, look around at the wagon and us, and switch their tails a few times. Again Father hollers, "Come, Red! Come, Bally! Time to go home!" Right off, kind of ducking and swinging their heads, they come walking slow and easy up to the wagon. Each gets on his own side of the tongue and stands still, waiting for Father to put the yoke on their necks. Even if he is fussing around the wagon a bit, they don't move. They don't care how long he fusses. They don't watch the sun to see how late it is. They don't care when they start for home or how late they are when they get there. Father says he wishes he could take life so easy.

He puts the yoke on their necks, next the pins in the bows so the yoke won't slip off. After that he fastens the chain to the yoke. It is the chain they pull by. The end of the tongue is put in the ring of the yoke, so the oxen can turn the wagon. "Gee" means turn right. "Haw" means turn left. Still they don't move. They might of raised some more cuds and are chewing on them.

But they don't move. They are in no hurry, just happy to be there waiting for Father to start them up, switching their tails and chewing cuds. Sam says cuds are made of grass and fodder which oxen carry around in their stummicks. After a while, when they got nothing else to do, they bring up wads into their mouths and chew on them. Cuds, Sam says, is the same thing as warmed-up dinners for us. Father likes to see them chewing. It makes them look satisfied and happy. There were times when almost the whole of Santa Clara was so hungry they would of give a lot to know how oxen manage that cud bizness.

After the oxen get hitched up, we climb onto the springseat and get ourselfs straightened out. I take ahold of the end of the seat so I won't get shook off. Father yanks the brake. He swings the long whip but don't hit with it, letting it drop soft and easy on their backs. "Go on, Red. Go on, Bally," he says. They give their tails a switch or two more, and we are off for home.

Horses won't do any of those things. You dasn't turn them loose to nibble brush on account of they won't stick around. They won't come to the wagon when you call them. They might not stand still while you hitch them up. They won't behave theirselfs till you climb onto the springseat and take up the reins and let them know who is in charge. Horses mostly don't want to do a thing you want them to. Sometimes when you're traveling along the road a big dead weed comes bouncing along from nowhere and dodges under their bellies, and horses will get scairt plum to death. They jump and kick and buck and try to bust the tongue off, else smash the wagon all to pieces, like they want to kill everybody in it. I seen them do this very thing.

I was standing by our front gate with Father and Jim and Earl's pa, who was talking about a calf of his which had been kilt in the mountains night before last, the second one in a week. He was sure bears done it, on account of the calves were all chewed up. A covered wagon was coming up the road from down by Ray Linn's ranch. I seen it making its way a while ago as they talked. It seemed to be moving along slow and easy-like in the hot sun, raising only a little dust, but I forgot it when I heard the talk about bears. Just then Jim hollered out, "Hey! Look quick! A runaway's coming hell-for-leather!" We all looked where he was pointing at. It was that wagon and its horses bolting straight up the road, pounding their hoofs, with the wagon bouncing and tilting behind them, ready to tip over. Already they had stirred up a great big dust cloud that was rolling right to our house.

You couldn't hardly see the driver. In no time they would be right on us. All together, Father and Jim and Earl's pa made a dive for the road, running fast as they could, and began waving their hats up and down and yelling loud as they could holler, "WHOA! WHOA! WHOA!" at the wild horses. Quick I hopped over the fence and looked through the slats. The runaway team slowed down a bit seeing so many hats waving and a string of men jumping up and down like they were crazy. But they didn't get plum stopped. Straight off Jim grabbed the bridle-bits on one horse. Earl's pa grabbed the bits of the other horse. Father was in front and kind of running backwards waving his hat and shouting "WHOA! WHOA!" Jim and Earl's pa slowed them down some more. Even with their boot heels dug in, they were being drug. They were still shouting "WHOA!" loud as they could. Lucky for them, a man over from Parowan came riding up fast, jumped off his horse, threw the reins on our fence post, and ran over to help.

The horse Jim was trying to hold was rearing up and pawing the air. His eyes rolled around and his nose holes looked red. The man grabbed ahold of the horse's bridle, same as Jim. Both of them together pulled the horse down, but he was all trembly-like. His skin shivered. When that horse came to his senses, so did the other. Soon as it looked safe to do it, Father unfastened the tugs so the horses would be loosed from the wagon. Then Earl's pa and the helping man held both horses while Jim and Father pulled and wiggled the driver out of his busted-up wagon. He wasn't moving at all. He looked about dead as nits, and bloody all over his shirt and head. But he wasn't dead, least not yet. He sort of croaked to Father that he'd been traveling with only the running gears and had slipped and got stuck between the double tree and front hound. That was probly what scairt the horses and made them run away.

Some of the men carried the man into our house, where Mother and my sisters and now several other women were watching with worried frowns on their faces. They got to work quick with setting him on the bed and taking off his bloody clothes. He looked awful bad. Then the helping man rode uptown to tell people about it. Right straight, Earl's ma and the Bishop's wife, which is the nurse in town, and two or three other women hurried down to our house with white cloths and plenty of salve and things to help. They washed the hurt man with warm water and clean cloths, and put salve on the hurts and bruises they could see, and tied up his chest with strips of cloth so he could breathe more easier. Earl's pa told the women it give him the cold shivers to look at the poor soul. But the women in Summit don't shiver so easy. They are too bizy. They pitch in and help each other do a job which is tuff. They knowed already it would take more than one woman to fix that busted man.

It wasn't long at all before there was a heckuva crowd on the walk in front of our house, some inside the fence close to our door, and some kind of stepping on our flowers. A couple more wagons had come down and stopped in the street. One of the men had picked up the hurt man's hat from off the road and left it on our fence. A bunch was standing by the wagon looking at the blood on the wagon parts. I tried to be near everybody to hear what they said, but they were scattered in too many bunches. Looked like most of Summit had come to see about the runaway. Earl and me probly knowed more about it than other people on account of our fathers and my brother had been the ones stopped the horses, and of course the Parowan man.

Sister Persis, the Bishop's nurse wife, and two other women stayed with Mother that night to help. And every night for what seemed like a month, usually at least one sister stayed to set up with the poor hurting man so Mother would not have to do it all. That would of been too much for her. Father slept on the shed with the boys and me. The girls took Mother and Horace into their room at night, when it was her turn to rest. By herself, it would of been too much for Mother. It was several days before the crowd stopped coming, and then every day was about the same. The man was slow getting better. Finally some of his people belonging to him, who got word about him finally, came down from over in the Sevier country and layed him in a wagon on some sheepskins and took him home. They couldn't say enuff thank-yous for all of us helping their husband and father. Nothing like that had ever happened in Summit before. That is what horses do for you. They are crazy things. Red and Bally would never pull a stunt like that.

If you're all tuckered out and you go to sleep sitting on the springseat, oxen won't jump at something along the road and run away, busting up the wagon and mebbee killing you. You don't worry about them, even go to sleep. They just keep going right along the road till you wake up, or till you get home. Course it would not look good for folks in town to see the oxen coming down the street with the wagon and you on the spring-seat sleeping with your chin down on your buzzum. Father and me would never do that.

We got another yoke of oxen. It takes two oxen to make a yoke same as it takes two horses to make a team. Our other yoke is named Buck and Blue. Blue was named on account of his hair is kind of bluish. Red was named for his red hair. Bally was named on account of his hair is red but his face is white. We call it a bald face. Buck was named after me. I didn't like it at first and asked Father why he named that ox Buck when he knowed my name is Buck already. I didn't want an old ox named after me. Grandmother Cragun says I am too nice a boy to have to give my name to any animal. I think, myself, Grandmother is right. Father said he couldn't for sure remember why he named the ox Buck, but he thought it could of been on account of Old Buck is the best ox he ever had, the best puller of all his oxen. He always does just what Father tells him to do, then gets the other ox to do it, too. If the other ox don't know how to do it, Buck shows him. When he named him, Father couldn't think of any other name good enuff for such a good ox. Father guesses that's the reason he named Old Buck for me. Well, I think, myself, that's a pretty good reason. Ever since Father told me that, whenever I pull weeds for Buck and the other oxen, I always pick out the juiciest ones and put them in Buck's end of the manger. Old Buck is a good ox, all right. No wonder Father named him Buck.

One thing about oxen is they don't like to stop along the road when they meet another wagon and the men talk back and forth to each other. We met a man driving a yoke of oxen same as us on the Parowan road. We each turned to let the other go by, but when we got even with each other, both wagons stopped with only a piece of the road between us. Father and the man talked back and forth quite a long while. The oxen began twisting and wiggling like they wanted to go on. Oxen don't start traveling till they are told to, else they would of started. The man told Father he thought the oxen wanted to go pretty bad, and that was why they were twisty and wiggly. Oxen know they walk slow and know if they don't keep right on traveling they'll never get to where they are going.

After we started up again Father told me he didn't think that was the reason. He said oxen just get tired of listening to the stuff most men talk back and forth to each other about. Probly they thought Father and the other man were just nattering. They wanted to go on, and so did he. Myself, I think Father and the man were both wrong. I been around oxen a lot, about every day. When oxen stand still out on the dusty road, flies gather all over them to suck their blood. Some flies are so big that three or four, mebbee five, can suck enuff blood in just one sucking to fill one of Mother's thimbles. If the flies had gathered on Father and the man, if their arms was bare, to suck their blood, I'll bet they would of got wiggly and twisty too, and probly cussed and swatted and gone on.

I think myself I'd ruther have oxen than horses any day. One wet spring day, Father and me and Earl were coming back from the field, and when we got close to our house we could see Jim and Bill turning into the yard with a load of wood. They had been up the canyon with horses and brought back a wagon-full. Inside the fence was a little ditch where water had spilled out over the ground since the boys had left in the morning. When their front wheels hit that mud, down they went and all wheels were in the mud. The horses tried to pull the wheels out, but they wouldn't budge. Bill was driving the wagon. Jim jumped off and put his back against the wheel and grabbed the spokes to help turn the wheel. It wasn't turning.

By this time we had come up even with the fence. Father and Earl and me got out and went over to their wagon. Bill had started whipping the horses, letting loose lots of cuss words with every stroke. "Bill!" Father yelled at him. "Stop whipping these horses! And stop that swearing, too! That is no way to get animals to pull."

Bill quit swearing, but he looked plenty sour. "Drive 'em yourself, then," he grouched, throwing the lines to Father. Bill was fuming mad. But Father wasn't paying any attention to him. He was looking at the wheels stuck in the mud and figgering. He turned and looked at our wagon. "You got the lines," Bill said to Father. "Let's see if you can do any better than I can." He would love to bust both horses with a club, I could tell.

"No, I won't drive the horses," Father said. "You unhitch them and I'll bring the oxen over and pull this wagon out."

"Those dum oxen can't pull good as horses," Bill grumbled. "Everyone knows that."

"The heck they can't!" I hollered at him. "Buck and Blue can pull the ears and tails right off your old horses."

"Shut up, you squeaky squirrel. Whatta you know about pulling?" Bill unhitched the horses. Father brought the oxen over and the long chain, too. Jim took the double trees off the horse wagon. Bill stood by holding the horses. Jim got his back against the wheel same as before. Father spoke gentle to Buck and Blue, letting his long whip drop easy on their backs. "All right boys, go to it!" Buck and Blue made half a step forward, then stopped and looked at each other a second or two.

"See! I told ya," Bill said to Father, kind of snickering.

"Wait a minute. Just give them time to think about it," said Father. "This heavy load took them by suprise."

I was standing to one side of the oxen by their heads. I could see their faces plain. I could almost tell what they were thinking. Oxen talk with their eyes, their ears, and their nose holes. Besides, they grunt a little and swing their horns. Buck and Blue looked at each other kind of suprised-like. Buck batted his eyes at Blue. Blue batted his eyes back at Buck. Buck said a kind of grunt or two at Blue. Blue said the same back at Buck. I said, "See, they're talking to each other. I can tell just what they're saying, too."

"What do you think that is?" Father asked, cracking a smile through his whiskers.

"Buck is telling Blue they got to dig into it this time. Blue is telling Buck he thinks so, too. He's saying we musn't let these horses get the laff on us." Next we saw them knock their horns together. "See," I said, "knockin' horns together is for oxen same as shaking hands."

Buck batted his eyes at Blue and wiggled his nose holes. He flopped his ears backwards and frontwards, then upwards. It looked like Buck was saying, "If the wheels don't come up this time let's pull the tongue off." Blue was wiggling his nose holes at Buck and flopped his ears the same. Once more they knocked horns together. "They are shaking hands on it. I'll bet if the wheels don't come up this time, off goes the tongue."

"All right, boys," said Father. "Let's get down to it this time."
You should of seen the way Buck and Blue went against the bows
on that yoke. They got their front and hind feet set just right.
They humped their backs. Their heads went low down. Then
they pulled. Seemed like both of them had stopped breathing.
The old wagon squealed like it was being pulled to pieces. Then
up came the front wheels out of that mud with a loud sucking
sound. Next, down went the hind wheels, kersock! But Buck
and Blue had their feet already fixed for it. Out came the hind
wheels, and they pulled that wagonload of wood over to the
woodpile like it was nothing—well, almost nothing.

When Jim was putting the double tree back on the wagon he
hollered at Bill, "Hey, come over here. See how that bolt is bent."

"Well I'll be," said Bill. "If that load had been one stick
heavier, the oxen would of pulled the tongue right off the
wagon."

Father took the oxen back and hitched them on his wagon.
Before he got up on the springseat he turned and gave me a
wave. And just then his dark whiskers split into another wide
grin. Then he went on up the street. It was Aunt Mary's week
for a day or two yet.

ANIMAL TALK

Why I could tell what Buck and Blue were saying to each other that time in our muddy yard is on account of you can't be around all the animals me and Earl been around in Summit's pens, coops, and corrals, and the ones we see in the fields and not know that animals talk to each other. Earl's brother Ray and my brother Sam ain't learnt this yet, even though they've seen lots more animals than us. They think animals are too dum. That is why they are called dum animals. Father says all God's critters talk to each other in their own ways, else how would they get along in their bunches together? They just don't do it the same way we do. We don't unerstand what they are saying most of the time, but that doesn't mean that they don't know what each other is saying. Mebbee we are the dum ones.

Earl and me know oxen talk to each other with their whole heads, switching their tails and grunting. They hardly ever bawl. We watch how they do it. Father's oxen don't seem to have much to say if they're not being asked to do something. When Old Buck and Blue had to move that load of wood for the horses, I know for sure they talked together about how they would do it, and then they just hunkered down and did it. We think our big brothers have a lot to learn about oxen.

Horse talk is mostly whinny and snort, but sometimes it is prancing around and kicking up their heels. That is what they do when they feel specially good 'stead of shouting. Cows moo and throw their big heads around, sometimes stand around lowing, don't know what for. They can have a lot to say. Our rooster sends up noises that make his chickens flutter and cackle and rush in and out of the coop.

Pigs and hogs seem more interested in eating and sleeping than talking. And a good thing 'cause they genny don't have any birthdays to speak of. Sows have their litters of piglets that snort little snorts, grunt little grunts, and snuffle right onto their mother's milky tits and begin eating and sleeping same as the big pigs until they are fat enuff to make into ham and bacon and sausage. In the spring again there will be more little piggies, and that is the way it goes with hogs. They don't have time to learn the talking stuff. They would never get to use it much before they wouldn't have any use for talking at all on account of they are already hanging in the smokehouse.

Rabbits don't seem to have much to say, either, but when we come at them on a rabbit drive with clubs and sticks to kill them in heaps, they squeal for help something awful. Folks that have rabbits in a coop never seem to notice them talking any other way than wiggling their noses at each other and waggling their ears. People think they don't have anything interesting to say, so they don't say nothing. Having to live only in a little pen probly don't give rabbits much to talk about.

Those are the animals Earl and me know most about, on account of we see them every day in our sheds and corrals and pastures. They are the animals folks in Summit take care of. But there are lots more animals living in the brush, like coyotes, and in the mountains, like bears and lions and wolves. I don't know much about them, only what I hear from Father, Jim, and other men what have seen and heard a few. These animals mostly hide, kill mostly calves and sheep, and are mostly hard to find, if you are looking for one, but mostly you wouldn't go looking.

I know something about coyotes on account of they are everywhere, and I have seen and heard plenty of them. I like to hear them singing out in the sagebrush at night. I wish Herk could do that 'stead of just standing there barking. And a coyote can smile. I know this with my own eyes. It looks friendly-like when he smiles at me, but probly I don't unerstand enuff coyote talk to tell if he means it or if he means Look Out. When they are in that smiley mood, they faunch around and look like they want to be friends with every other coyote, mebbee even with you. But Earl and me never even think of stepping out to try to pet one, smiling or not.

A man alone in the mountains, Father says, can feel his heart drop into his feet when a mountain lion lets loose in all that silence just one of its hair-raising screams. I should be glad I never heard one do it. I never heard or seen one, but I have scratched my head thinking about how a mountain lion mother talks to her little cub. Does she scream at it, or does she lay in her den and purr like mother cats do when they're taking care of their kittens? Can't say I ever heard, either, what a bear does to talk with another bear. But Earl's pa has told him that a bear has a terrible deep voice that can lift a man straight out of his boots. There is still lots Earl and me need to know about animal talk, you bet, but I think myself I have a pretty good start with it.

We don't have cats, but there are plenty around. They have a few kinds of talk with their meowing: "Feed me," "Don't come near me," "Tickle my chin," "Let me come inside." I know never to pick up a cat what has its ears layed back and is ready to scratch your eyes out. Dogs are differnt. I know all about dogs myself. They talk a lot together, but not in a polite way. When dogs meet they have to sniff each other and show their teeth and call each other names. It sounds just like cussing. Then usually one jumps on the other and starts to chew. I don't blame him. I would fight, too, if a boy my size called me names and dared me to fight. I would make him take it back, else bloody his nose. And a little dog don't even seem to care how big the other dog is. He fights him just the same. If he gets chewed up a bit, he shakes hisself and struts away thinking anyways it was a mighty good time. When a dog is friendly to you he whines a little and yaps or yips at you in puppy talk. You can usually tell when a dog is feeling good on account of he lets everyone know he is by wagging his tail to the left side and slobbering on you with his red tongue, or rolling over for you to scratch his belly. I know what Herk is saying to me, and he unerstands what I say back.

One day Earl and me went out beyond our field a long ways to where the prairie dogs have their town, which is a lot of holes in the ground kind of close together. We dasn't go too far, or Injuns might come steal us. Only one prairie dog was in sight, standing still by his hole. Guess he was the watchdog for the whole town. Soon as we stopped walking that dog started yack-yacking loud and fast. Of a sudden, two or three dozen prairie dogs poked out of their holes and stood up to look at us. They didn't yack any, only stood up and gawped. It made a scary kind of feeling to have the whole prairie dog town gawping so steady and still at us. A few of them showed us their teeth. Sam says their teeth are so sharp and stout they can bite a finger or toe off easy as nothing. They can bite a chunk out of a bone easy as I can bite a piece out of a biskit. After a minnit or two that watchdog started yacking fierce and loud again. He was going like sixty.

"Know what that dog's sayin'?" Earl spoke up.

"Not for sure. What you think he's saying?"

"He's asking what them two boys are doing way down here in our town. They ought to go back to their own town."

That dog quit yacking a second or two, then started up louder than ever and lots more fierce. "What's he saying now?" I asked. Earl is better than me at prairie dog talk.

"He's tellin' all those dogs if we don't get away from here mighty quick, they should take after us and bite our ankul bones till our feet drop off!" Just then the whole town stopped gawping and started yack-yacking. Now I could tell just what they were warming up to do. Away we went back through the brush fast as we could run. We didn't dast to even look behind us, but I thought I could hear their little claws scrabbling over the ground. When we got to Father's field he was just hitching up to go home and said we looked a little puny and might like a lift home. A good thing we got there in time, and a very good thing that Earl can unerstand their talk, else we might not have any feet this very minnit.

Earl's brother Ray says sheep are dum as hogs, but he only knows sheep about as much as he knows red bull calves. Mebbee reggler sheep don't have any more sense than hogs, but Earl and me have found that buck sheep are differnt from other sheep, like ewes or lambs. Buck sheep are he-sheep with big horns curling backwards. They are smart, all right, a whole lot smarter than boys like us, and they can talk. They showed us.

Henry is one of our friends, bigger than us, but not mean. He herds his father's buck sheep, a small bunch, and he don't

take them far off. His father won't let him. Coyotes could easy
run in and scare one off and kill it. He may be a buck and tuff,
but he is still pretty good eating for a hungry coyote or two. So
Henry herds them in the brush around the edges of town, like
out where the Injuns camp, when they ain't there, and down
towards Ray Linn's ranch. Sometimes Earl and me go with him.
He has a couple he will sometimes let us ride. Usually we don't
ride very far. A buck is hard to sit on 'cause his skin slides over
his body in an awful slippery way. A horse's skin slips only a
tiny bit. It stays on his back where it belongs. But a buck's skin
won't do that. It slips as if there's nothing underneath to hold it
anywhere on his back. You make just a little jiggle and it slips,
and when it does, you slip with it. This time we climbed up
on their backs and gripped our legs against their sides, which
don't do any good without you sit steady and straight up and
not jiggling. The first time you lean to one side, the top skin
you're sitting on has already slipped clear around, almost under
the buck's belly. And there you are on the ground. Mebbee the
buck's stepping on you, or mebbee there's a prickly pear bunch
close by, and you had better be careful not to stick your hand
on it. Good thing prickly pears are mostly close to the mountain and not so many down by the fields.

Those bucks acted like they wished we were someplace else
and not on their backs, as if they couldn't carry us and nibble
weeds at the same time, or that they didn't want to. We could
see it made them mad, but they didn't know right off what to
do about it. Lots of times we don't ride more than mebbee just
one minnit on account of we fall off, so they don't have time
to get mad at us.

We had just got started riding along with some other bucks
among the brush, when our two bucks moved close to each

other. They went around a big bush, one buck going one way, the other the other way, and came face to face. Right straight they quit nibbling. Each one looked at the other. Then my buck looked at Earl and his looked at me. Guess it was the first time a buck had ever seen a boy riding on top of another buck's back. We could tell by their eyes and noses and the wiggle of their heads they were talking about us, but we didn't catch what they were saying. We knowed they wanted us off before we even got on. But I don't think the bucks knowed how slippery their skins were and how easy they could wiggle it and off we'd of been on the ground. But no, they had to knock horns to make a plan to knock us off. If Earl and me had been smart as buck sheep, that's when we would of got off.

They stood still a minnit or two, each looking at the boy on the other one's back. We laffed and laffed at their funny faces. That's 'cause we didn't have as much sense as bucks. Then they batted their eyes at one another and wiggled their heads kind of fast. We knew they were talking to each other about what they were going to do. It wasn't reggler sheep talk. They were kind of grunting, too. It was buck talk. Reggler sheep probly wouldn't of unerstood it, either.

"See!" said Earl. "They're talking back to each other just like your pa says they do."

"It's the same as the squaws do with their hands and fingers when they're out begging," I said. "I know squaw-talk pretty good, but I can't figger these doggone bucks."

"Baa-a-a, baa-a-a, baa-baa," said Earl's buck to mine, twisting his nose around like he was making faces at mine.

"Um-baa-a-a, Um-baa-a-a, baa-baa," my buck said back, flopping his tongue out and around his nose like he was making fun at Earl's buck.

"Sounds like he could be mad at us, or mad at each other," I said. Each of us was sitting up straight as we could and gripping our legs tight against the bucks. Our fingers were dug into the wool by their necks. We were still sitting straight and steady. Mine stamped his foot at Earl's and then stepped back a step or two. Earl's buck stamped same as mine. Each took another step or two back. They had made up their minds what they were going to do. Still we only laffed at them. We were so dum. Each buck ducked his head quick. We knowed then what that meant, right enuff, but it was too late to get off. They made for each other quicker than a dog for a cat. KER-BONK! went their heads together.

I don't 'member another thing about it. I must of gone to sleep and woke up kinda slow-like. My head was laying on Earl's leg, and he was laying on his side, one leg stretched out, the other doubled up. His head was 'cross his arms. My head was on his doubled-up leg. It took quite a while for me to tell where I was at. Then I wiggled onto my hands and knees. My nose had been bleeding all over Earl's pants. I could tell it was my blood, 'cause I could taste it, and I rubbed some off on my fingers.

I shook Earl to wake him up, but he didn't wake so easy. Scairt, I shook harder. That woke him up. He turned over and sort of sat up, but said he was dizzy. Now that I knew he wasn't dead, I could feel a sore place on my head, hurting something awful. Holding our heads between our hands, we didn't feel glad that we weren't dead. We were mad at those gol-durned bucks! We let loose with some real cussing, which was all right on account of there was nobody to hear us. That made us feel better.

"They done that on purpose, dang 'em!" Earl shouted. "I'd like to kill 'em both! Gosh-all-over! My head hurts! And just look at that blood on me. Where'd it come from?"

"From my nose," I told him. "We been sleeping here in the brush quite a while, mebbee longer than that."

"Well, if we hadn't of been sleepin', then we been dead. It hurts more to of been sleepin', but I'm gladder," Earl said.

"What a black eye you got! It's all red inside and black outside," I said, giving him a good once-over look.

But Earl was too bizy looking around for those bucks to care about his eye just then. "Where's the dang bucks? I'd like to bust their horns off with a big rock. That's what I would." We stood up and looked around. He couldn't see very well with his black eye and kept one hand over it and looked with his good eye. There wasn't a buck anywheres. All we could see was sagebrush. Linn's ranch wasn't so far off, but town was closer, so we set off for home.

"Look where the sun's gone to, Earl. We been layin' here like a couple of dead rabbits."

"Yup, and anything could of come along and et us both up." We looked at each other when Earl said this. We hadn't given one little thought to getting into trouble out here. It gave us the fantods. Right off we knowed that wolves or coyotes could have found us laying there looking like dinner. And what if a bear had come along down from the canyon! We began running towards town even though it made our heads hurt to run.

"Henry must of thought we had gone home, so he took the bucks back to town," Earl panted. We hurried.

At supper when I told Father about the bucks, he looked serious at me and didn't laff. He said we could of easy got kilt. It was a real buck fight, and not just because Earl and me were on their backs. We were a pair of lucky boys. Mother said I better not try buck-riding again if I was serious about growing up. Earl's eye didn't stay black more'n a few days. By the time it cleared up we had talked about our bucks quite a lot with Henry. Now we know real bucks fight the same as men, standing on their hind legs and butting with their horns. Our bucks had talked and made up a fight just to get us off their backs. All they had to do was run at each other, bang horns hard, and we were dumped and asleep. We should of been listening more to all that buck talk. That's what Earl says, and I say so, too.

RABBIT DRIVE

It is getting on to warm these days. Sam and Bill have already flang out of the door to join other boys and men from Summit and Parowan for another rabbit drive. They are carrying clubs and spades and anything else they can hit with. Not so long ago we had one, but the rabbits have already got so thick and pesty we shouldn't wait to clean them out again. Ackcherly, we have several rabbit clean-ups a year. If we didn't, rabbits would eat all our crops, and then everyone would be hungry. Rabbits always move in where folks make the land green.

Crops need a heap of tending without rabbits coming in and eating what we have planted. Wheat and corn in the fields and carrots, beans, onions, and such like in the gardens take a lot of work, too, specially watering and weeding. Father says we are lucky our fields in Summit are on the high point of the valley so the land slopes away just enuff downhill for water to run easy in the furrows. In gardens, rows are short, and you turn in only a little stream and watch so no sticks or trash get in the furrows to make the water run over the edges and drownd the plants. Out in the fields water runs slow and soaks into the ground. Then things grow good, but it takes a lot of water to bring up crops. There is never enuff snow in the mountains to keep creeks full or enuff rain to do the job by itself, Father says. Him and all the other men hope they can get by without a drout, or even mebbee hunger. It's the critters give Father the most work. Grasshoppers and cutworms can strip a field before you even know they got started. Can't do much about the flying and hopping and crawling critters, they are so many, but we can do something about rabbits.

We have these drives and kill hunnerts and hunnerts at a time. A rabbit drive is when it seems everyone from Summit, Parowan, and Paragonah get out in the sagebrush west of the fields and spread out in a long, long raggedy line which looks to stretch from Summit all the way to Parowan and probly Paragonah. Everyone pitches in. Some drives, even men from Cedar City will come join us to drive rabbits out of the brush. They all carry clubs and scatter out and about so as not to whack the person next to them when they swing down on a rabbit. Boys and girls carry big sticks which can mow a rabbit down, even kill it, if they swing hard enuff. Girls usually don't like to do that. Sometimes men choose up sides, batchlers against married men, or one family trying to outdo another family. Sometimes whole towns are the sides. Father says when they do that, the losing side genny has to make a party or a dance for the winners. A rabbit drive is a good time for folks to get together. Shouting and laffing probly scares rabbits into bounding around as much as anything.

Everyone starts walking out through brush whooping and yelling loud as they can. Mostly us kids have got cowbells and old tin pans. I carry my own stick. We shake bells and hammer on tin pans and make a heckuva racket to spook rabbits into running so we can start hitting. Sam and Bill and Jim hike out ahead with Father. I go with Sarah Ann, Emily, Ellie, Eliza, and Laura. Mother stays home with the littles. She doesn't like shedding of blood, even if it's only rabbits. Laura and Emily are good at yelling and tin-pan banging. Sarah Ann likes to swing a cowbell. Ellie and Eliza mostly just swish their sticks back and forth and laff. It is like our own party.

It is not long till we have about a million rabbits scurrying and leaping around in front of us. We drive them toward Little Salt Lake, which is quite a ways out across to the other side of the valley. Mostly men and big boys boom ahead towards it. Me and my sisters don't go far as most folks on account it's too far for us, and anyways Ellie is limping some and gets tired and has to sit down and rest every now and then. So I don't know if the men push them out into the water to drownd or if some men are already waiting there with wire nets to trap them for easy killing. Sam says I don't know how many rabbits is a million. Anyways, a million is the most I can think of, and I can't think of more rabbits than what are running and squealing around us.

They leap up and down and crossways right in front of us. Sometimes in their craziness they knock each other down. They do not even know which way they are running. Some try to run back of us. That is when us kids bust them with our sticks. At least we try, but they are skittery and fast, and we have to watch out that we don't bust each other. When we get out of breath we just sit down and look at each other and laff some more.

A whole herd came running straight at me. One went between my legs. One jumped over my shoulder. I busted one with my stick. Another tried to jump over me same as the first had done. He was so excited he didn't jump high enuff and gave me a hard bunt right under my neck. Over I went on my back. Two or three of them ran right over my stummick. One stepped on my cheek, and his sharp toenails made a scratch clear along my cheek, and it bled a little. I dropped my stick when I got bunted, but jumped up quick and grabbed it off the ground and beat on more rabbits. I could see Earl near his pa ahead of me, and past Earl I could see Rebecca swishing her club back and forth sideways by her big brother Jed. I was wishing that smart brother of hers was close to me. I would sure bust him one with my stick. I ain't forgot him.

There was a fattish woman in the crowd close to me. She could not dodge or jump sideways very much. Mostly when she struck at a rabbit it jumped ahead of her stick or easily sideways, so she missed. One big swat I saw her take when her feet got crossways with each other and she staggered a little and fell down. A rabbit running past did not see her or think she was going to fall so quick, so he was in the way of it. When the woman rolled over she saw she had kilt that rabbit deader than nits. Soon as she got straightened up, she took her rabbit and waddled slowly back to her wagon. She must of been plum tuckered out, but she had caught her supper.

After the drive, we have plenty of rabbit meat to eat. Out in the brush buzzards and crows have all they can eat and more. And at night coyotes move in and help theirselfs to all they want. We hear them yip-yipping. Father says it is feast after famine. We eat a lot, too. I like rabbit meat about the best, specially when Mother fries it. Sometimes she simmers it in gravy. One of the old batchlers in Summit won't eat rabbit at all. He says when a rabbit is skinned it looks too much like a "bobby." That is Hinglish for "baby."

When the big boys got home they were still talking about the drive. Jim said he heard a man say that they must of drove mebbee six thousand rabbits into Little Salt Lake that day. I can't hardly think of all those rabbits. Bill heard a man say, "If I'd of kilt just one more rabbit that would of made two." Father said that fellow probly hadn't walked a foot past the start, because rabbits were throwing themselfs at the clubs.

That evening, before we sat down to that good-smelling feast, Sam reached into his jacket pocket and brought out a little brown baby cottontail and gave it to me. I could tell it was still scairt from all the day's racket and blood. Probly its own ma had been kilt along with the jacks. She might even be the meat we were going to have for dinner. Sam took me out to the cowshed and made a little box pen for it, with fresh hay and weeds for it to burrow in and a few carrot rounds to nibble on and a little lid of water. Sam is a terrible tease and has an awful smart mouth, Mother says, but he has a soft heart. I know for sure he does. I had that little rabbit quite a while till one day he slipped out of his box and shed and probly ran off into the brush by hisself. I hope he headed for the mountains and not the fields, and hides somewheres safe when he hears cowbells clanging.

PEDDLING

One summer day when Father's corn came up only to my knees, a wagon loaded with boxes and bundles stopped at our front gate. When Father came out to greet him, the man unloaded three boxes and a sack to leave at our house. I was watching by the gate, and Mother had come out to watch same as me. She said he had come a long ways to get here and looked like he still had some ways to go before his wagon would be empty. Father paid the man some money. Right quick the freighter was on his way toward Ray Linn's ranch. Those boxes were full of things he will peddle, which he had ordered from Salt Lake City, small things like thread and box matches, hard candy, rolls of ribbon, packages of tea and coffee, and plugs of tobacco which he would never use hisself. These things don't take up much room in the wagon, which will be loaded with candles and bags of flour and salt for his next trip. Father said, "Buck, it's time I take that peddling trip over to Pangwitch I been talking about. I want you to come, and we will take Laura along, too. Emily would like to go with us, but this time Mother needs her help with Horace and Martha. Ellie can't do as much as she did."

I been peddling over there before, and so has Laura, Aunt Mary's girl, who is old enuff to help Father with campfires and meals on the way and can handle quite a bit of the peddling. I can go with her to the door and help show the goods, and ask folks if they want to buy candy or matches. There's hardly any stores over by Pangwitch, and not a lot of farmers, either. We peddle our candles, which is why we make so many of them. Matches are fifty cents a box. The tea is a dollar a package. The coffee is just the green berries. Everyone has to roast their own. Father brings candy on account of everybody likes it, specially the red-striped kind. Us kids don't hardly get a stick of store candy for ourselfs, so we like to lick it slow to make it last when we do.

About a week after the boxes came, Father loaded up the wagon first with sacks of our flour. He said people living over on the Sevier River where we are going don't always have enuff flour in their houses. Most of them will be glad for a sack. He has a few sacks of salt and even some sacks of sugar. He put in a box filled with the small things. I plan to keep my eye on it. Then he put in oats for the horses to eat, and cured ham and bacon for us to eat. Over these he spread blankets we would be using to wrap up in at night. We went to bed early the night before we left. It seemed I just layed awake waiting for morning to come, which it did in a hurry which suprised me. Soon as we had breakfast, we waved goodbye and started on our trip. Father was taking the horses for this trip. We picked up Laura at Aunt Mary's house. There was room on the springseat for her, too. The horses stepped lively down the track.

First we went through Parowan, and we were there lots sooner than we would of been with Buck and Blue doing the pulling. We kept moving right along. It was not even noon when we got to Paragonah, which has red dirt and red rocks and not many people. Father met with a man he knowed that asked us to stop a while and have dinner with him and his family, which we did. When we came out to hitch our horses, a bunch of his children, which was mostly boys, were standing around our wagon. I looked at them. They looked kind of funny. My clothes looked good as theirs, mebbee better. But Mother cuts my hair a lot shorter than theirs was. Guess that's why they looked funny. Mebbee they don't have sizzors.

A little ways past Paragonah we went into the deep canyon which is called Red Canyon on account of it is red all over and has big red ledges and rocks and not many cedar trees. A stream of water named Red Creek runs down the canyon, but the water is not red, just reggler water same as our creek has. Sometimes the creek was close to the track, sometimes not so close. The mountains were steep and red and rocky on both sides. When the creek and mountains came close to the road at the same time, there would not be room for wagons to pass each other if one came along.

Up this canyon a ways, all of a sudden, here came a long band of Injuns stringing down the road towards us. Soon as we saw them Father turned the wagon off the road as far as he could and braked it to let them go past. Rock was hanging right over us. There was just room enuff for the wagon and horses. Even so, the wheels were almost slam against the ledge on his side. My side was on the side of the Injuns. I bet I could touch their horses as they went by, but I didn't dast. I was just glad there was room for the wagon. Their men were riding horses.

"Is it Old Wibe's band?" I kind of whispered to Father.

"No, they do not belong to him," he said, which made me feel a lot better. "They look to be some from over on the Sevier.

Guess they are moving to another camp spot on our side of the mountains." Once and again as they passed by, Father would raise his hand and say "Howd'do" to them. They would answer back with "How." Sometimes when they passed they would look at me straight in the eyes. It made me jumpy to be so close to them. This was even closer than when I was out at the Injun camp. I thought to myself there was enuff of them to scalp everybody in Summit.

The Injuns had long poles dragging behind some of the horses. On top was piled blankets and tents and baskets and poles for their wickyups. I saw bunches of buckskin, too. Behind one of the horses a squaw was sitting on some blankets. She looked too old to ride a horse. But then I didn't see any of their other women riding horses, either. They had dogs which barked at us as they went by. I was glad Herk had not come along. He can't bide the smell of Injun dogs. Once when squaws came begging at our house they had a dog with them. He took one smell and it was more than he could stand. In a jiffy he had jumped on that dog and was chewing on him. It took Jim and two squaws to pull the dogs apart. That Injun dog knowed how to fight good as Herk, I have to hand it to him.

Soon as the Injuns passed us by, Father started our horses and got the wagon back on the road. We went on up the canyon same as they had come down it. I kept looking backwards, wishing there was another road we could take, but there wasn't. I thought sure some of them might change their minds about us and come back and scalp me. Earl's pa says you never can tell 'bout Injuns.

When it was coming close to dark we camped on a nice level patch of meadow not far from the road. Father said we were getting near the head of the canyon, but we had spent too much time eating in Paragonah to get through it today. The road had been hard pulling for the horses, too, which also slowed us down. Father said he didn't want to work the horses too hard the first day out. We made our bed on the ground. Laura helped Father make a supper. It was about dark when we pulled the blankets around us. I didn't go to sleep quick, but stayed awake listening for Injuns. Couldn't tell what might happen if I went to sleep. I didn't want any of them killing us in the night without me knowing it. I could hear the little low fire crackling. I could smell its smoke. I turned over and opened my eyes. Father was setting the fry pan on the coals.

"Pile out of it if you want any breakfast, Buck. Laura is already up and stirring some eggs." I was ready in a jiffy on account of I sleep with my pants and waist on. I didn't have any shoes. All I had to do was put on my old straw hat. Father sent me to the creek to wash my face and hands in its cold water.

That same day we drove into the Sevier valley and stopped at a few little ranch places. None of them seemed to have much in the way of livestock on their pastures. At all of them, folks were needing our things and glad to see us. A ranch is a farm you live on with the family and is a long ways from a town. Mostly on a ranch there is lots of cattle and horses, mostly cattle. Genny they don't grow wheat and oats and corn like us farmers over in Summit. They grow hay. Ray Linn's ranch is too close to Summit and more of a kind of a farm and ranch together, which don't make it a reggler ranch, and he raises wheat and oats same as us, too, besides hay.

We drove on to another ranch which seemed a bit bigger. These folks bought matches, a sack of flour, some sugar, and some coffee. The man of the ranch needed a plug of tobacco. The little girl there begged her mother to buy some candy. The grandpa asked for a bundle of tea, which is called a package by most everybody else. He must be Hinglish. It was in the afternoon when we had come to this ranch. After we had got through selling things to them and talking with them friendly-like, the man told Father we had better stop for the night. It would soon be too dark to go on. So we put our horses in the stable and gave them plenty of hay. We had supper with them. They had lots of beef meat and gravy and butter for hot biskits. They wouldn't take any pay, same as we don't when campers stay over with us. We had breakfast with them, too. It felt good to be filled up. Then I was ready for more peddling.

That ranch family also bought two pounds of sugar. After we got away Father said he did not think we should sell so much again to just one family, but scatter it around, one pound to a family. That way everyone would get a little of it. About noon we got to Pangwitch, a funny name. Sounds like Injun to me, but I didn't ask Father. He was too bizy peddling. We stopped at doors till almost sundown. When we got to the front of a house Father would ask me to go to the door and find out if they wanted to buy something. He didn't dast leave me with the horses on account of that runaway team and what they done to their driver. Then Laura would come with me and run back to the wagon to bring the little things, like tea or tobacco or matches. At first I was kind of jittery doing it, but soon I wasn't. I just walked right up and told the folks what we had to sell. Father said I was a good peddler 'cause what I told them seemed to bring someone out to the wagon to find out about it. I think, myself, I am a pretty good peddler.

That night we stopped with some folks who had camped at our house a few times. The man wouldn't take any pay, either. That's the way it is everywhere. At this place the man bought a sack of flour, a package of tea, half a plug of tobacco, and some candy for his kids. Most everybody buys a box of matches, and he did, too. After we got through peddling there we still had some stuff left, so we went on down the valley a ways. Wish folks at home had cash money like they do in Pangwitch. Don't know where they get it.

After a while we came to a place where a little house was quite a ways off the road. There was a mudhole right across the road to the house, so we stopped our wagon by the main road. Wouldn't want to try that mudhole. The house looked kind of shabby, as if really poor people lived in it. Father asked me to go over there by myself to find out what they might want. He did not think Laura should try the mudhole or go around it. Her skirts would surely get dirty. A red-headed boy 'bout my size was sitting on the ground by the door. He saw me coming but didn't say a word, just looked. His nose was dirty, and speckled with tiny brown spots. So was his whole face. I said "Hello!" to him friendly-like. He didn't say a thing, but stuck his tongue out at me and twisted his dirty nose up. That made me sour, but I went on and knocked at the door, anyways.

"Oh, it's a little boy, ain't it?" said a young-looking woman when the door went open.

"We got things to sell over there in our wagon. Father thought you would like to buy some," I told her, just as I should. She gave me a kind of queer look, but still nice.

"We got sugar and tea and coffee . . ."

"Uh-uh!" she said quick before I got through talking. She shook her head. "Don't want any sugar. Wouldn't know what to do with the stuff. I ain't tasted it only oncet or twicet since Ben and me been married six or seven years ago."

"Well. We got tea and coffee . . ."

"Uh-uh! I should say not!" she said, shaking her head hard side to side. "Wouldn't have 'em in my house, neither of 'em."

"Some folks like them . . ."

"We don't. Wouldn't let our hogs drink that stuff. We drink Brigham tea. Ben finds it in the mountains growing on a bush. We don't have to pay money for it."

"We got matches. You got use for matches?"

"Oh! You got matches, have you?" opening her eyes wide at me. She had red hair same as the speckle-faced boy, only lots better looking. It wasn't hard at all talking to her.

"You bet we got matches. They're bran new, too."

"Matches are little sticks, ain't they?"

"Yup, little sticks with hard stuff on one end."

"I've heard of matches, but only seen one or two. Ben's talked about 'em. Do they come in bundles or boxes or what?"

"They come in boxes, good-size ones 'bout like your hand, and are only six-bits a box. Mother says if she didn't have any matches she'd give a whole handful of six-bitses for only just one box."

"Are they easy to work?" she said, kind of bending down at me. She had pretty blue eyes.

"Easy as nothing. You give one a quick scratch on a rock or a board or something hard. Father doubles up his leg and gives them a long straight scratch on his pants, like this." I showed her. "Oh my!" she said, smiling. Guess she never seen a man strike a match.

"Soon as you give it a scratch, the stuff on the end starts to fizz and smoke. Then you hold it a minnit."

"Why?"

"So it can fizz and smoke some more. Then you tip it upside down another minnit, like this." I showed her.

"Why upside down?"

"So the heat will come up the match. Then you twist it around with your thumb and finger like this." I showed her.

"Why?"

"So the fizzing and smoking will get on all sides of the match. Then you hold it level and kind of still, like this." I showed her.

"Why?"

"'Cause in a minnit, if the fizzing and smoking ain't quit, the end of the stick busts out in a hot yellow flame of fire."

"Oh my! Is the flame hot enuff to start a reggler fire?"

"You bet it is. If that blaze hits your finger you got a blister on it quicker than scat. That blaze is so hot it'll fry the grease right out of the finger if you leave it in too long. Father says one match can burn our whole house down. They burn things up something terrible. He just as soon let us kids play with shotguns and butcher knives as with matches." The redhead had come in, sticking his dirty nose up at me. His mother was looking at our wagon and couldn't see what he was up to.

"I can see we got to have some matches," she said.

"They're awful handy if you want to make a fire right quick."

"Sometimes we don't put enuff ashes on our backlog," she told me. "Then the log burns up. Sometimes we put too much of the ashes on it, then the fire goes out and everything is cold in the morning."

"Mother has said it used to be that way with us, and then we would have to go borrow fire."

"Well, out here we can't borrow fire. We have to use a flint and steel. Sometimes it's more'n half a day for me makin' the doggone thing work." She picked up a little purse and went out the door and toward the wagon.

I walked behind her. Her dirty-nose kid walked behind me. I walked slow and easy so he would catch up. He walked slow so he wouldn't. I went slower and slower as if I couldn't get enuff of looking at their mudhole. I could hear him real close behind me. I whirled around to bust him on the nose, but he wasn't as close as I figgered. Back to the house he went on the run. I took after him fast as I could go. He outrun me, but I was close behind. Another jump or two I would of had him. He slammed the door right in my face, almost slammed my nose. Quick I grabbed for the latch string, but he was quicker than me again. Before I could grab it the string was jerked inside.

I started back to the wagon. At the mudhole I met the mother coming back. She looked smiling and happy. She had a box of matches in her hand, but she didn't stop to talk. "See, I got a box. Soon's I get in the house I'll try one out." She kept on walking.

I could see Father was turning the wagon around and Laura was sitting in it waiting for me. I started to run. "No use going any farther, Buck. We better get back to Pangwitch and find someplace to sell what little we got left."

Which we did. Father figgered it was much too far to the next town. Probly that would of been Orderville. We would go down some other time and bring back their good fruit and other things they grew and made there. Laura told me she had been there with Father and Emily already. It was a clean and tidy town. Folks invited them to dinner, and the whole town showed up in one big room where everybody ate together. They eat that way all the time. Every meal is like a bankwit, she says.

On the way back to Pangwitch we passed a shingle mill going like sixty. We did not stop to see how they did it. Father and me figgered the men would push a board of lumber into the mill just far enuff for one length of shingle, then a knife would cut the end off, which would be a shingle. So I made a little pome about it while we were sitting on the springseat:

Is that the way the shingle mills do,
Go a little farther and whack it in two?

Father and Laura laffed at my pome all the way back to Pangwitch.

Folks like this woman we just done bizness with, living not too far from Pangwitch but on just a little hardscrabble place, don't have any money, Father said. Town was the best place for that. We hustled there and sold out the rest of the stuff we had brought before we headed for home. In little more than a couple of days we turned into our lot with a empty wagon, 'cept for some of the ham which we couldn't eat all of on account of we had taken meals so often at places we stopped at. Laura and me had a good time with Father. We sang some songs on the way home while the horses stepped right along. I just wished I could of popped that speckle-faced kid one on his nasty turned-up nose. My fist twitched to do that.

BUMBLEBEE POISON

When we got back from peddling it was quite a bit after dark. Next morning Earl could see our wagon had come home. Not waiting any longer for me to get back, he lit out for our house soon as he could do his chores and eat some breakfast. We been thinking of going out to look for baby cottontails. Just before we left for peddling, Earl's pa had spotted some around Snake Hill. But Earl is just like me; there is no fun having a good time all alone. So he just stuck around waiting and waiting till he thought we were never coming back.

He wanted us to go up to Snake Hill right away, figgering him and me could easy get a couple each of these little rabbits this time, and when they got big enuff we could grow cottontails to sell to families in Summit and make lots of money. Him and me don't like jackrabbits so much. They're big and strong and mess up our gardens and fields, kicking and scuffling if you try to grab one, and then leaping away probly laffing at you. The only time we ackcherly touch a live one is with our clubs in a rabbit drive. They are only good to eat.

On the way we saw lots of bumblebees bumbling around weeds and squatty flowers which layed close to the ground. Earl says Injuns claim when there are a lot of bumblebees in summer it is a sure sign there will be plenty of pine nuts in the fall. Sam says Injuns have signs for everything. Injuns like pine nuts better than 'most anything. I don't blame them; I do, too. Injuns pound on them with a pounding rock to gather the nut parts. Mother has us crack them for her. You have to do an awful lot of shell cracking with your teeth to get at one small pine nut, but I figger it is worth doing. Pine nuts have the most nuttiest taste I know. Mother cooks them with squash.

We didn't see any cottontails. But lots of bumblebees bumbled around our heads. And of course now we wouldn't of chased little cottontails if we had seen any on account of Mother says not to run from a bee. It makes them twitchy, and they go right after you. We had to go easy on our toes for a while. So we looked for arrowheads and not for cottontails. The bumbling kept on and began to sound angry. We dasn't twist our heads around or even stoop to pick up an arrowhead if we spotted one, which we didn't, on account of we might get stung in the bum. Criminy, what is the use finding things if you dasn't pick up what you find?

The bumbling got so loud we just stood still as a dead tree. Bumblebees are one thing we are scairt of on account of they are so big and their buzz sounds louder and madder than a reggler bee's. We were sure they were mad at us for being in their flower-smelling place. But after a while we thought mebbee they were not really so mad. Might be they only wanted to smell our smell. But we weren't taking chances; we just stood still, like Earl's pa said to do if we found ourselfs in the middle of bumblebee bizness. He said to just stand still and don't wiggle too much. Soon as the bees get your smell they will beat it away from you. But you have to be careful on account of if a

bumblebee smells the kind of smell some people carry around
with them, which they might not even know about, which he
can't stand, he will right off jab his stinger into that person,
which is why boys our size should never go out among bumblebees till their mothers have scrubbed and cleaned them up.
Ours had. Mother said she was just scrubbing off the dust of a
week in the wagon on the road.

Bumblebees are bigger than reggler bees. They have a worser
poison. If they hit you with their stinger in the right place, down
you go with just one sting. Earl said his Uncle Gideon was stung
by one, right under the nose on that kind of bare spot where
each side of his mustash starts growing the other way. He was
just walking along the sidewalk calm as calm when that bee
came out of a apple tree loud and bumbling, and bang! Down
he fell to the ground like he been shot and didn't come to hisself
for it seemed nearly a whole hour. It even blinded his eyesight
when he did come to hisself. He couldn't see to walk steady or
straight frontwards till he got home. Seems they like to sting
you on bare places where there is not much hair.

Our dog Herk has got hair all over but for his nose, and
that is where a bumblebee stung him one day. It must of been
only a little bumbler on account of it didn't knock him flat.
But you ought to of seen him jump up and down and whirl
around like he'd gone plum crazy. A couple of times he acted
like he was trying to put his nose in his mouth, then rubbed
it in the dirt and scratched it with his paws "Stand back! Run
away quick!" Sam was yelling at me. He had just come around
the house and seen me standing close to Herk. He thought our
dog had dog-madness till he came up to where I was at and
could see he didn't have any bubbles coming out of his mouth.

I told him it was only a bumblebee sting. Then he laffed to see that poor old dog cutting up so. After that, the grumbling of a bumblebee would scare Herk more than thunder and lightning scare me, which is a lot.

We sneaked away very slow from Snake Hill and its big bees, not turning or stooping, toward where the Injun camp is when they come. On the edge of the clearing was a patch of bluebells and red bells and a few larkspurs. When we got to the flowers the bumblebees had quit circling around our necks and ears and gone over to the flowers, where soon they were thick as honeybees on our currant bushes. Never saw so many bumblebees close together. You could hear them from quite a ways off. They were tired of us and our smell, we guessed. We just stood and watched them.

Butterflies were flicking among the flowers. A little yellow butterfly sailed over and lit on a pretty bluebell near us. It sat there waving its wings up and down kind of satisfied-like. I know, myself, bumblebees are mean to butterflies, and sure enuff, right straight there came a bee bumbling along like a bully straight to that bluebell. He saw that butterfly waving its wings slow and gentle, and bang! He dived straight for that butterfly and almost hit it, but it fluttered away just in time. Then he bumbled some more, sounding like he was cussing that butterfly for getting on his bluebell. That made him feel better, and he lit into the flower his own self and started sucking the sweetness of it. Earl was mad at him, so was I. There was plenty of flowers to go round. He didn't need to bully that butterfly away.

"Doggone that ornery bumblebee," Earl hissed to me. "Just watch him a minnit and see where he goes. I'll get a switch and bust the living guts outa him." He went over to the brush and was back in a hurry holding a brush switch. The bumblebee was still hard at it on the bluebell which he had stole. Earl sneaked up close, raised the switch up slow and careful and WHAM! He gave a slam that kilt it deader than nits.

"There!" Earl said. "Guess you won't chase no more butter-flies off any more flowers!"

"Serves him right!" I said. "Serves him right for all the buzzing those bumblebees done to us today, too."

There layed that bumblebee on the ground. We got on our knees for a better look at him. Funny, he had got kilt without looking like he been hit, not sqwished at all. He had long woolly legs, sort of hairy. He was ugly all over. I didn't know they looked so awful fierce. If I was a butterfly I would be more scairt of him than of Old Wibe. I found a switch for myself so I could turn him over.

"Gosh, Buck! No wonder Uncle Gideon was knocked blind. I'll bet one of these tuff-lookin' cusses could almost blind a ox."

"Mebbee make it stagger," I said, touching the ugly thing with my long stick.

He had big starey eyes that seemed to see us even if he was dead. We turned him around so he couldn't stare at us. But when we did, it seemed like his big eyes could see backwards and forwards at the same time. We looked at his stinger place, but the stinger was out of sight, back up in his insides. We didn't dast touch him with our fingers, only the sticks. "Let's bust him open and look at his insides," Earl said. "I've seen the guts of most everything but bumblebees, pisants, and spiders."

Earl pulled him apart in the middle. He broke awful hard. We sqwished all his insides out and made a reggler mess of him. Earl took his switch and slammed another bee. He was big and ugly same as the other one, and just as fierce looking, too. This time we were braver and used our fingers, keeping them away from his stinger place. We didn't know for sure if a dead bumblebee stinger could sting or not. This one broke apart easy. There inside his hind half, back up a ways from his stinger and just inside his broke place, we could see a little lump of whitish-looking stuff.

"Look out, Buck! Look out! That's his stinger poison, all right." Earl hollered. Now he was looking close at that whitish thing, and in a second leaned back on his heels. "Yessir, that's his poison. Better look out. Pa says poison always looks whitish or creamy."

With some long, slim slivers we wiggled the whitish thing out a bit. Didn't look like it could stand us wiggling it much. "Let's bust that thing," I said, picking up a longer sliver and poking kind of easy at it.

"Hold on, Buck, don't you do it. It might get on your fingers and blister them something awful. They could rot clear off if that poison gets on them." He put his hand on my arm.

"Ah, I ain't scairt of blisters. And not scairt of my fingers rotting off me, either," I bragged, pinching that poison thing a little hard. Earl was watching close. The whitish thing was big as a pea, but kind of flat. It broke easy with the first real punch. Some stuff clear as water came out, kind of slow. It was only the skin of the thing which was white.

"So that's what he jabs into folks to sting with," Earl said, like he'd just found something he had been looking for.

"Gosh, Earl, looks there is enuff poison to knock down every man in Summit. If we put that stuff in our bellies we would have cramps and bellyaches," I said, feeling a little squiffy just thinking about it.

"If Ma was around she would make us eat mustard so we would puke to get rid of it. If we didn't, we would probly get fits and die," Earl said while we stared at the poison. First time we had ever seen real poison. "I'll bet our folks never seen what we are looking at," he said.

"I know my brothers ain't," I said. "They would of let me know about it by now if they had. Wonder what that stuff tastes like."

"Tastes like poison, of course," Earl said, speaking kind of loud and mean.

I dipped the end of my sliver into that bit of clear stuff and kind of stirred a little and held it up. We looked and looked at it. "It don't look so good," Earl said. "But if it wasn't poison it wouldn't look so bad, either, would it?"

"Let's give it a taste," I said.

"And get us both kilt? No, sir, I won't taste it. Don't you, either."

"Ah, bumblebees don't kill folks, they just knock them down. That's all."

"Taste it yourself, then, Buck. I ain't that crazy." He stood up and walked away a step or two.

"Ah, come on back. Let's draw cuts."

"I won't draw cuts with nobody to taste bumblebee poison."

"Then I will taste it myself. I want to see what this stuff tastes like."

Earl was back, on his knees now, watching. "You might get fits."

"Course I won't. Won't take enuff for that. Just watch." I put the sliver in the little pouch again, then put it to my lips, careful-like. Earl was watching me close and holding his breath.

"What's the matter?" he hollered after a bit. "Are you poisoned?" He was getting scairt, I could tell. I had been staring at him with wide-open eyes and licking my lips a queer way, not saying a word, just staring and staring.

"Uh-uh, I ain't poisoned," I said kind of slow, but still staring.

"What you lookin' at me that way for if you ain't poisoned?" He looked terrible ankshus.

"Say-y-y! If that is poison, then poison tastes a whole lot better than I thought," I said between licks across my lips.

"Poison don't taste good. Pa says it tastes bitter or puckerish."

"It tastes better coming outa his guts 'stead of outa his stinger. And see! I ain't had a fit yet."

"That's 'cause you didn't take enuff. You dasn't do it again?"

"Yes I dast." This time I took as much as I could get on my sliver. It had mostly run away into the insides of the bumblebee. I put it to my lips kind of brave this time. "Hey!!" I busted out at Earl. "I'll bet that's honey!" I gave my lips a lively licking.

"Course it ain't honey. It's poison. That's what it is." Earl stood by his claim.

"Bumblebees have honey same as they have stingers, don't they?"

"How do I know? I ain't seen their honey," Earl said, not wanting to let go of the poison notion. By this time the thing had all flatted out. There wasn't any more juice of it left for Earl to taste. He was willing to give it a try now, but only just a little. "Could still be poison, anyways. Might just take longer to work, same as Ma says vinegar does."

Soon we had another bee and pulled him apart. There in the same place was the little white bag. This time we got a longer sliver and slow and careful-like Earl dipped it and put it to his lips. "Watch my eyes, Buck. Pa says eyes turn green when you're goin' into fits." He took quite a while getting it all off his sliver. "I'll bet that is honey!" he said, suprised, licking his lips and staring at me same as I did him. "And right there by his stinger. Seems to me he'd get his honey and poison mixed. This tastes awful good."

"Let's kill more bumblebees," I said. "We can have a reggler feast of this bumblebee honey or whatever it is." Which we did.

When we left for home quite a while later, seems our lips were puffed up big as sausages, looking red and meaty, too. Mine felt both big and heavy. When I came through our front door Mother was at her spinning wheel, her back to me. I sort of banged the door when I shut it. She turned around and stared at me and stared at me. "Oh-h-h! Homer!" she almost screamed. Stopping the wheel, she hurried to the door and grabbed me. "What on earth has happened to you! Have you fallen off a house?"

"Uh-uh! I never fell off anything. Just been stung by bum-blebees," I mumbled through my thick lips. She stood me on a chair to see more clearly how I been mangled. "Oh, dear! What a face! What a face!" She was shaking her head and looking at me as if she been stung 'stead of me. She pulled me into the kitchen quick where she put some white stuff all over my lips. "Why didn't you run away from bees? What did you or they do to your face!"

"Couldn't of done that. Didn't need to. It was dead ones what stung us."

"Dead bees! What are you talking about?"

"It was dead ones, all right," I said, kind of slow on account of my lips were getting bigger and more sore every minnit. They wouldn't or couldn't move fast. Felt like my whole face had swoll up. It was getting worse and worser. I didn't feel a bit like me. I thought my whole body would swell up like a big bag.

"Tell me how it happened! What a face! What a face!"

"Earl and me kilt bumblebees and pulled them apart so we could suck the honey out of their insides. We had to quit when our lips got so big they couldn't suck anymore."

"Sucking insides out of dead bees? Why, you nasty things! It almost serves you right."

"Well, you take insides out of chickens, don't you?"

"But I do it to get the gizzard and heart and liver for soup makings. I take them out with my hands."

"Mebbee if they tasted sweet as bumblebee honey you'd want to suck them out same as Earl and me did."

"Just tell me, Homer, how could dead bees sting up your face like this?"

"We had to suck the honey out of its little bundle in their guts, else we would break it and lose the honey in it."

"How did they sting you?"

"Seems every time we put the bee's broken end to our lips, the stinger would flip around and jab us in our lips or chins. Least that's how it seemed."

"Why didn't you quit?"

"On account of we wanted that honey. And after the first sting or two it didn't hurt so much," I told her. "And how did we know dead bee stingers could sting?" Mother just sat and looked at me and kept on looking at me. "We must of sucked a lot of bees."

I couldn't tell if Mother felt bad for me, or if she wanted to laff at me, or if she would ruther give me a hard spanking for whatever it was we had done.

It took a long several days for my lips to be mine again and my head not to hurt if I moved it. In the meantime, the whole family had to look to the side of me when we were bizy in the house or out at the field. They had to look at their plates at dinner or they would bust out laffing. It helped if Mother had me sit at my little box while we were eating so no one could see my bumblebee lips.

AT DAN HARRIS'S WHEAT STACK

I do not know any boys my size in Summit which swear much. That's something big boys and men do. They don't seem to care even if it is wicked to swear, specially if they mean it, and they usually do, but if Bill hits his thumb with the hammer and cusses out loud right then, he only means it for that minnit when his thumb is hurting like blazes. Boys like Earl and me say pertend swear words like "heck" or "dang it," or "dadburn it," or "doggone it," or "consarn it!" We sound like old Brother Sherburne. Sometimes "geeminy whiz" or "geewhilikers" pops out. Mostly I just say "gosh," which I think myself is too tame to be any kind of cussing. Bigger boys, when they get bunged or mad or even just excited, shout "Judas Priest!" None of us knows for sure what it means, but sounds like something big. I dasn't say it at all on account of Mother claims that is skating right on the edge.

I know a woman in town says "dam" quite a bit but only in a friendly way, like "Mighty dam fine morning, ain't it, Buck?" when she is glad to see me come to get her ripe orangey plums for Mother to make that good jam for her warm biskits. Most of the time Earl and me don't cuss at all, just only when we are hurt or awful mad at something, like stubbing our toes. Seems to me sometimes a real cuss word is the only one that helps my toes stop hurting.

Some folks dasn't cuss and swear even if they are terrible, awful mad and want to cuss so bad they almost bust with it. That was the way with a man from Paragonah traveling through Summit one day. I heard him tell Father how he almost cussed and swore like a Gentile, but he took hisself in hand and prayed the Lord to help him overcome his weakness on account of he is a Bishop and has to set a sample for others. He said it was only a few days ago when it happened, and he was still a good deal shook up about it, but not enuff to cuss anymore. He had a big puffy rag on his fingers which showed he had got hurt bad.

Late in the afternoon he had put a twenty-dollar greenback in his outside coat pocket. His pants pockets had holes from the nails and bolts he carries around, never knowing when he might need one. He didn't want any money to slide through one of the holes. He had sold some pigs to get that twenty-dollar greenback, which we know is a lot of money to have all at once and in just one piece. That night he went to bed leaving the twenty-dollar greenback in his outside coat pocket.

Early next morning he thought that any man which had twenty dollars on him could afford to be nice to his cows and give them a few fresh ears of corn. So he went to his little patch next to his orchard and broke off some ears and put two of them in each coat pocket and carried a few in his hands. He fed them to his cows, one ear at a time. They were standing loose in the corral, like everybody keeps them. Only there was a shed close by for his cows to get under when it rains or the sun gets too hot. He went around giving each cow an ear of juicy corn. One of his best cows is Old Liney, named for the white stripe all the way down her back. He handed her an ear of corn from his coat pocket, and darned if the twenty-dollar greenback, which he had forgot was in this pocket, was stuck to the husk of that corn. She grabbed that ear of corn so fast that only a little strip of the money was sticking out from between her lips. He held on to that ear of corn. Old Liney held on to it, too. He hit her on the nose with his fist to make her let go. She only shook her head and pulled harder on it. He wiggled his fingers into her mouth to get ahold of the greenback. One finger got between her jaws and was mashed. He kicked her on the shins and hurt his toes so awful he thought he broke them.

His finger was hurting and bleeding so bad he had to quit using that hand. His toes were hurting so bad he had to stand almost on only one foot. Still he pulled and jerked at the corn with his other hand. Old Liney pulled at the corn and jerked her head, which knocked the man down in the munoor. When he scrambled up, Old Liney was chewing the corn and the greenback, looking plum satisfied as if nothing had happened. He could see a few green bubbles between her lips. And then corn and greenback slid down her gullet like swallowing her cud. Only this was a twenty-dollar cud and worth more than the cow. That is egzackly when he needed to cuss and swear and grab a club and mash Old Liney's jaws, only it wouldn't do any good now.

He said he never wanted to swear so bad in all his borned days, but it wouldn't of done for folks to hear a Bishop cussing his cow a streak. They would of lost faith in him. Besides, he didn't believe in swearing. It's against the Bible. 'Stead, he grabbed ahold of the top fence pole with his good hand and as much of the hurt hand as he could wrap around it, gritted his teeth a minnit or two, then shouted, "Multipliers and Horse Radish! Multipliers and Horse Radish! MULTIPLIERS AND HORSE RADISH!" fast as he could. "I kept on saying it so I wouldn't choke to death with the madness what was burning me up. They are the hottest and strongest things I could think of, next to real swearing. I kept on sayin' it till I cooled down enuff to breathe."

Sam told me multipliers are little onions half as big as my little finger that grow in bunches. When you pull one out of the bunch, he says two and a half more grow in its place. They're so hot that half a bite, if you chew it, will make you see stars in broad daylight, and your breath smells worse than a skunk's. Multipliers and Horse Radish sounds like it would do the trick for me. I plan to shout it the next time I feel a cuss word coming on. Father said to him, "I don't know what I would do if a cow chewed up a twenty-dollar greenback of mine, mushed my finger, stomped on my toes, and then rolled me in the munoor, besides."

"It's a tryin' sitchyashun, Brother McCarty," the man said, shaking his head and his face looking like he was in Sunday School.

"I don't know how to cuss very well," Father told him. "I'm afraid I'd be like a horse with a tight collar. I'd choke right down and go into a faint for want of breath."

"And mebbee roll in some munoor yourself," I said, kind of laffing. But little boys should keep their mouths shut when their fathers are talking to other men. Right off, that is what Father told me.

Dan Harris is a sort of a batchler which lives in Summit, only not a reggler one like Brother Sherburne and Brother Oakley. They live alone. Dan Harris lives with his mother and his sister.

Not so long ago Dan Harris had cradled his wheat. I mean he got Father to cradle it. Dan does not have a wheat cradle. It was a good-size stack, all right. Him and his mother and sister will have all the bread they want when winter comes. If we run short of flour in our house we will get some of his wheat. He had it stacked on his lot close to the edge of town. A big patch of sunflowers was growing on every side of the stack, all blossomed out in bright yellow flowers.

On a hottish sunshiny day Earl and me were playing in those sunflowers. Don't know how it was we were there, but there we were. We thought sunflowers look more pretty when you are not too close to them. The big sunflowers were so high we had to bend the stalks down to look right at the flowers and we were breaking off the biggest blossoms. Sunflower blossoms don't break off so easy. We should of had a knife to cut them off, but most times Earl nor me don't have a knife. There is lots of gummy stuff on sunflower stalks, we found out.

After a while Earl had some sticky stuff on his hand and between his fingers from the stalks, which there was a lot of. He cussed the sunflowers for it. He only cussed in fun. He didn't mean it. He was not mad at all, but he said words we don't make reggler use of if we don't want soap between our teeth. We both laffed at that. We thought it sounded funny to swear at a sunflower. But things which stick your fingers up like sunflower stalks do ought to have something said to them. Cussing was just the thing to say. Then I used some swear words I have heard, myself, and plum forgot about trying on Multipliers and Horse Radish. We thought we were smart. I cussed my flower on account of it didn't have enuff sticky stuff on it.

It wasn't long till each of us was cussing sunflowers with all the words we could think of. I gritted my teeth and shook my fist at them. I let them know just who was talking to them. The longer we were at it, the more we liked doing it and the smarter it sounded, and the more daring we got. We would bend the stalk down and cuss the flower right to its face, cuss it that it didn't grow any bigger, cuss it that it had too many bugs on it. Sunflower blossoms always have lots of bugs. They crawl and hop into your hands, getting stuck in the sticky stuff. Next thing you know they are on your wrists and crawling up your arm on the skin under your waist sleeve. It took a long time to run out of reasons for cussing them.

When the sun got too hot to stand out in it, we each broke us off the biggest sunflower we could find, then went over to the shade of the wheat stack to sit and cuss our flowers some more. We would look at the flower in the face and cuss and then bust it one with a fist. Pretty soon quite a few sunflowers were all smashed in a heap. We throwed them away and went on swearing without anything to swear at. First we cussed at the same time. We cussed the sun. We cussed the wheat stack for not making more shade. But that wasn't the stack's fault. After a while we looked each other straight in the face and cussed, both at the same time. Earl cussed me. I cussed Earl.

When we got tired we stopped for a while, rested a bit, and chewed some wheat. We had to shell it in our hands. We couldn't shell much at a time; our hands were too covered with sunflower sticky. Licking them didn't help much. While we chewed what we had shelled, we shelled some more. Then we layed on the ground and cussed some more, only not so fast. We almost choked on the wheat in our throats. We sat up quick. Earl said I wasn't doing it right anyways. I could easy see Earl was outswearing me. I was saying the same words too many times. Earl could use more differnt words quite a while before he said the same ones over again. Soon as we took turns, Earl showed me how to do it right. When it was my turn he watched me close, and if I got it wrong he would stop me quick and show me how his pa said it. Once when he stopped me, I said, "Well, that's the way my brother Bill swears it. He's a good cusser, too."

"Aw, Bill can't hardly cuss. I hear him when he's driving Bally and Red out to the field."

"You can't tell only by that," I said back. "He just says things to make them feel he doesn't like them."

"Yah, but Bill's only a big boy yet, ain't he? He's just got fuzz. My pa's a man. He's got whiskers. He's done it a lot more."

"Bill's almost a man. One day when he was chopping wood a stick flew up and hit him on the chin. If you'd of heard him then, I'll bet you would say Bill is a right good cusser."

"Same as us, boys only swear when we get hurt like that, else mad at something. Men swear right along same as they talk, don't they? Boys don't do that."

"You're probly right." I quit sticking up for Bill's swearing. It wasn't any use. Earl could outtalk me same as he could out-swear me.

We started all over again. I got better right along. I got so good I could swear till Earl would have to stop me so he could have another turn. It got to noon awful quick. We been having so much fun we did not notice it had got to be time to eat, and we were hungry. Eating a little shelled wheat did not keep us from getting that way. We made a bargain to go home, eat quick as we could, hurry back to the wheat stack, and spend the after-noon in its shade practicing some more before time to help at home with the chores. We had found a new game, a differnt kind of game, and lots of fun 'cause we were doing something we both knowed we shouldn't, but only in fun. We weren't ever going to really swear. Still, we were glad there wasn't anybody around to hear and go blabbing to our folks.

We chewed a little more wheat and then started for home. When I got there I could tell it was later than we had figgered, and folks were already sitting at the table. I slid onto my stool and ate in a hurry. I wanted to get away soon as I could. I was scairt something might happen to keep me from going back. Mother might come up with something she wanted me to do. Worse, Father might ask me to pull weeds for the pigs. I had heard them squealing when I came into the house. And Mother was just telling Father the weeds were awful high out there in the carrot patch, so high she could hardly find the carrots. I didn't like that kind of talk. Then, too, Mother might ask me to pick threads at the loom. I got off my stool and was leaving.

"What's your hurry, Homer?" Mother asked.

"Why, you haven't eaten half your potatoes and gravy," Father said. "Are you sick or something?"

"Uh-uh! I ain't sick," I said, shaking my head. "Only not so hungry, either. I just want to go out for a few minutes." I slipped out of the room, still quite a bit hungry. If I didn't get back to the wheat stack in a hurry, Earl might think I wasn't coming. Then he would go home, and the whole day would be wasted. I wanted awful bad to spend the afternoon at that wheat stack, not pulling weeds in any old carrot patch.

He was eating wheat in the shade of the stack and gave me some he had shelled out. After that we sat down in the shadiest side, squared ourselfs on the ground, and started up swearing. We found there are lots of things you can do with hell. Just by itself it doesn't sound so bad. Besides it's all over the Bible, and no one says a word against reading it. When you put it with kind of helping words, it can roll off your tongue quick as a wink, like hellfire, or hell's bells, or that one I hear from tired travelers on their way to Dixie who say it's like going to hell in a handcart to get there. Mother says I should leave it alone all together. She doesn't want me to say Judas Priest, even if Bill occasionally does let it pop. Father says that's just a sly way of saying Jesus Christ and we only say that when we read scriptures or pray. We have to be careful not to use the Lord's name in vain. I can't think why goshdarn or goldarn are just another way of saying something you are not s'posed to, even if it only sounds a tiny bit like what you are not s'posed to say. Boys my size use them quite a lot and don't mean a thing by them. We don't even know all the words that these words are another way of saying, but freighters can let rip with everything in the bag. I've heard some. They can thunder, but Father lets it pass.

We drawed cuts to see who would start. Earl won. I never was lucky drawing cuts. I don't see why. This time we took longer turns. Earl cussed me 'cause my father has long legs and big feet. I cussed him 'cause his mother is fat and cannot run very fast. He cussed me 'cause my little sister is a crybaby. I cussed him 'cause his little sister has a sloppy nose most all the time. Between cussings we rolled on the ground laffing at the smart things we could think of, and we were mighty pleased with hell and dam. They don't hide any other words. I tried on gaddamit for a fit and was glad Father couldn't hear it. I knew egzackly what he'd say and do to me.

"Mebbee, Buck, we could swear better if we got mad at each other," Earl said.

I did not know what to think. We never were mad at each other. "But we promised never to get mad, didn't we?" I was scairt he might really be meaning it. "I can't," I said. "There's nothing to be mad at."

"Course we won't ackcherly get mad. I didn't mean that. I just said it."

"We are going to be friends forever and ever, ain't we?" I asked him.

"Yup. We're going to be friends till there ain't any world for folks to live in," he said kind of serious-like, swinging his arms around.

"Wheww-y! We'll be friends till there ain't any stars for folks to look at," I said back to him, pointing my hands at the sky and feeling lightness in my chest.

"Let's shake hands and mean it," Earl said, getting up and reaching to me. We took ahold of each other's hand, but we didn't laff anymore, on account of we meant it. We just looked each other in the eyes. That afternoon went quicker than the morning had. Before we even thought about it the sun was settling on the hills across the valley. We took one or two more short turns, had another good laff, then each went home and figgered it a happy day. I guessed Mother had saved some chores for me to do, even if it was too late to do them now. I also guessed she was probly mad as heck, which I know is just polite for hell, and my supper would be cold potatoes and a scrap of meat.

I was so hungry it tasted good anyways. Just as I finished I felt a hard hand on my shoulder and looked up. Father's eyes were glinting at me from under his brows. "I know that if you can't or won't tell me what you and Earl been up to today, then I know it is something that shames you and would shame Mother and me."

"We were teaching each other how to cuss. We didn't mean anything by it."

Father leaned down and brought his lips to my ear. "You are just a small boy getting too big for his britches. If I hear just one of those words from you I will whup your britches till they smoke." That made it much more easier for me to hold back when I was itching to sound off with something that would take care of any itch.

HANDS, FEET, AND MY MOUTH OF SHAME

It is funny about my hands and feet. Sometimes they act like they got sense, and sometimes they don't. My right hand and foot know how to do things better than my left ones do, probly on account of they are doing things all the time and are more used to doing it. My left ones only know how to keep from getting hurt, which I wish my right ones knowed as much. Seems I am right-footed and right-handed in most everything I do. If there is anything on the path where I am walking which looks like a toe is going to stub against it, my left foot stays behind a step or half a step. It always lets the right foot go ahead and bang the thing. Could be a rock or a piece of board, whatever is sharp and hard.

My big toe sticks out in front of all the others. It is the one the right foot does the banging with and gets most of the punishment. Seems the left foot goes along just to be there when the right big toe bangs something. Then I can hop around on the left foot while I try to hold the hurting one in my hands. If the hurt is really bad I sit down and try to put the bloody toe in my mouth. It helps if I can kind of suck on it.

My right hand, same as my right foot, gets in trouble lots more than my left one. It is my right hand which goes farthest under a slab or piece of timber or something else we are lifting. Then if the slab slips back, my right fingers get squoze the worst. One time the nail on one of my fingers got took off that way. It did grow back, but took a long time to do it. Seems it is always my right hand which grabs ahold of stinging nettles, not on purpose but just 'cause it is the habit that hand has. Left hands don't do foolish things like that.

One night Father was out in the yard doing some chores in the dark. The big boys had gone to Parowan to a dance, and it was up to Father to do the chores by his lonesome. A wind came up and blew his old hat off his head. Everything that was loose was whizzing up in the air. If a wind sends things up in the air it is a whirlwind. I know all about whirlwinds and straight winds. It was a whirlwind took off his hat and sent it sailing. Next morning he could not find that old hat, which did not worry him. It was just old and good for nothing. Mother had told him if his hair grew straight up like his whiskers grow straight down it would stick up through the holes of that hat like a pair of mule ears.

Just the same, if Father had not of had that old hat down at the Little Salt Lake when we were salting, he would not of been able to wrap up both my burnt chappy feet that I dunked in the danged saltwater. I am glad he wore it then. But he was sort of 'shamed of it and only wore it when neighbors could not see, or down to the lake, or up in the hills when he went for wood, or in the canyon when he cut poles. He needed a better hat for church. When he came into the house that night and told us his hat had finally blown away, Mother said she wished it would keep on going to the other side of Paragonah.

But it turned out the hat wasn't so far away as everybody hoped. It was only around the corner of the corral and stuck in some stickery bushes on the side farthest from the house. After a few days of nobody looking very much, I was the first to find it when I was snooping around looking for a bird's nest. A mother bird had been flying back and forth with worms in her mouth. I poked in the weeds, and there was Father's old hat, looking dirty and mussy, but not much more than it always looked. When I saw it there in the weeds, my left hand did not care a thing about that hat. But my right hand was differnt. It wanted to see what was under that mussy old hat and in a hurry to find out. My left hand was willing to hold the weeds apart.

My right hand dove down and kind of wiggled the hat upside down. There in plain sight was a mouse nest. I could not see any babies in it. Guess the nest wasn't ready for them yet, else they were covered up with that furry-looking stuff. My left fingers would not go down to feel around. They stayed back and only held the weeds. My right fingers reached down and wiggled the furry stuff to one side. SNAP! My finger was bit! Quicker than scat the mother mouse which I hadn't seen had jabbed her teeth into my finger, clear to the bone, it felt. She beat it as soon as her jaws done their work on my finger, which was already bleeding and hurting so bad I could of kilt every mouse in Summit if I could of got ahold of them. I jumped up and down on that old hat till I had tromped it to pieces. If there were baby mice, I did not care. Even being barefoot I did not care about the stickery weeds. I was not thinking about stickers.

I ran back to the house, holding my bloody finger in the air for Mother to see. She looked a little worried on account of she was thinking I might get lockjaw, but I didn't. She cleaned it up good and tied a little rag around that finger and told me to stay away from mice and gofers and other critters that bit. Which I do, with gofers. I always have a stick with me. Everybody knows they can take a finger off with one bite. I should have a stick to kill mice with. All they want to do is bite you and give you lockjaw if they can.

My right foot is worse than my right hand getting into trouble. Mostly, without even watching, I know where my fingers are going. I do not need for them to get bit or stung, not if I watch out. It is differnt with feet. I cannot be watching my feet all the time. Seems they are always moving. I want to see things around me when I am walking, things on the ground and in the air, things a long ways off and close by. If I have to be watching my feet all the time, how can I see buzzards or bees, jackrabbits or flowers? How can I see people or cattle or houses or mountains or anything but my feet? I could just as well stay home.

Not long ago I was chasing a little pig to get it back in the pen. No one saw it but me. Little pigs can run mighty fast, and I was holding my breath and running hard as I could, watching that pig close as I could 'cause it might jump sideways. Little pigs are that way. I did not see a cedar post laying in the weeds. Even if I was running fast, my left foot was watching out for itself, hanging back a little. It must of knowed weeds have lots of stuff laying in them that will hurt a bare foot. Sure enuff, the big toe of my right foot banged that cedar post, KERWHACK!

Over I went, sprawling in the weeds and hollering bloody murder. I took ahold of my right foot, trembling something awful on account of the big toe was bleeding a reggler stream. I tried to put it in my mouth. That didn't help a mite. My whole foot and leg and everything inside me was hurting so much I wanted to die right then, stay dead a whole day or week. Finally

I was able to half limp, half crawl to the house. Mother was in the kitchen washing pans and things. She had been washing the churn, which was why she hadn't heard me hollering. Right quick she got a basin of water and washed the blood off my face and wiped my waist best she could. She soaked my foot in clean water and put the salve and a cloth on my busted toe. She guessed the nail might come off, but it hung on for a while more. She let me lay on her bed while she went out to slop the squealing pigs. When she came in the house she told me the little pig had come back by itself and got into the pen. It was just too bad, she said, I had hurt my toe for nothing. That made me so mad at the pig that the hurt started up all over again. Good thing I did not have ahold of his leg with the left hand and a club in my right hand, or I would of give him a whole lot worse than a stubbed toe.

Earl and me talk a lot about our feet and all the hurt they are to us. Mother says our feet would be just fine if only we put them into shoes reggler and do our running around in them. Right now she says she doubts I will grow up with two working hands and feet. I can easy tell that could happen. Sam says a big toe hurts so much on account of it does not know how else to feel. Wish I could laff like him, but he is not the one getting stubbed. I walked around on my heel. Even to think of stubbing it again made me almost sick. I kept the toe sticking up in the air out of reach of stones and sticks and other things laying around waiting for feet. I didn't go uptown. Rebecca might see me walking on my heel. I only limped around the yard.

Earl came over every day about, and we sat by the coop or under the shed and played ginny peg. I had to be careful with every step to let the heel down to the ground slow and easy. I looked funny when I walked. In the house I felt more safe, but the toe was not sure about things there, either. It seemed to know I could bump against a chair leg or the corner of the door or the spinning wheel leg. It wanted to stick up even in the house. It knowed there could be trouble, 'cause trouble follows me.

We got a old rag carpet in our front room. Mother made it when I was too little to pick threads. It has got ragged spots in it where it is always walked on between the front door and the kitchen. You can easy see the walked-on places. About in the middle is one of the ragged spots, a strip of loose warp all doubled up in a little loop, just big enuff to fit a boy's toe, but I did not know the loop was there, and Mother did not know either, on account of it was hard to see if you were just walking on the rug. Afterwards she said she thought that loop had been hiding, just waiting for me to come along with a sore toe. I know, myself, it did. The spot is close to the spinning wheel where Mother walks frontwards and backwards spinning the yarn. Her wheel is the tall kind, taller than her head. She walks three steps forwards, then three steps backwards, and keeps doing that all the time she is spinning. She has told me that even if she did walk nearly all the way to Salt Lake City when she was just a tad older than me, she has gone twice that far just walking her walk by that old spinning wheel.

One day when that sore toe and me were out in front of the house just fooling around, I got thirsty and walked slow and easy into the house for a cup of water. My toe wanted to stand up, but I wouldn't let it and made that toe lay flat down same as the others were doing. That was when my toe had more sense than me. I started along the path on the carpet towards the kitchen. The water bucket always stands on a bench there. My tender toe had layed down and was doing what I wanted it to do. In full swing of a step that toe caught the warp loop. I mean the warp loop caught my tender toe BANG! under the nail, and down to the floor I fell, grabbing ahold of my bleeding, murdered foot.

I ripped out three or four verses of my wheat-stack cussing, and I did it in one long screeching rip. Mother's eyebrows shot up into her hair, and she fell into a chair as if someone had hit her, for the while that I was rolling on the floor like a chicken with its head chopped off, damming and hell-firing the carpet, the warp, the spinning wheel, and everything else in sight. Earl and me had learnt to swear just in time. Right at the top of my swearing Mother ran over to me and cried out, "My boy! Where on earth did you ever learn those awful, terrible words?" I heard what she said, all right, but I did not care, and she did not seem to care that I had been good as kilt before her very eyes.

Once more and lots of times after, I let out a sight more of that wheat-stack talk as fast as I could yell them. I kept those words busting all over the room. At first Mother must of been scairt to even try to touch me, I was so wild. After what seemed a long time my screaming and swearing got to be fainter and fainter on account of I ran out of breath and could not do more than squeak a whisper. I knew then I was dying for sure. I could just barely tell that Mother was putting something on my toe smelling like tar off a wagon wheel. She wrapped my toe in soft cloths that felt so good after all the hurting. I layed still and let her do all these sweet things. My face and mouth had got bloody, too, where I tried to jam that toe in my mouth. She wiped me off with a warm wet cloth. Then she wiped the blood off the carpet, too. I was all wore out. Mother took me over to her bed in the corner, and I went to sleep.

When I waked up, Mother was walking back and forth at the spinning wheel. She could see I had waked up, stopped her wheel, and came over to me. She did not scold, as she could of done. I could tell she felt bad for me. She gave me a kind of nice talk, like she always does when I have forgot the rules. She told me how sorry she was I been hurt so bad, but how wicked it was for me to use that as a reason to swear the way I did. It was worse than awful, it was terrible! It hurt her ears and heart.

I did feel bad about all that cussing. I had not meant to let it out. Earl and me had learnt it just for fun, but we were not going to use it and really swear, not ever. I would not of done it, I knowed for sure, if it hadn't of been for that hellfire crazy carpet loop. Mother gave me a sharp look. Quick I promised her I would never, ever use such words any more. I would forget how to swear. When Earl came over to see how my toe was doing we talked about it. We thought we could quit as easy as we learnt it, and we made a bargain to never swear again anymore, anywheres, anyhow. But that is a hard bargain to keep. Sam says it must be the Irish in me.

A WONDERFUL THING

A Wonderful Thing is coming to Summit. Earl came running down to our house to tell us. Bolting through our front door, which was open, he nearly fell into our loom. Mother has the loom where she can have more light to work by when the door is open. Course we don't keep the door open when it's cold or wet or windy. But when I pick threads I need good light, too, and I was helping her when Earl came busting in to tell us about the Wonderful Thing, which he said is going to be in our schoolhouse right away. Earl was about out of breath when he started telling us of the Wonderful Thing which would be a very special occasion for everyone.

Mother asked how he knew about it, and he said his ma just got home from Brother Bartlett's place where the man is camping who is bringing the Wonderful Thing to Summit. Brother Bartlett said that over in Parowan the man had to show the Wonderful Thing three nights so all the town could get a chance to see it. Lots of folks went all three nights.

"Hold on a minnit," I almost hollered at Earl. "What is a Wonderful Thing?"

"Ma says it's a Panner-rammer."

"Well, what in tarnation is a Panner-rammer? I never heard of such a thing."

"I'm same as you," Earl said. "All I know is Ma thinks it is lots of pitchers of things to look at. My Aunt Lillie saw it in Parowan and says it is the most wonderful thing that will ever come to Summit, and anyone who doesn't go see it will only show they don't have good sense. Ma's going, and so am I. You can count on it."

"What kind of pitchers does it show?" I asked soon as he quit talking a second.

"Things all over the world and in history, that's what. Lots of pitchers are of things so far off there's nobody ever seen 'em yet. That's what my aunt says. And things which happened long time ago and not so long ago."

I had a sudden hankering to see things which nobody else ever saw. "Do we just see or do we have to pay?"

"You bet we do. My aunt says big folks pay two bits. Kids size of us a dime."

Mother stood up from the loom and said she would go get the details from Earl's mother so she would know if the Wonderful Thing would be worth the cost. She learned a lot. A woman told Earl's ma the Panner-rammer would be better than a whole year's schooling to the Young and Rising Generation. That's what boys and girls like Earl and me are, the Young and Rising Generation. When we are big and married we will be farmers, carpenters, shoemakers, blacksmiths, and teachers. Then our children will be the Young and Rising Generation. That is the way it goes with human beans.

If anybody don't have the money, the man will take hen eggs, dime a dozen if the eggs are fresh. That is what the man had told Mr. Bartlett. Earl's aunt says a person shouldn't miss seeing it even if you have to go out and steal the eggs. "Course," his aunt said, "I don't mean you had ought to go right out and really steal eggs. That would be downright stealing. I only mean it would be worth that much to anyone to get to see such a Wonderful Thing."

Mother said if I want to go she would give me the dime. Sam and Emily will want to go, too. She would like to see it herself, but she'll have to stay at home with Ellie who is feeling so poorly Mother doesn't think she should leave her. Ellie's feet and legs are swoll up so she can hardly step out of bed and to the table to eat with us. "Homer can tell me all about it afterward," she said. I smiled quick at her. She knows I like to tell about things.

Soon as the men with the Panner-rammer got set up at the schoolhouse next day, Sam and Emily and me went over specially early to find a good place to see. When we got there it looked like most of the town had come early also, only earlier than us. The room was full, lots more folks inside than comes reggler to Sunday School. There was a big bucket full of white eggs and brown ones standing on a little bench close to the door and a woman taking the money. Folks were all talking to each other and laffing and making a heckuva noise. Children mostly were running around the room, dodging benches or scuffling for seats. It was the first time any of us been to a thing like a Panner-rammer, and there wasn't anyone knowed egzackly how to act. We were all plum excited, only it's a differnt excitement you feel when you don't know what it is you are feeling excited about.

While Sam was paying the woman at the door our money, I saw Earl on a bench just behind the front row trying to hold a seat for somebody and having a tuff time keeping other boys away. I knowed right off that seat was for me. Quick I left Sam and Emily and made a dive through that noisy crowd and flopped myself down next to Earl. Just in time, too. A bigger boy had seen the place and was on the run to get it. I could tell it was Abner, one of the Bishop's bigger boys and a bully. He grabbed my waist and tried to yank me off the bench. But I don't yank so easy. He pulled and yanked, but I held on to the bench with both hands.

"Git off this place! It's mine." He gave another yank

"I got here first. It's mine, and I won't get off it." I gritted my teeth to hang on.

"It's Buck's place," Earl said. "I been saving it for him."

"You shut up, you little feist, or I'll pull your nose."

"Just you dast," Earl said quick back to him, jumping up and giving him a shove. I twisted around and gave him a punch in the belly. "Let go my waist or I'll bust your snoot." I drew back my hand to hit again.

"Well, I ain't gonna fight in here on account of it's the Sunday School house," he said in a growly voice, "but just wait till I catch you runts outside." Off he stomped into the crowd. Folks laffed when they saw the set-to. He was bigger than us, but there were two of us and only one of him. Earl and me could of knocked the stuffing out of him same as we did Earl's brother.

Only little children were in front of us, and we could easy look over their heads. The Panner-rammer would be right in front of us. Up on the platform where the Bishop and other men sit when we have meetings or Sunday School and where the members which do the singing sits, too, we could see a long piece of cloth wider than a man is tall. Each end of the cloth was wrapped around a smooth pole higher than the cloth was wide. The poles stood up straight, one pole at one end of the platform, the other close to the other end of the platform, and back from the edge about a foot or two. There were three or four big candles on the edge. I could tell they were ready to light on account of someone was snipping the tallow off the little ends.

While we waited for the show to get going I could see somebody moving behind the white cloth. Still nothing happened. I turned around to look at the people in the room. I know about everybody in town and wanted to see which of them had come. I had to stand up on the bench to see over the folks sitting behind us. It was darkish in the room on account of they did not have enuff candles on the walls. All of a sudden—oh m'gosh!—there sat Rebecca and her mother, a little ways from us off to one side. Quicker than scat I sat down, not letting on I had seen anybody. Folding my arms I looked straight ahead at the Panner-rammer cloth.

After a few seconds I turned my head sideways, careful-like, to look at Rebecca. She was looking in my direction. We looked at each other, and she kind of smiled, at least that is what I think she did. My heart quit beating. Felt like everything in me had quit, too. But no matter, it felt good. Soon as everything got going inside me again, I sat up straight and looked in front of me, only I had my eyes shut so I could see Rebecca without turning around. When you shut your eyes they can see things good in your head, a long ways off or close by. You can see them in front of you or behind you. Now I was looking at someone behind me, Rebecca.

"If you people will come to order we will open the Panner-rammer with a word of prayer." I opened my eyes, but only for a jiffy. It was the Bishop standing at the edge of the platform. When he said, "Come to order," I knowed he didn't mean me on account of I was already in order and had been ever since Rebecca looked at me. And I was going to stay in order from now on, too. I didn't care how long the man prayed. I have heard him pray before, and he gives long ones. While he was at it I looked at Rebecca in my head. When he quit praying, which was quite a while, Earl's Uncle Lorenzo lighted the candles on the platform and asked someone to blow out the candles on the walls. At the same time someone put out the light behind the cloth. Now everything was dark except for the candles at the edge of the platform in front of the poles, which would be enuff light for us to see what would be on the cloth. I was glad we had such good seats.

Two men stood by the poles, one at each pole. The part of the cloth we could see between the two poles was plain white, without anything on it to tell us what the Wonderful Thing would be. The pole which had only a little bit of the cloth wrapped around it had a handle same as a grindstone handle, only longer. The other man stood by the wrapped pole and held a long slim stick. Just then, when the candles on the walls got blowed out, the woman who had taken our dimes at the door started making music on a little organ box that stood by the pole with the grindstone handle. The man bent his back and used both hands to begin winding the cloth from the other pole. I held my breath. Everybody sat still. We all bugged out our eyes to see what we might see. The music and the moving cloth made us all feel queery.

The edge of a pitcher started unwrapping itself from around the first pole. Out it came and out it came till there it was, a town with houses close together, with strange-looking pointy roofs. People were on the street, all wearing big clumsy shoes that looked like they were made of wood with sharp toes pointing upwards. The men wore funny wide pants. The women had red cheeks and white aprons. A few chickens and a dog or two were on the street with them. The man with the stick said these people were in Holland, which is far, far away from Utah Territory, and across a big piece of sea water besides, the Atlantic Ocean.

The man with the stick started talking and pointed things out with his stick that we should look at in the next pitcher. He pointed out a man coming down the street leading a jackass which had a load of sticks on its back. Earl and me looked at each other. We did not think the pitcher amounted to much. After a pitcher or two came one where a man was riding a little jackass along the road all by theirselfs. The jackass looked so awful tired he couldn't hardly keep going. The man was so big his legs reached almost to the ground. Next pitcher, they had met another man, this one walking. Right straight he told the first man he ought to be 'shamed riding a little jackass till it was all tuckered out and him so big. The man with the pointer was telling us what the men said to each other. If he hadn't, I would not of knowed. The walking man told the riding man he ought to carry the jackass a while till it was rested up enuff to carry him some more. Next pitcher, the jackass was riding on the back of the man, who looked just as tired as the jackass had. Now the man's knees were bent and looked trembly. We could tell the jackass was hee-hawing for all he was worth. The cloth jiggled a little and made the man look like he was going to fall over with the jackass. People busted out laffing at that.

Then the stick man hollered out, "NEXT, SEVEN WONDERS OF THE WORLD!" Everybody was making so much noise talking about what they had just seen that the man had to holler good and loud. A pitcher was crawling out from the pole of a tall, round house, taller than round, with lots of doors and windows in it. People were looking out of them. You could tell it was awful tall 'cause it leaned way over to the side and looked like it would fall over any minnit and smash people standing under it.

"What a big lie that is," I whispered to Earl.

"Course it's a lie," he whispered back at me. "Anyone leanin' over like that would fall and bust his head if he didn't grab ahold of something." Pretty quick that pitcher rolled past us and wrapped itself around the pole with the handle.

Right behind it came "ANOTHER OF THE SEVEN WONDERS OF THE WORLD!" This pitcher was a great big man, sort of gold-colored, standing up straight like a stachoo. He looked to be reaching the sky he was so tall, and he was astraddle a big water place. Could of been a lake, mebbee even bigger. His straddle was so wide and his legs reached up so far before that a tall pine tree could of stood between them without it scratching his skin, and it looked like he was wearing only a kind of little short skirt. He 'peared to be holding up a big ball into the clouds.

"That's another big lie," Earl hissed at me. "I'll bet Pa will tell this man what he thinks if he keeps on showing big lies."

"How could any stachoo get so high up as that?" I hissed back.

"Don't see how we're s'posed to learn anything if it's all lies," Earl shot back.

"When I tell Mother 'bout these lies, she will be glad she didn't come," I said and squinted a look over at Rebecca. Seemed like she'd been looking at us, too, 'cause we were being noisy. We quit whispering then for quite a while. I sat up straight and looked at the stachoo man. Might be Rebecca was looking at us yet. The light from the candles in front of the cloth made it so I could see people good close behind us. Back a ways it was darker.

After a few other pitchers had gone by there came one about a big battle. The man with the handle stopped turning when the pitcher got in front of us. He wiped his forehead with his big red hankerchiff and wiped behind his ears and under his chin which did not have many whiskers on it. He had not rested for quite a while, you could tell. "THE GREAT BATTLE OF WATERLOO!" hollered the man with the pointing stick. The pitcher jiggled a little. Soljers were fighting each other, stabbing with swords and sharp-pointed knives on the ends of their guns. They were wearing soljer clothes with white pants and black knee boots. Men, some of them all bloody, were falling off their horses. Dead men were layin' all over the ground. There was blood all around. Some soljers did not seem so dead as others. The horses had bulging eyes and red nose holes and looked scairt to death their ownselfs. One man was wearing a sharp-cornered hat and sitting on a fine white horse which had wild eyes and stuck his head frontwards and bared his teeth like he wanted to bite somebody. This man held a sword in his hand, but he was not fighting anybody. His horse was standing still, and a good thing he was on account of the man had his other hand shoved under his coat and on his buzzum. Don't know how he stayed on his horse. He was wearing white pants which fit his legs tight and shiny black high boots. Some men standing on the ground close by looked like they wanted to talk to that man on the white horse, but he only looked straight ahead at what was going on and did not notice the soljers a bit.

"NAPOLEON BONE-APART!" shouted the man telling about the pitchers. He pointed his long stick at the man on the white horse. I could not unerstand how he could be there with that awful battle going on around him and not use his sword or take his hand out of his buzzum or even notice what was going on when all the soljers were dying. It looked like everywhere men were trying to kill each other and horses were running around without anyone in the saddles, looking wild and scairt. The man on the handle worked his long handle fast as he could, which made the cloth jiggle and jiggle, while the woman made music on her little box organ louder and louder, which made the soljers and horses look like they were fighting like sixty.

"Do you believe this, Buck?" Earl whispered. "What a awful fight!" The pitcher was winding up around the pole.

"Gosh, I can't hardly believe what we are seeing. Wonder if old General Johnston's Army wanted to fight like that and kill all the men and horses in Salt Lake City." But we didn't know any more about him than about this Bone-apart.

When that pitcher got wound on the other pole, right behind it came a pitcher of another army. The man with the stick called out, "The Famous Mormon Battalion!" We looked at each other at the same time. We did not know there were so many armies, and now here comes another one we have not heard about. Mebbee Father or Earl's pa never heard about it, too. Then Earl whispered, "If the Mormons got a Battalion Army, why didn't it fight old Johnston's Army right there in Salt Lake City?" Somebody's hand tapped my shoulder hard from behind, and we quit whispering.

Right there in front of us was the Mormon Battalion. We could see it was a long line of soljers with guns on their shoulders. They didn't look much like soljers, more like plain raggedy men, and some of them plum barefoot. They had plenty whiskers on their faces and wore funny flattish caps which fit close down on their heads and had kind of like little porches in front to keep the hot sunshine out of their eyes. They were walking two by two. Earl's pa calls that marching. The men who had charge of the marching men rode horses with saddles and had on nice clothes and high-top boots. If I was a Mormon Battalion soljer, I would ruther be riding a horse and wearing good clothes. This army had mules to pull their big heavy wagons with, and it seemed to take two or three spans of mules to pull only one wagon. Don't know what was in it, but it must of been heavy.

These soljers marched by the side of a good-size stream of water which had lots of trees and willows growing alongside. We could see a bunch of wild bulls standing in the trees looking at that army marching past their willows and stream.

Next pitcher showed the soljers, marching right along behaving theirselfs, minding their own bizness, when all of a sudden, out of the trees and willows charged that herd of wild bulls. The pointer man was telling all about everything which was happening. These were specially mean and wild bulls, with terrible long horns. Never seen any like them and would never wish to. The bulls were mad, you could tell, and wanted to fight. Before those soljers knowed what was up, the bulls were hooking the stuffing out of their mules and pitching them over on their backs and boosting them up in the air. With their long horns they were tearing them to pieces. One mule which was pitched high in the air had its insides falling out.

Next pitcher the men shot off their guns, but didn't seem to hit many of the bulls which were tipping the wagons over and chasing the men. Some men were climbing trees to get out of the way, some were hooked by those horns awful bad. No one looked able to shoot the bulls, but I think it was on account of they had buck fever, which is when you get so wound up with the jitters that you cannot shoot straight. After they had got their guns loaded again they started shooting the bulls right on target. By that time some of the soljers were hooked in their legs and even in their bodies, and some looked almost dead. Some mules had to be shot. A lot of bulls were laying around plum dead. What bulls did not get kilt were running back to the trees and willows, and men were starting to climb down out of the trees.

Still another pitcher showed one man shooting a big black bull which was coming at him in a wild, mad gallop. He had got really close before the soljer shot him in the head, and the bull dropped, dead as nits. Even the pointer man got loud and proud telling us about the big bull fight. Sam told me later that bull fight was the only time the Mormon Battalion fired its guns in their long march all over the Territory clear to Californy. No wonder the pointer man was loud and proud.

"This is the best thing, all right, what has ever come to Summit," I almost said out loud.

"It's the best thing whatever to come to any town," Earl agreed.

"Just like your Aunt Lillie said. This is better than going to school a whole year." I felt like crowing. Even Sam told me later that the Panner-rammer was really something to see, specially since he already knowed this bit about the bulls and probly quite a bit more about the Mormon Battalion.

Then came "JOSEPH SMITH'S FIRST VISION!" Everyone got very still. First of all was a pitcher of tall trees and a boy about the size of Sam laying on his back among them and looking up at a couple of men with long white whiskers and wearing those long women's clothes like they do in the Bible, standing in the air above him in a burst of bright light. One of them was God, the man said. It was the first time I ever seen God. His pitcher is not in our Bible. I had looked for it. Jesus was the other man, and he was old, too, lots older than his pitchers in the Bible. His hair was white and so were his whiskers, just like God's. They looked just about the same.

Earl and me stooped our heads down a bit to whisper. We did not like to think God was getting old. People die when they get old. He must of been getting old a long time, but Jesus must of got old quick to have so much white hair and whiskers. "If God dies, who will be God after him?" Earl whispered.

"Guess Brigham Young will. He comes next to God, don't he?" I whispered back.

"Pa says he would like to be God for just one day. If he could he would straighten things out a whole lot better than what they be."

"I bet he would, all right. Your pa is right smart."

"Ma tells him she is mighty glad he ain't God. 'It is tuff enuff to live with you now,' she told him."

"Sometimes fathers and mothers talk back to each other, don't they?" I whispered.

"Uh-huh. Sometimes Ma and Pa do. I've heard it lots. But Pa only says the first words. Ma says all the rest."

"I heard Father say he is glad he ain't God on account of he has more than he can handle with only a couple of women and a pack of children. He says if he had all of them on his hands all the time, he would go crazy before the sun went down."

"That's my folks, too. Ma told Pa she can't see why all the women which have to live with men haven't gone crazy years ago."

"Martyrdom of the Prophet Joseph Smith!" hollered the man which talked about the pitchers. Quick as cats we straightened our necks and backs and quit whispering. Seems we had missed some pitchers. Now the Panner-rammer was showing a big house which didn't look like it but was a jailhouse. Joseph Smith was a growed man now and looking out of a upstairs window. On the ground close by the house were lots of men and soljers with guns standing around looking up at Joseph with mean looks.

Next pitcher the men and soljers were shooting their guns at Joseph, and he was falling out of the window. Next pitcher some men had pulled him over to a well and leaned him against it. He was dead; you could tell by the blood where they had shot him. A man with his sleeves rolled up and waving a long butcher knife in his hand was hurrying toward Joseph to cut his head off. Which I guess he would of, he was still so mad. But a bright light flashed from heaven, quick as lightning, and struck him dum, and he fell over in the next pitcher like he was dead. Some others of the men and soljers who were standing too close to the light got struck dum, too, and were laying on the ground looking dead. Some staggered around like drunks and probly could not see a thing. The pointer man told us that God would not allow any of the mobbers what had just kilt Joseph Smith to do any more hurt to him. If he had not told us, I would not of knowed what everything in the pitcher meant.

In the last pitcher all the men and soljers were running away fast as they could, throwing down their guns and hiding their faces. And then all the pitchers were wound up on the pole, and the man with the stick said the Panner-rammer was over. Earl's grandpa, Brother Throstle, stood up in front of the candles and told us all to come to order. He has white whiskers, too. Soon as we all sat still he held up his arms and prayed. Old men pray longer than young ones do, lots longer. After he said "Amen," one of the Bishop's bigger boys, but not Abner, jumped up and grabbed one of the candles in front of the Panner-rammer and lit the candle above the door, then blowed out the one he had in his hand. Right straight people started crowding toward the door, talking to each other and telling someone else what a wonderful thing the Panner-rammer was.

"My, oh my! Wasn't it just wonderful!" a woman said to Earl's Aunt Sophie, who had come because her sister, Aunt Lillie, said she ought to. "And so instructive!" Aunt Sophie nodded and wiggled her head back at the woman.

"I'm so glad to see so many of the Young and Risin' Generation out to see it," spoke up a short and chunky woman.

"There's lots of things in this old world we don't know about, ain't there?" Brother Oakley, the batchler what lives in the little dug-out house, said, putting his crumpled hat on his head and waddling kind of slow behind the big jam of people towards the door. No one but Earl and me heard him on account of he was talking to the backs of everybody. Everyone knows his feet are awful sore. That is why he waddles when he walks and had stayed behind the crowd. I don't blame him. I would, too, if I was him and had his feet. When you got only one sore foot, you limp. If you got two sore feet you can't limp on account of you don't have a well foot to stand on while you limp with the hurting one. Then when you walk you have to waddle along slow, same as a duck. You sort of favor one foot and then the other. Earl and me were already watching where we walked so no one would step on our bare feet, which I think, myself, would make us limp or even waddle, too.

We had been gawping too much at everyone pushing towards the door. When I looked for Rebecca she was not anywhere I could see in the crowd and probly was already on her way home with her mother. Doggone it! Wished I had not gawped so much. But I could not see so good anyways, with everybody standing up and the room kind of dark on account of the candle above the door did not make much light. Some other barefoot boys and girls in the crowd were minding their feet same as us. After a while we stepped outside in the cool, fresh night. Earl's Aunt Sophie walked away with him, and I saw Sam and Emily by the door waiting to take me home. We had lots to talk about on the way.

My mind was whirling with all the wonderful things I seen. There was so much it was kind of a jumble. I wondered what Summit folks would say if a man in wide blue pants and wooden shoes walked into town. I wondered how long the stachoo man holding up that big ball had been doing it and where. But mostly my mind was full of wild bulls with terrible horns and soljers trying to shoot their guns at them. I wondered what would of happened if that fancy Bone-apart had been there with them, if he would of just sat there in his fine saddle and not raised a hand to help those soljers, like he was not doing before. And I don't unerstand, if the Lord did not want any more hurt give to Joseph Smith when he layed dead in front of the jail, why he let him be kilt at all.

Sam already knows a lot of things and told me the Battalion was a army of Mormons in 1846, before Brigham Young got out here to Zion, which the American guvment asked to go with some reggler army all the way across the big desert Territory to Californy making trails for them. The guvment thanks was to give Mormons part of that Territory for Zion when they came west in 1847. After it was took from Mexico. Sam guesses no one else was crazy enuff to be interested in that desert land. After that, the Mormons had to take their Territory from the Injuns, same as the guvment done from the Mexicans, but not as soljers. Still, Injuns don't give up so easy as Mexicans. They are still mad and kicking about it. Guess that is why they scowl and look fierce when they come to camp by Summit and have to go begging. The Panner-rammmer showed me it's a long haul before I will have sense to unerstand all the things I think I know.

PART TWO

TO PIOCHE AND BACK

STARTING OUT

We've had the Fourth of July. Men had horse races and foot races. Some wrestled each other, and some boxed to see which could knock the other man's hat off. We had a meeting in the schoolhouse where the Bishop and several more men gave speeches about the flag and how good it is to be an American, a Saint, and to live in the Territory. We hurrahed a lot, and outside some of the big boys and men shot off guns.

In the afternoon us children had a dance in the schoolhouse. I been waiting a long time for another dance like the one Earl and me went to first. My striped waist and spotted galluses didn't look so fresh as they did that first dance on account of I been wearing them reggler, and you can't wear clothes all the time without they get to looking kind of old. Mother washes my waist every week for Sunday School. Usually she just brushes up my pants, unless I have got them greasy, like riding bucks with Earl. She only just brushed them for the dance. She said I didn't need to dandy up to look handsome.

Just as I was hoping, Rebecca was there, and wearing her pretty blue Sunday School dress. This time I think I would of asked her to dance, but bigger boys pushed and got in the way and stepped on my toes. I couldn't of felt worse. But I didn't let on how I was feeling. All of a sudden the leader of the dance called out, "Girls choose partners this time. Make it snappy!"

Right off, Rebecca came straight across the room to where Earl and me sat. I could see her smile the sweetest smile what ever was. I'll bet lots of those boys thought she was going to choose one of them, but she said, "Buck, will you come dance with me?" Would I! My insides liked to bust with happiness. She must of forgot my blowed-up valentine. That was the best Fourth of July I ever had.

The weather is hot now. Father figgers he better go over to Pioche with a load of chickens and eggs and other things while the sun is shining. By and by it might storm. He doesn't want to get stuck in gumbo. He's been buying a lot of old hens and young roosters. Our coop is plum full of chickens, and we got a lot more in a pen by the corral. In the morning all the roosters want to crow at the same time. You can easy tell when our big red rooster crows. His crow goes high and all around in the air. He knows how to do it. Young roosters don't crow, least not a reggler crow, only a kind of squeak, like their throats are too thin.

Besides eggs and chickens, Father will take a load of cured hams and bacon. He'll take sacks of flour, too. Folks always have to have flour and meat, specially hungry Pioche miners, Mother says. Flour and meat are heavy, but they don't take up much room in the wagon. Room in the wagon is what he's scarce of.

At breakfast he said he would try to load up tomorrow and be off next day or the day after that. He wants to get there and back before it rains. He says the 'Scalanty desert is a terrible place to be when the road is mud and gumbo. It's a hunnert miles to Pioche from Summit, mebbee a little more. He doesn't use the ox team to go over there on account of horses move faster and get you through the heat sooner. Pioche is in Nevada. Summit is in Utah. Father says Nevada towns are wild and woolly, but Utah towns are pe-cool-yer, and that's why Nevada is a State and Utah is a Territory. I never been to a State.

All the way to Pioche it's desert and dry hills. There's water only once after Iron Spring and not a thing to see or hear along the whole road, only wind and dust. The horses sweat like sixty, and you sit on the springseat and sweat same as horses. Father knows, he's been out to Pioche lots of times. He says if he can't teach school, he would ruther peddle or freight than farm. Laura and I have gone peddling with him when he went east through the mountain road over to the Sevier country and then south to Pangwitch. He has been as far south as Orderville with my sisters. They say it's pretty down there, green cedar hills and red bluffs. Usually Sam or Bill goes with him to Pioche. There's lots of men who freight and peddle there. Earl and me see wagons every week heading down our road towards Johnson's Fort and the desert trail. Seems folks out there in Nevada don't grow things, only dig them out of the ground, gold and silver mostly. Father says that's a good thing for Utah farmers. They can take grain and hay, flour and meat and chickens, fruit and salt, wine, lumber and timber and shingles out to the miners and bring back money, which we don't grow enuff of for anybody to notice.

After breakfast Father said to Mother, "Jim and Bill are working at Ray Linn's ranch this week, and Sam has to clear the sty for Aunt Mary and repair her roof." Mother nodded and looked at him. "Buck's good company," she said, giving me a wink. "So he is," said Father, with a little laff, "and I'd like to take him with me on this trip if he likes to go." I did and I went. You bet I went.

It was a lot of work to get ready. Mother helped Father pack the eggs, which was the biggest part. Eggs are always packed in oats in wood boxes. If any break they stink something awful. First you put in a thick layer of oats in the bottom of the box. It has to be thicker than the eggs are tall. Then you smooth the oats with the backs of your fingers. Then you stand the eggs on end snug and tight. They can't even wiggle when the wagon's jolting. After you got the whole layer standing on end, you pour in more oats and make a layer on top of the eggs. You smooth this down same as the other. Then you stand up more eggs, but just only on their little ends and make new rows stand in between the rows underneath. You have to be careful the whole time. Sometimes when Father has drove the last nail in a box he will lift it to one side and say to Mother, "There, that con-founded box could roll down a mountainside and never bust a single egg." Everybody packs eggs this way. You got to have things just right when you haul them a hunnert miles over bumpy roads through hot sunshine.

Jim, Bill, and Sam all helped load up, while Emily and Martha stayed out of the way in the yard and held on to baby Horace. Ellie handed things to Mother as she could. Bill said he was awful sorry he couldn't come along to show me the proper sights of Pioche. Mother frowned and told me it would be hot there and I was to be sure to wear my hat. It was after dinner when we finished. She wanted us to wait till morning, but Father said in this hot weather he would ruther get a head start now and travel this first stretch at least in the evening cool.

Mother made a place for me on the bedding folded under the cover where I could lay down if it got too hard on the spring-seat, or if I got sleepy. If it's not too hot I like sleeping under the wagon cover when the wagon is traveling along. I was ready, but first I hurried up to Earl's house to tell him I was going to Pioche. He said he wished he could go someplace like that, but mebbee he'd be glad he didn't go when I told him how dum it was after I got back. It was afternoon when Father told me to jump aboard, then climbed up on the springseat next to me, gathered up the lines, and the horses started off. It was mostly downslope and easy on the horses.

First night we camped quite a bit beyond Johnson Fort at Iron Spring where there's a nice stream of water. Good thing daylight lasts and lasts a long time. Still, we didn't pull in till well after dark. Three other wagons were already camping there. We could see beds on the ground and all the people in them. Everything was still. The moon had just come up over the mountain behind Summit and Ray Linn's ranch, making scary shadows everywhere I looked. Moon shadows are the scariest of all. You never can tell what's in them. It was too late to build a fire, so Father and me sat on the wagon tongue and ate the bread and meat and piece of sweet cake Mother had put up for us. We didn't make any noise. When we talked, it was only whispery.

Father made our bed on the ground same as the other men had. Soon he was snoring like them, only not so bad. The worst was coming from the man closest to me who was strangling. He had marbles in his throat and couldn't get them out. On account of him I layed awake looking at the stars and thinking about Earl who I knowed would of give anything to be heading out with me. Coyotes started howling, and I listened. Some were close, some quite a ways off. When they all got going together it sounded like music to me.

ASA HANKS AND THE WILD HORSES

Next morning everyone cooked breakfast on the same fire on account of wood being scarce. It wasn't a good fire, too smoky, but the men took turns with their frying pans on the hot coals, and everybody laffed at the smoke. Guess that's the way with freighters.

One of the wagons was pulled by a span of yellowish mules. The owner was a big man with lots of bushy black whiskers and a good-size voice. You could hear him anywhere in camp. He had a double-barrel shotgun with him, leaning against his wagon wheel closest to the fire, on the side where he was at. He had his little girl with him, called Lucy. Father already knowed the man and told me he was Asa Hanks, from Paragonah. The other two wagons came from other places in the Parowan valley, but Father didn't know their names right off. They were all heading for Pioche, too. Our four wagons would be traveling out together. That's the safest way to go.

Soon as we left camp I found out Lucy drove their mules! Her father sat on the springseat by her side and kept the shotgun on his knees. That girl was a good mule driver, all right, I have to give it to her. She knowed how to handle the lines and brake and everything. Father told me she had learnt from her father. Everybody's wagon had a big barrel strapped on each side close to the middle to carry water for horses and people to drink when they got out on the desert.

When I looked back at where we camped, our mountains by Summit looked lots smaller on account of the mountains right behind them which we mostly can't see very much of are so much bigger. Ahead of us were some low hills. All the wagons stepped out onto the desert early in the morning when the air was shivery and gray and started towards them. It's called the 'Scalanty desert on account of the white man who saw it first a long time ago was named that. After we traveled the road a while, there wasn't a hill anywhere, only behind us. Far ahead we could just make out a little line of bluish mountains. They were almost too far away to see without squinching your eyes. Pioche is somewhere out by them, Father said. Our wagon was the last one, behind Lucy's. If our horses walked fast sometimes we'd be close to their wagon and dust. I couldn't see Lucy or her father on account of the cover was in the way, but sometimes the sun flashed on the shotgun barrels sticking out past the wagon cover.

When we camped for noon there was nothing but sagebrush everywhere on the ground and nothing but sky everywhere above our heads. All the wagons turned off the road a little ways and stopped close together. Nobody stops on the road, in case some other wagons might come along needing to use it. Right straight, the men jumped off their seats, unhitched the horses, and tied them to the wagon wheels. Men take the harness off horses at noon so the horses can rest better. Father said, "Buck, you can gather up a big pile of brush for a fire."

Sagebrush is easy to gather, and soon I had a whole bunch. While I was bizy, everybody gave their horses a drink from the barrels. They tied nosebags on so the horses could be eating their dinners, too. Soon all the men were cooking coffee, frying eggs and pork, same as breakfast, talking and laffing. People sure do like company on the road.

We had one fire, same as in the morning, only this was a big one, what with all the brush. Seemed like everybody wanted to talk to everybody else at the same time, even through the smoke and heat.

I could see that Lucy was a bit older than me, like Rebecca is, only a little bigger. She had hair like Rebecca's, only mebbee a little bit red. If it hadn't of been for Rebecca I think I would of liked Lucy best. But I'm differnt from the other Summit men. I can't like two girls best at the same time. And I liked Rebecca first and longest.

While the men were cooking dinner, me and Lucy went hunting flowers. Red Indian flowers were growing in the brush not far from camp, and we found some desert lilies nearby, in soft sand, called sego lilies. I was barefoot. Lucy had on shoes, of course. You can't expect a girl to go all the way to Pioche without shoes on. All of a sudden she said, "Wait! Wait! What's that noise?" Quick I stopped to listen. I could hear a low-sounding noise, but not like thunder. It didn't stop. We ran back to the wagons. The men had stopped talking and jumped up to listen, same as us. One man was holding a frying pan in one hand, a fork in the other. No one spoke a single word. No one could tell where the noise was coming from. It was coming from every-where. Just then Mr. Hanks yelled out good and loud, "It's wild horses! Coming this way! Run for your teams!"

Everybody beat it, each to his own wagon where his horses were tied. The man with the frying pan dropped it on the fire but hung on to his fork as he made for his team. We dropped our flowers. Lucy ran for her wagon, I went for ours. Quick I climbed up on the springseat and looked around. I could see something off on the desert making a big cloud of dust and a rumbling noise that shook the seat under my feet. If Lucy's father said it was wild horses, it must be wild horses! Father was seeing to it that the ropes were tied fast around our horses' necks and rubbing them around their ears. The horses could hear that awful noise their ownselfs. They could tell it was coming our way, all right, and began to act up. Above the rumbling I could hear Lucy's father shouting, "Hold on to them tight, men! They'll try to pull loose, sure as shootin'!"

When the wild band got close, all the teams were excited, prancing around the wagon wheels and jerking at their ropes, whinnying, and showing the white parts of their eyes. Guess they figgered it would be nicer to run around that desert, same as this wild bunch was doing, than pulling heavy wagons over chucky roads. Which I don't blame them for it. I would, too, if I'd of been a horse. Father gritted his teeth while he held on to the ropes. I could tell he was excited, too. Our horses pulled and reared. The horse band was coming fast, with pounding hoofs and flying tails, closer and closer to the wagons. Then like a big blast of dusty wind they thundered across the road in tumbling brown-gray-black-red.

A slick-looking black horse which was in the lead of the band left his herd and came pounding toward camp, his head high and his mane standing straight up. His nose holes were wide open and red as blood. He stopped a second or two and looked us over, gave a loud squeal of a whinny, pranced a little closer, and snorted a couple of times, then reared up, snorted some more, and came down pawing the ground like a bull. Seemed like he was expecting our horses to run out and join him. Every man hung on to his ropes for dear life, digging heels into the sand. Then just as quick, the stallion swung around, kicked at our camp as if to say he didn't care for our old tied-up horses anyways, and went for his band like a racer. They were already just a ball of dust out on the desert. I watched till he got far down to where his horses were running. Last I could see of him he was still chasing the dust of his band.

When all the wild horses were out of sight, our teams got quiet again. Then all the men started in talking. "You can bet your bottom dollar that stud left his band to steal our horses away." Mr. Hanks punched his hat back on his head. "Why, even my old mules wanted to go with him."

"I never saw a horse so fine looking as him," the younger freighter said.

Mr. Hanks drilled a little hole in the sand with spit. "If I could of let go my mules I'd of give that foxy chap a dose of buckshot."

"Not me. I'd never shoot a horse handsome as him," Father said quietly.

"Oh you wouldn't, Jim?" Mr. Hanks's loud voice had everybody listening. "We shoot men for stealing horses, don't we? And wasn't this horse trying to steal ours? Can't see how a horse could be better'n a man, if they both be thieves. Ever'body knows it's a old trick of these wild studs to lead their bands close to other horses just to drive them away." Lucy's father sure knowed a lot about things. I was glad he was with us.

The men walked back to the fire again. Mr. Hanks clapped a strong fist on my shoulder. "Well, Buck, don't you go worryin' none. One of these days that stallion will get his needin's.

A younger stud will tell him he's led the herd long enuff, and there'll be a fight. The old horse will either get kilt or have to leave the band."

"What happens to him then?" I asked.

"Oh, he'll wander about the hills and desert alone till he dies, which won't be from old age. He'll be meat for wolves, and then coyotes and buzzards'll finish him up." He laffed a little.

I looked across the empty desert where the dust had rolled away. I could almost see that big black horse running at the head of his band, running with his mane standing up and tail flying. He wouldn't be meat for wolves or buzzards for a long time, I knew. Not him.

FREIGHTER TALK

Then we all got back to work on dinner. Someone stirred up the fire. The man who dropped his frying pan picked it up and put his bit of bacon back on the fire. Now I saw that all three freighters had pistols on their belts, and another man besides Lucy's father had a gun leaning against the wheel of his wagon. After we had dinner and all the men had their fill of it and were talking about wild horses, Lucy's father took his pistol out and began cleaning it. The other men watched him. Soon two freighters drawed out their own pistols to clean as well. Lucy's father put new loads in his. While carefully doing that he said, "On this here Pioche road you want your gun to go off when you pull the trigger. If it misses fire, your freightin' days is over." When he was through with the pistol he put it back and took up his shotgun, and after cleaning it up and down and in and out, put new red caps on his shots. It looked mean and ready to go off any second.

Father and me didn't have a thing to shoot with. We got a shotgun, but it was back home in Summit. Jim shot off a load for the Fourth of July. Sam hunts rabbits with it. I got a sling which Sam made for me, but we came off and left that even. I never seen Father with a gun. The freighters already knowed that he was a particler man.

When all the wagons were ready to be on the way again, Mr. Hanks stood his shotgun in the corner of his wagon box in front of the springseat and climbed up next to Lucy. He took the gun over his knees again. Lucy jerked off the brake, shook the lines at the mules, and they were off. Father started, too. Our load of eggs, flour, chicken coops, ham and bacon, bedding, and grub box filled our wagon plum full. In the hind end it was heaped up. Back under the covers and close to the seat was the place Mother had fixed for me with the quilts where I could lay down if I got sleepy. But shoot, I didn't want to. I wanted to see things. I didn't know the desert had so many things to hear and see.

Every little while I spotted jackrabbits in the brush and wanted to get out and throw rocks at them, but Father wouldn't stop the wagon so I could. He didn't have to stop, I told him, I'd crawl off behind while the wagon was going. Then soon as I hit a rabbit for supper I'd run and catch up. But he didn't think that was a good idea. He said he might lose me, and if he lost me here on the desert and didn't bring me home, Mother would give him one terrible scolding. Which I know myself she would.

I asked Father why him and me didn't have pistols strapped around us same as the others. "I'll tell you, Buck," he said. "Pistols are made to kill people with. If we never carry one we'll never kill some other person with it." Stands to reason that's good sense, but what I don't see is why Father is the only man in camp thinks that way.

Besides sagebrush and rabbits, seems like the desert was full of little whirlwinds about the size of a wagon wheel hub. They were kind of white or yellow and looked like I could easy reach my arms around them. Father said we weren't seeing the real whirlwind, only the dust in the wind on account of we can't see air. Mostly these whirlwinds spin around like sixty but never go anywheres, not like the ones in Summit which can get big as a house and come roaring into our yard and corral and upset things something awful.

When we camped that night it was like being out in the middle of nowhere. Summit was far away on one side and Pioche still so far away on the other. The sun was about down when we stopped. Everybody started unhitching their horses. All the air was still. In a few minutes there wouldn't be any sun. Seems you get a queer feeling when you camp in a place big as this. All you can do is look and feel, only you feel mainly with your insides. The sky wasn't red and it wasn't yellow, it was both of them, in between and mixed up and so pretty I thought I could live out here all the time just to look at the sky. Never saw a place where there is so much air as out here on the desert.

After supper it was dark. We made a big fire which sent orangey-yellow blazes straight up in the night, and then we all sat around the fire and talked. To be honest, they all talked but Father and me and Lucy. She had already gone to bed on account of it wouldn't be right for a girl size of Lucy to sit by the campfire when freighters were telling bloody stories, which they were doing. The other freighters and Lucy's father took turns. Mr. Hanks knowed the best ones hands down, and for sure he knowed the most. Father didn't tell any stories. He likes to sit and listen to other people, same as me. Besides, he don't much care for bloody stories, and I could tell he didn't like me to hear them either. He nudged me to go to bed.

"Aw, let the kid stay," the older freighter said.

"Sure, Jim, let the boy stay," Lucy's father said, smiling at me through his black bush. "How you expect him to become a man?"

So I stayed. I pulled some more brush for the fire to pay the freighters back. Their stories could of been bloodier, I thought. After a while the coyotes started yelping all around us. After a while more, when the stories died down and the coyotes heated up, one of the men asked Lucy's father if he had a story about keeping that shotgun so close and handy. Mr. Hanks spit into the fire and said we could put money on it that he did.

"This road has a bad repytation for highway robbers and horse thieves," he said. "A man goin' over to Nevada with his wagon full of freight don't run too much risk havin' his load lifted. Like us here, f'r instance. It's the man alone with his pockets full of greenbacks and gold and with his wagon empty on the way home that invites attenshun. Yessir, behind any one of them little cedars in the hills between Desert Spring and Panaca you can easy expect some scoundrel who don't fancy an honest day's work for hisself to relieve you of your hard-earned cash. Some ain't so very respectful goin' 'bout it, neither. There's no angels on this road, believe me. I oughter know. I helped to make it.

"A few years ago I had took a load of long timbers to Pioche and sold them to one of the mines. You know how Pioche is, swarmin' with all kinds of folk, a few honest ones but more that ain't. I felt good 'bout my trip and even better 'bout the money in my pocket. Only a few miles east of Panaca on the way back, when the mules and me were havin' an easy time on a little downgrade, I was kinda drowsin' in the sun and not keepin' my eyes peeled as I should of done. In those days I had with me only my white-handled pistol which I kept in my boot top. But I wager that pistol beats a rifle any day for quick short-range shootin'." Mr. Hanks stopped and spit into the fire a spit or two. Seemed like too much talking made his mouth water.

"Just then two men with bandanas tied 'crost their faces rode out from a bunch of cedars onto the road with drawed guns and grabbed at the bridles of my mules. 'Hands up!' they ordered. I didn't have a chance. I knowed they meant bizness and I was as good as dead already. But if do say so, I can be cool as a new-dug potato if I have to. Quick I dropped down from the seat onto the tongue hounds, pulling my pistol from my boot top, and fired at the near man who fell from his horse dead on the road. The other robber was alongside the wheel mule and reached back to get a shot at me, but his horse was crowding the wagon, so I stretched and grabbed his bridle reins and gave a jerk. The horse reared and jumped sideways. He fired at me, but when his horse jumped it throwed him off aim, and the slug went wild. I shot him in the chest. He dropped his gun, put spurs to his horse, and got away as fast as he could. A few days later the sheriff found him in the hills where he had fallen from his horse and bled to death."

Lucy's father looked at each of us before he spit into the fire again. "Ever since that day in the cedars, I tell you, I been on the lookout for road agents. There's many in these parts, and ever' one of 'em knows a bushel of money comes down this road reggler, and that's why I hedge my bet and keep this double-barrel shotgun 'longside of my white-handled pistol. There's nothin' puts fear of hell into a robber quicker'n a double-barrel shotgun, yessir."

The men all laffed, and the older one said, "Asa Hank's told Heavn's own truth 'bout that shotgun. I'd sooner be shot by a cannon than by that shotgun." This kind of talk gives me the jimjams. Myself, I'd ruther not be shot at all.

When we pulled away next morning the sun was just coming up and shining from behind the wagon, which made the springseat shady and cool. It's funny on the desert. In the day it's so hot it almost burns you, but at night you need lots of covers. Last night I leaned into Father mostly to keep warm, but partly on account of I was thinking about road agents, with bandanas over their faces, crawling into our wagon.

DESERT SPRING

Father and me didn't get away soon as the others, on account of he had forgot to water the chickens and had to wait for them to drink. If we started too quick, the water would of slushed all over the coops, and when chickens get wet they turn sick. So we stuck around camp for a while. When we started out I was cold sitting on the seat and feeling kind of dull besides. Couldn't hardly see any dust from the wagons ahead of us. There wasn't a thing to see or look at. Father wasn't feeling to talk much. I know how he is. He'd ruther just think to hisself, which doesn't call for talking.

The desert is a long ways across, and it looked about the same all the time as if we'd been just standing still 'stead of traveling right along at a steady pace. Seemed to me we been in the middle of the desert ever since the band of horses scairt us all to death, 'cept Lucy's father and me, and Lucy who was only scairt a little. She's real brave to be a girl. Just when I was yawning and thinking it might be a good idea after all to slide into the box onto the quilts for a spell, I was looking at a couple of coyotes trotting along together in the brush. Couldn't tell where they had come from, but there they were, plain as could be. Funny how things sneak up that way and you can't tell where they came from. Father said coyotes have learned that sneaking bizness better than any other animal.

I could see their eyes close up. If they had opened their mouths I could of counted their teeth. Coyotes don't seem to be panting all the time, like dogs. They keep their mouths shut more'n they keep them open. Their ears stuck up straight, and their tails reached behind pretty as could be. Going the same way as us, they didn't seem scairt of the wagon or anything. Father said probly they were interested in our chickens, which they could surely smell. They would raise their heads up and look at us. Guess they couldn't figger out what we were doing on their desert. We kept right on going, same as them. Soon as we got past a little ways, they quit looking at us, dropped their heads, and jogged along till they were even with us again, circling around in the brush smelling at everything. In all that smelling they didn't heist a leg once, no sir, which dogs always do. They didn't seem to be in a hurry any more than us and moved more like they might be hunting up something they had lost, since they weren't about to get our chickens.

It's kind of tuff for coyotes. They go hungry for every meal till they hop out and rustle it up. Father guessed these two belonged to that gang which had yelped and howled last night around camp. Now they were hungry. If I was a coyote I think I'd be hunting something to eat 'stead of spending the night howling. I know I could howl better if I had something to eat. But I have to give it to the coyotes. Mostly at every meal they eat up all they have. Nothing is left for anything else to eat, 'cept mebbee crows and buzzards. Earl and me think if there's only stink left, crows and buzzards will try to eat it. Next to chickens, Father says, coyotes like rabbits best. If it wasn't for rabbits, these coyotes on the desert would just about starve to death. At first I thought they were sniffing for our chickens, but then while I was watching, up jumped a jackrabbit right under their noses and went lickety-cut through the brush. Both coyotes charged after him, but the rabbit had a good start. One coyote went straight for him, and the other started running, too, but quick went off to one side. What a crazy fool way of chasing rabbit, I thought. Why didn't he go after that rabbit same as his chum? Father said, "They're not dum, Buck, they're smarter than most human beans. Just keep your eyes peeled and you'll know why." Still, I begun to feel sorry for those dum coyotes. Suddenly that rabbit made a fast turn to his left side. He didn't go around bushes, he jumped over them and never slowed for anything. But the poor rabbit didn't know he was running straight at the other coyote. Quicker'n scat I knowed it's the rabbit that's not got any sense, on account of he ran smack in front of that second coyote, which grabbed him just that quick. I have to hand it to Father. He knows his coyotes and his rabbits. The first coyote stopped when he found he'd lost the rabbit. To see better, he jumped high over the brush looking to find it. When he saw his pal had it, over he went on the run, and the two of them had their breakfast. I bet they laffed at how easy it was done. Just the same, it took two coyotes to catch one jackrabbit. How smart is that?

After we had drove on and caught up with the other wagons, I kept looking around in case there was something else I ought to see. Finally I did spot something, which I'd been kind of thinking I was seeing for quite a while. Way off in the brush on my side of the wagon, I thought I saw a covered wagon. In a little while I was sure it was a wagon, and there was a white spot in the air above the wagon cover. I showed Father. Same as me, he thought it was a wagon, but he didn't see the white spot. I was probly just seeing things. Boys can't argue with their fathers, so I just kept on looking.

It wasn't long till I could tell for sure it was a white cloth on top of a stick. The cloth wasn't waving on account of there wasn't any breeze. I wiped the sweat off my face and out of my eyes with my sleeve and looked again. There it was, plain as anything, a wagon with a white cloth on a tall stick. "Look, Father! Now you can tell."

He took a good squint. "You're right, Buck, something's wrong out there. Hope the men in front see it too."

The other wagons must of seen it, on account of they stopped, too. We all climbed down and without anybody saying anything went over to Mr. Hanks's wagon. The other two freighters wanted to unhitch their horses and ride out there to see what was the matter. Mebbee someone was sick or dying. That's what Father thought, too.

"What, go out to that white flag! You'd be danged fools!" Mr. Hanks said in his loud voice, shaking his head hard. Most always he had to say "dang" when he talked.

"Why not?" the younger freighter asked.

"There ain't nobody sick or thirsty out there, and I know it." He wouldn't even get down from his springseat.

"But someone must need help. That's what white flags are for, ain't they?" the younger freighter said more firmly.

"Whoever it is, I can't go by leavin' some poor soul to suffer on this desert," the other man said.

"Yes you can," Mr. Hanks said. "It don't mean any of them things to me, not when a flag's so close to the wagon. Nobody's sick out there. Just think about it. Anyone could put up that flag could come down here to the road and stop a wagon 'stead of waiting for some simple soul to come out to him. Don't you know that's a old trick of road agents, to separate our crowd?"

Everybody looked at the white flag just hanging out there. "I ain't freighted this danged road all these years without learnin' a few things about it. Why, I'll wager my mules that flag's not for us anyways. It's meant for some other outfit coming back from Nevada loaded with greenbacks, and I could guess they might be along sometime this afternoon or evening." It must be true if Mr. Hanks said so. That wagon out there was chock full of highway robbers and guns. "Best thing for us is to move right on," he said, turning to Lucy. "I wouldn't go out to that wagon if a dozen flags was flyin'."

That seemed to settle the white flag stuff. We went back to our wagons and were on the way again. "Even so," said Father, "I don't like the idea of just going on. Lucy's father might be wrong. It wouldn't hurt if two men had gone out to see. Mebbee we really are leaving somebody out in the desert who needs help." I could tell Father thought about it for quite a while. He kept turning on the seat to look back at the lone wagon. But pretty soon we couldn't see it anymore at all.

It was late in the afternoon when we reached the other side of the desert and the hills I'd been looking at most of the day. Myself, I was glad to get across it. I was kind of tired of desert now. Just ahead I could see a good-size frame house up on the bench by the first hills. Close behind it was a wide corral with a long stable. Father said this was Desert Spring. A spring is there with good clear water in it, he said, the only water on the way to Pioche after Iron Spring. All the freighters fill up their barrels there going and coming. Father said it would be two more days on to Panaca or Pioche, and by now our barrels were almost empty.

In a hollow not so far from the house was a long deep box full of water, called a tank. Everybody filled their barrels from the tank through a hose big around as the little part of my leg. It had a crooked iron snout on the end of it which we put into the bung hole of the barrel. In Summit we fill barrels with a bucket. When we do, we slush water all over the barrel and ground and everything, and it takes a long time. At home that barrel-filling bizness is a reggler job. Jim and Bill are good at it. At Desert Spring it was differnt. You didn't waste a bit of water. Soon as the barrel was filled you quick yanked that iron snout out of the bung hole, else the barrel would of got too full and might bust itself. Then what would you do going back over the desert with only one barrel of water for you and the horses?

Father said Desert Spring belonged to a man named Tasker, only he wasn't home that day. His wife was taking care of the water bizness. She had to do that quite a lot, and all the freighters knew her. I took notice of her right off soon as she came out of the house. I could only see a little of her skin, her arms and face, but they were darker than any Injuns I have saw, somewhere between brownish and blackish. Father said that is the reggler color of Negroes. I never seen a Negro before, never seen skin so dark. Our Injuns by Summit are dark, all right, but not what you would call black. I would have to call her just about black.

I was kind of scairt of her at first, but in only a little while I wasn't. The freighters joked with her and called her Maggie. She joked back and helped them with their barrels. When she laffed her mouth was bright pink on the inside and black only on the outside, and her teeth were the whitest I ever seen. She smiled and laffed a lot. The men got along fine with her even if her talk was differnt than theirs. It wasn't Hinglish, like they talk in Summit. It wasn't hardly American either. But I could easy unerstand what she said when she came up to me. "Hey theah, young fella, Ah sholy could use a lil boy just yo size to stay heah wif me and hep out. Yo kin see Ah got lots to do. 'Sides, Ah gits pow'ful lonesome on dis ol' desert when mah man away so much of de time." I hung on to the springseat with one hand and to Father's arm with the other.

She had a long buckskin purse tied around her waist which I could see was more than half full of money. You have to pay to let the horses drink from another tank. I never heard of people paying for water. When folks come to Summit they can have all the water from our stream and ditches for nothing. Tasker's Maggie said she would let me carry her purse if I would stay and be her little boy. But I shook my head and said I would ruther be my mother's boy. Then she laffed and patted me and said I was a good boy to like my mama so much. I liked hearing her laff and talk. Her voice went up and down like singing. She asked how I would like to stay with her "jist till yo papa gits hisself back from Pee-oche." But I told her I wanted to see Pioche for my ownself. That was why I had come along with Father. She could tell then I was set to go on and didn't ask anymore.

A little while after we had drove up to the spring another gang of freighters pulled in on their way home from Pioche. They said they lived over on the Sevier. While they were waiting till our barrels were filled, I heard Lucy's father telling them about the covered wagon and white flag. "Now don't be danged fool 'nuff to go out where that wagon is. It's a good bet your bunch are the very one they're layin' for."

"Don't sound too good, does it?" one of the Sevier men said to his friends, but he didn't look worried none.

"Better set out a guard tonight," Mr. Hanks said. "Fact, wouldn't hurt if your whole danged crowd stood guard." The Sevier man nodded. They had guns enuff to take care of the job, I could see.

Our bunch pulled away from Desert Spring while the other freighters were still watering and went quite a ways before camping for the night. Father said wise freighters don't camp at the spring. Too many horses get lost there, and men have to pay old Tasker two dollars a head to find them in the hills. Most always he's able to do just that and bring them back, which is passing strange, said Father, no matter how you look at it. He didn't trust Tasker far as he could lift our wagon, which I knowed was not at all.

ALONE

Where the road forked, we stopped. One road went straight ahead towards Panaca, which was where the other wagons were heading. The other turned to the right, which Father said was a shortcut to Pioche, and we would follow it. Some bunchgrass was growing close to our camp. We hadn't seen any since starting on the desert. Wood was plenty because of cedar hills close to us. By the time everyone had unhitched their horses and taken off the harnesses, Lucy and I had gathered a good pile for a fire. One of the men struck a match to start the fire by hitting it on his pants, even though there were handy rocks. We ate our supper while dodging the smoke. Everyone wanted to talk.

The horses were hobbled out till it was time for everybody to go to bed. We didn't dast leave them out all night. Lucy's father said we were in the country of robbers and horse thieves who wouldn't think twice 'bout stealing our horses while we were sleeping. The young freighter laffed and said that was probly why Tasker was away from home so much.

After supper everybody sat around the fire and told more stories. Lucy got to listen on account of there wasn't hardly any blood in them. When we rolled into our quilts, Father went right to sleep, I could tell by his low snoring, but I layed awake hearing the nick of hoofs on the rocky ground when the horses shifted legs. Finally I got tired of waiting for a horse thief to sneak up on us and went to sleep, too.

Next morning Father told the other men he figgered it would be best for him to take the shortcut to Pioche as he was in a hurry to get there and back.

"Well, of course that's the shortest road, right 'nuff," Mr. Hanks said, "but I think it's always best to travel with comp'ny. Still I guess there's not a whole lot of danger you bein' held up till after you've sold out and got the cash."

"I'd like to stay with you bunch," Father said, "but I haven't the time to drive over by way of Panaca and Bullionville this trip. My load could spoil."

"That shortcut road's a little ruff," the older freighter said, "and it's got one mean steep hill. But I think you can make it all right. Your wagon ain't too heavy."

"Buck and I will get along fine," Father said and shook hands with the freighters.

After breakfast I sat on the springseat watching everybody getting ready to break camp. The lead wagon had a horse with a loose shoe. Good thing the freighter had brought his horse-shoeing tools along. Soon as he had that shoe tightened he looked over at our wagon and came up to us. He told Father he noticed last evening that our off-horse had a loose shoe also, and while he was at it he just as soon tighten it for us. Father thanked him for doing it and said it was mighty nice of him to do a good turn like that.

It wasn't long till everybody started putting on harnesses. One of Mr. Hanks's mules kept acting up and wouldn't behave hisself. He gave that mule a stiff kick in the ribs and "danged" at him. Then the mule stood still. Mr. Hanks looked around at us. "The on'y way to treat a danged mule is to let him unerstand he is nothin' but a danged mule."

In a little while the lead wagon started, then the next, and then it would be Lucy's turn. Before she climbed up on the seat she looked at me and waved her hand. I waved back at her. Next she throwed me a kiss! That made me feel good, awful good. Gosh! If Rebecca throwed me a kiss like that I believe I would fall over on the ground just from sweet feelings.

Lucy's father got up on the seat and layed that shotgun across his knees, same as always. Lucy yanked off the brake and shook the lines at the mules. In a jiffy or two, Father and me were in camp alone, and everything had got still and differnt. Wagons were gone, people all gone, no one talking, no one laffing, no one fixing a horse's shoe, no one kicking a mule or swearing at him. Nothing but stillness. The whole world had got still and littler too, and Father and me were in the middle of it. Felt like Father and me were the only people in it, just us, our horses, and chickens. Everything else had dropped plum out of it. Being alone makes everything differnt. I wished Earl was here. I wished Lucy hadn't of left. I could still see the wagons going along down the road, and I wished we were going along behind them same as yesterday. Once or twice our horses gave a loud whinny at the wagons going steadily away. Seems horses get lonesome, same as boys. Folks get lonesome for folks, horses for horses. Nothing likes to be alone.

Before leaving camp, Father thought of the things he had to do after the others had gone. This morning he didn't forget anything, only he stepped on his whip handle and broke it. Now the handle had to be spliced and wrapped with strings cut from our piece of buckskin. It's a good thing everybody takes a buckskin with them when they go traveling. Then he hitched the horses, and when he was ready he climbed up alongside me. "Well, Buck, it's our turn now." He jerked off the brake. "And if we want any stories tonight, we'll have to tell them ourselves." I could tell he had a little smile inside his whiskers.

It wasn't long till we drove into patches of cedars on both sides of the road. The road wasn't so good, all rocky and jolty. I had to cling on to the seat. Father's legs reached down where his feet could rest on boxes. My feet hung in the air, but I didn't have shoes on, so my feet didn't hang heavy. They only flopped around, same as me. Big black and brown flies buzzed around the horses, sometimes around us, too. Once in a while Father would stop the wagon, get out, and kill flies by banging them with his hand. When he came back on the wagon his hand would be bloody clear up to the wrist. But the flies just kept at it. I could see the horses' skins shivering and wrinkling when the flies bit too hard.

We went on at a easy walk, and the road went steadily up, but not steep. We had to stop a few times to give the horses a drink. Father would take water out of the barrels in a good-size bucket and hold it up to their noses and let them drink with the bridle bits in their mouths. This way they don't push the bucket over and spill the water. You can't afford to lose water in desert country. If you lose too much of it, later on you might choke to death for just one drink.

We stopped for noon by a tallish tree where there was shade. The horses rested and ate their oats. We watered the chickens. Father fried some pork and made coffee. The coffee was just for hisself. Myself, I won't drink the stuff. I don't want to be stunted. But Father wouldn't let me drink it anyways, not even if I wanted to. I drank water, same as the horses.

It was kind of late in the afternoon by the time we got to the bottom of the steep hill we been waiting for. Even though the sun was still higher than the hills, Father said we would camp right where we were on account of the horses were too tired to pull a heavy wagon up that hill at the end of the day. Father already knows about this hill. He said we would be going to bed quicker than we had before on account of it was up to only us to tell the stories, and we would be done pretty quick. No matter, he said, we need the extra rest because the hill will be a job and a half to do with just the two of us.

He was bizy unhitching the horses and feeding them, when I heard rocks rattle up on the hillside. I looked and saw a crookedy old man leading a little jackass loaded up with stuff. Father had got the nosebags on the horses when the man got to the wagon.

"Hello, pardner," he said to Father in a gravelly voice, like he didn't use it very much.

"Hello to you, stranger, howd'do?" Father said back to him. The man had long gray hair and gray whiskers with a yellow streak down the middle, I guess on account of the tobacco juice didn't always get away from him when he spit. His jackass, also gray and dusty, was loaded with bedding and cookware. Under the ropes I could see a pick and shovel, and there was a gun tucked under the ropes.

"On the way to Pioche?" he asked.

"That's where we're headed, all right," Father said. "This is a pretty tuff hill here, so I figgered we'd camp for the night and pull up it in the morning."

"Wul, I like to see a man's got thoughts for his animals," the old-timer said. "I wouldn't think of im-posin' on Jinny here jis 'cause she belongs to me."

"Won't you stop and take supper with us?" Father asked. "Mebbee camp all night here, too. We have plenty to eat." Father sounded a little lonesome his ownself.

"Nope, can't do it," the old man said, biting off a chaw from his plug and handing it to Father.

"Don't use it, but thanks just the same. My boy and I would like you to stay if you will."

"Thanks, pardner, but Jinny and me ain't got the time. Been a big strike t'other side of Panakie, and Jinny and me is makin' a run fer it. Aim to stake some claims. But if you got any water to spare, ol' Jinny and me will drink with you. My canteen's 'bout empty." Father got out the bucket and drawed enuff water for Jinny to drink. He took our coffeepot and poured enuff water for the man to drink and to fill his canteen.

After he had a long drink, he tied the canteen onto the ropes around the bedding and spit a big spit the other way from us. "Mighty nice of you. Not so fur down the road is a little coyote trail which saves us time. Jinny'n me will take it long as we kin see. So long, pardner, and thanks for the water." He and Jinny plodded away. I could of walked lots faster.

Father loosened a couple of slats to reach his arm back where the egg boxes were. We were going to have some for supper. While he was working on that he said, "These hills may hold swarms of robbers and road agents, Buck, but you will find many more men like him, prospecting for gold and silver, hoping every hole they dig will be the one to make them rich. Never yet saw a rich one."

Just then out flopped a big red hen and scooted for the rocks and bushes. Up I jumped and took after her. I knowed it was my job to catch her. Chickens are good runners when they get out of the coop like that. They sort of half fly and half run. I chased that old hen up and down hill, over rocks and through stickery bushes. Every time I reached to grab her she'd up and run some more. At last she tired out and layed flat down under a scrubby tree, her tongue hanging out, breathing hard, plumb tuckered out same as me. I grabbed her quick and took ahold of her legs. She was too tired to even squawk or flop her wings. I didn't have a single stubbed toe and only three or four, mebbee five or six slivers sticking in my feet. Father yanked those out easy as nothing. I didn't feel to tell him my feet were kind of hurty for a while.

After supper Father smoothed off the place where our bed would be. We always made our bed by the wagon tongue. That way we didn't have to carry our bedding so far and back again in the morning. We put out the fire. The sun had gone down behind the hills, but it wasn't all dark yet. There wasn't a sound in the hills anywhere. I knowed that even if it was still now, it would be even stiller after dark. It would get cold, too, but that didn't matter, we had plenty bedding. The ground was kind of bumpy where Father had spread the quilts, but we're used to hard beds. I could tell I would miss the stories, but I would think of Rebecca, or I would think of Lucy, or I would think of them both together. Rebecca is the sweetest girl who ever could be. Lucy is the bravest girl what ever was. Seems I like them both the best.

Sometime in the night I waked up. Don't know why. There I was laying wide awake while Father snored next to me. I listened to him sucking in his breath and letting it out in soft mumbles. I found my legs hadn't got rested yet from chasing that old hen, and I stretched them out to make them feel better. "Whiz-z-z-z! Whiz-z-z-z!" Great Honk! I knowed that sound. Earl and me have heard snakes shake their rattles at us when we been playing around Summit Creek. It was a rattlesnake laying at the foot of the bed where I wiggled the covers.

I just held all of me quiet and hoped he would slide away. Of a sudden Father quit snoring, took a deep breath, said "Uh-hum" twice, and turned his head a little on his pillow. Right then that old rattlesnake gave a "Whiz-z-z-z! Whizz-zz-zz! Whizzz-zzz!" so close to Father's head it sounded like the rattle came right out of his whiskers or his hair. Up he jumped, taking all the covers with him, grabbing ahold of me and pitching me up into the wagon like a sack of flour. Next after me came the bedding in a heap, and right after that Father came with a leap.

"Great Caesars! Didn't you hear that? It was right against my cheek! Thunder and tarnation! That was a rattlesnake!" Father's cussing ain't a patch on the cussing of Lucy's father.

"Aw, that's nothin' to get riled about. I heard him rattlin' but figgered if I didn't bother him he would crawl away," I bragged.

"Blast the snake! And confound you! Don't you know he might have kilt us!" Father shook his head, grumbled some more cusses, and began untangling our quilts to make our bed all over again in the wagon, which wasn't a very good place on account of all the boxes and things we were packing along. Some of the boxes wouldn't budge. The moon was up by now and shining silvery over the little trees and rocks, but it was dark as a cellar under the wagon cover. I was in the way and so was the springseat. Father didn't dast get out on the ground to take the seat off, so he raised it up and let it slide to the ground over the wheel. It tipped when it hit the ground. He told me to stand on the double-tree place while he made the bed, but I should hang on to the endgate post so as not to slip off onto the ground and get bit.

"No one can tell where that rattlesnake might be," he told me. "He might be under the tongue waiting to grab us." I knew when the biting started I'd be first for being the cause of all this trouble. Finally when we slid into bed, the edge of a box poked my ribs, and if I turned my head I got a corner sticking me in the neck. Father kept breathing hard and muttering to hisself even after he pulled the quilts up over him, and he was still at it when I went to sleep. But I didn't really sleep so good the whole night. Mebbee that rattler was just waiting for me to step off the wagon. It was the worst bed I ever had.

THE STEEP HILL

Father was up soon as it was light. He couldn't stand that bed any longer either. After he made a fire, then I got up. I couldn't wait to eat for the smell of frying ham and boiling coffee. After breakfast but before the sun had come into our eyes, Father went in among the trees and cut a good-size piece of dead cedar, almost big around as me but not so long. I asked him what it was for. He said it was to block the wagon wheel when we started pulling up the hill. Dried cedar is not so heavy as pine. He was lucky to find such a good log. When we were hitched up we drove not far at all before the uphill of the road got started. It looked to be ruff, like it hardly got used. Father stopped the horses to look at it. "Buck, every pound that can walk up that hill will be just that much help to the horses, and I can see they'll be needing it, too."

He tied the lines to the endgate post, leaving the lines loose so the horses could bend their necks and swing their heads around. Him and me got off the wagon. Then he took the chunk of cedar from behind the springseat where he had put it before we started, and said to the horses, "Git up, boys! Go on! Buck, you stay well behind, hear!" The horses stiffened their backs and got right down to pulling. Up went that wagon. This first stretch was easy. Father kept close behind with the piece of cedar over his shoulder. I hung back and walked slow. After we'd gone a ways he yelled out "Whoa!" The horses stopped, and Father slammed that cedar bang! against the hind wheel. The wheel leaned back against it hard, but the wagon held good.

The horses rested that way for a bit, then he stooped for the cedar, yelling "All right, all right, boys! Go on!" They toed into it again, and up went the wagon, jolting over loose rocks and tight ones stuck in the ground. Father had been slow picking up the chunk, and he had to hurry to catch up with the team. The horses kept on pulling until he shouted "Whoa!" and slammed the log against the wheel another time. Carrying and catching up and shoving that block against the wagon wheel made him out of breath. Looking back down the hill, I would of hated for the wagon to slip off and roll back. It would roll all the way to Desert Spring.

Now Father leaned over to take ahold of the cedar once more. "Try it again, boys! Go on!" Up went the wagon. He grabbed up the block and soon caught up with the wagon. He shouted at me to stay a bit more behind else I might get hit with the stone flying from the hoofs. I knowed myself I might, on account of once or twice a little rock gone whipping past me. "It's a long hill, Buck, but we're getting along good as I expected."

That's the way we kept going, pulling and resting, then pulling and resting some more. Every little ways we had to give the team time to rest and get their wind back and some water. They're no differnt than human beans. They'd drop dead if they couldn't stop and breathe once in a while. When we were more than halfway I could see that Father was getting wore out. Hefting that cedar and having to catch up with the wagon, all uphill and in the hot sun, was taking the wind out of him, and he was sweating hard as the horses. He said that chunk was lots heavier now than when we started. I could see he was letting the horses rest longer these last stretches.

"Let's go, boys! Go on!" The horses buckled into it once more. They sure knowed how to pull together, same as if Father was sitting in the springseat guiding them with the lines. Just then Father stubbed his boot against a rock and went down all spraddled. The block of cedar got away from him and went rolling down the hill straight for me. I knowed I had to fall on it if I was to stop it before it would get past me and sail down the hill. Lucky for us I did, just like catching ahold of a runaway chicken. I reached for it, fell over on it, grabbing it against my stummick. Father jumped up and came running, picked up the cedar quick, and hurried back up to the wagon. Still on the run he hollered "Whoa!" loud as he could but not as loud as before. Good thing the horses heard him anyways and stopped, on account of he was plum tuckered out and couldn't of run another step. When he pitched that cedar against the wheel this time he just layed on the ground and puffed. When he got his wind back he sat up and hugged me. "Don't know what I'd of done if I didn't have you along, Buck. You are one good helper." He was feeling pretty good again and seemed he'd forgot about cussing me last night for the rattlesnake's rattle. In a while he said we'd better get on the way again or we'd never make Pioche by dark.

We kept on starting and stopping as before, till by and by we topped the hill and the road was kind of level again. There we stopped for a long rest. Father was glad to sit down in the shade of some little trees. While all of us rested he told me that sometimes when he's been on this road with other freighters, they pull up at the bottom of the hill and unhitch all the wagons. Then they take them up the hill one at a time with double teams of horses, or even more, on account of many timber loads are too heavy for just two horses to pull up this grade. At the top they unhitch the wagon, leave someone to keep an eye on it, and walk the teams back down to pull up another. It can take most of a day to get a large party over this hill. The freighters all use cedar brakes like ours for going up. On this road, without them, they'd never get to Pioche. Coming back empty, if they come back this way, they drag a tree behind the wagon to brake on the way down the hill.

"I tell you, Buck, if our load had been one chicken heavier, we couldn't of made it. A good thing we let the horses rest all night, rattlesnake or none." He watered the horses good and us, too, and throwed that chunk of cedar up behind the spring-seat. He said it would come in handy for a campfire. Both of us finally got up in the wagon, glad we were on the way again.

For a while the road was pretty good, but soon the cedars petered out and things sort of flattened again into another desert. No rocks, no hills, no trees, nothing but sagebrush, blue sky, and dirt. Pioche still looked a long ways off. The sun didn't let up any, neither. We sat on the seat and sweated. There wasn't one thing to look at, not one thing to talk about. Only when you sit still and sweat you're not sitting still, you're wiping eyes and neck and behind your ears. I pulled off my hat and fanned my face with it. While you're doing this you're thinking of something you've seen or heard. Thinking like that helps you forget sweat and stillness.

Guess Father had started thinking like that hisself. It must of been about rattlesnakes, on account of I could see he was frowning. Stands to reason a rattlesnake would be hard to get out of your mind, specially when it had crawled right into your whiskers. I couldn't wait to tell Mother how Father jumped right off the bed and pitched me headfirst into the wagon, then the quilts and things like a whirlwind blowing.

I started thinking about Rebecca. The more I thought about her, the better I felt. But it seemed like the more he thought of that rattlesnake, the madder it made him, which I don't blame him for. I would of got mad myself if anybody let a snake crawl into my bed and rattle right in my ear. After a while Father was thinking out loud. "Of all the darned little fools!" He said it gruffly, like last night, scowling down between the horses. Gruff is not how Father mostly is, and his words made something catch in my throat. I piped up, even though I know boys shouldn't never go up against their fathers.

"But I wasn't such a darned fool when I stopped that cedar chunk getting away from you, was I? And didn't I catch that old red hen for you?" Father turned towards me, and his eyes and my eyes looked into each other at the same time. This time he spoke in a low voice. "Oh, son, of course you're not a fool. If there be a fool, I'm it. A fine big one, to boot. You are my dependable Buck, and I'm right glad you came along on this trip." He squinted up at the sun. "Here it is, long past noon, and we're pretty close to Pioche now, and we don't want to be rolling into town tired and hungry and thirsty."

So we stopped. The chickens needed wheat and water, and the horses were thirsty after all that pulling. There wasn't any breeze. Everything was hot and still. Don't see how the chickens stood it. Father put fresh water in the coops. The ground was hot. The wagon tires were burning hot if I touched one. Father poured some water on the tires so they wouldn't come loose.

I forgot the patch was off one side of my pants when I sat on the ground to rest. Up I jumped and quick sat on the wagon tongue, but it blistered through the hole in my pants. Couldn't find anyplace to sit down, so we didn't stay long, not even to scratch up something to eat, and soon as we could we hitched up and went on to Pioche.

PIOCHE

At last! Don't know what I thought Pioche would be like, 'zackly, but what it was was just a spindly town stuck on dry hills, with some streets going mostly up and down, and it didn't have a single tree or even bush growing anywhere. Father said any timber which had been there was long used to build the town and the mines. He drove up a dusty street and stopped in front of a place that he said was a store. Looked to me like all the houses in Pioche were stores. There weren't any yards or mothers and children. After tying the horses to a long tie-post where some other horses were tied, Father went into the store. He said he would be back in a minnit. I stayed on the spring-seat and looked around.

What a lot of people coming and going everywhere. Only everyone in Pioche was a man. I could see plain they all carried pistols stuck in their pants or in holsters. Pioche was some kind of tuff town, all right, and it had a bad smell. Don't rightly know what was rotten, but it stuck in my nose soon as we drove in. I could see little trails going between and behind some of the houses. Where there were sidewalks, like in front of the store Father had gone into, they were covered with boards which thumped when the men walked on them with their boots. It didn't seem a very homey place. Who would want to live in a town like this?

While I waited for Father I saw more men than I ever saw at one time in my whole life. I'll bet all of Summit, all of Parowan, and all of Cedar City don't have so many men as Pioche. But I didn't see a single boy or girl, or woman. I wondered who cooked for the men and kept their houses clean. Must be a funny sort of town where everyone is a man.

Right off we sold all our chickens to that store. I got down and helped Father carry the squawking coops back behind the store. We had to squeeze through one of those little trails between houses. The chickens made so much noise that men passing by had to say something to each other about it. Still, it seemed they wanted chickens and eggs mighty bad. I heard the store man say to Father, "Pioche just can't hardly get enuff chickens and eggs these days. Don't know what we'd do if it wasn't for you Mormons. Thanks to old Brigham for that much, anyways." He said that last bit kind of sneery. I wished Father would bust him one on the nose, but mebbee they would kill us if he did. Father heard the man, all right, but he didn't say anything back, just let on like he didn't hear. Guess that man was a Gentile. Pioche looked full of Gentiles. Wonder if they knowed Gentiles go to hell.

By the time all our chickens were out of the coops, and Father and the store man had figgered everything up on a slate, and Father been paid his money, the sun was low behind the hills where the mines were, and it was time to make our camp somewhere. We drove down the street to where lots of other wagons were camping in an open spot with a water trough for horses. He fitted our wagon in among the others and stopped not far from the street to have a little room around us. We made our bed on the ground on the side next to the street so's Father would know if anyone tried to get into the wagon. But I didn't sleep much that night, nor Father. I would lots ruther been sleeping with Earl's old cow like we did once and listened to her chew her cuds all night.

Men stomped up and down the boardwalks all night, whooping and yelling like they been drinking Dixie wine. Bang! Bang! Pistols sounded next to our ears and jolted us awake from such sleep we could manage. Lots of stores were still doing bizness after dark, men shouting and cussing and laffing inside them. Some stores had doors which swung both ways and you didn't use a latch. More Bang! Bang! And a gang would come by clomping and stomping. I was scairt one might stomp on me. Seemed the dark just kept everybody up raring, hooting, and shouting at the tops of their voices.

I nearly busted out of my quilt when some of them swept by us singing in hoodling voices: "Whoopee, there, my Susannah! Why doncher come to me? Fer I'm goin' down to Dixie with my banjo on my knee." They sang it two or three times near my ears to be sure they knowed it, fired their pistols in the air, and stomped away. But that's how I learnt that song, and I would show Earl how to sing it soon as I got home. Father said folks sang it in St. George, on account of them being southeners theirselfs, and he had knowed it in Kentucky.

But I'll bet if those Pioche wildcats went down to St. George and shot off guns and yelled like that and sang that song, those Dixie men would chase them off with sticks and pitchforks.

"Pile out of it, Buck. We got to sell our stuff and get out of here soon as we can. I can't stand another night in this place."

I was suprised to find I had slept a bit after all. Father had a fire going and had started on breakfast. It's a good thing we brought along that cedar block with us, on account of there wasn't hardly any wood to be had in Pioche. But we didn't get sold out soon as Father figgered on doing.

The wagon stood in front of another store for quite a while. I sat on the springseat looking down the street which was full of men. All of a sudden it sounded like a hunnert guns going off faster than you could count and not far down the street. Quicker'n scat, the men started pushing and shoving each other trying to get inside stores or behind horses or a wagon. Father ran out of the store, yanked me off the seat, and dragged me into the store. Soon as we slammed the door behind us, the shooting stopped. The storekeeper peeked out the door. "Well, I guess it's all over with," he said. "It's kinda early for this kind of 'citement. It could be somethin' new to you, though. Why don't you and your boy go see what it is?" Father took a firm hold on my hand and down the street we went with everyone else. Not far away a crowd had come together that filled the whole street, and every man of them was shouting and talking about the shooting. Father and me wiggled in close where we could see something or someone was on the ground. He put me on his shoulders so I could see over their heads.

On the ground a man was laying on his back. Plain as day, he was dead all right. His shirt had quite a few red spots on it. Blood was coming from one of them, and there was blood on the ground, quite a lot of it. Someone had put a hat over his face. Three or four men with pistols in their hands and stars on their shirts stood around the man, telling everybody to stand back and keep away. The crowd didn't pay any mind to what they said and almost shoved Father and me over on top of him. "Hang on, Buck. I'll try to get us out of this jam. Wish we hadn't got into it."

On the way back to the store another man walked alongside us and told Father the man had done something he shouldn't of. The men with stars on their shirts had gone to see about it. The man had run into a house and started shooting at them. They shot back, and all of them could shoot faster and more than just one man. "See, that's the house," he said, pointing a little ways from where the dead man was laying. The door had been busted down and the window smashed in. Father set me down on my own legs. "For a little boy you are seeing a dangsight more than you should of. Don't know what your mother is going to say about it." I think myself this shooting in Pioche is more bloodier than the stories which the freighters told around the campfires. Now Father and me had a bloody story our ownselfs.

"Let's get goin' on this egg-countin' bizness," the storekeeper said when we came back. He didn't seem to care what happened out in the street. He turned his head and spit close to his right side and cut a plug of tobacco with his plug-cutter for a man with short whiskers who was standing by. The co-op man in Parowan has a plug-cutter same as this Pioche man. Most every man wants his plug cut on account of when he carries a whole plug around in his pocket it sticks up too high above the pocket and looks like a thin piece of board. Someone could easy jerk it out of the pocket when he wasn't thinking about it, and it be stole, specially in a big crowd like what was out to see the shooting.

"If we had a daylight killin' half a dozen times a day," the storekeeper said, spitting to his side of the counter again, "every sonofagun on the street would have to go see it like they just done." He looked up at Father. "Course, I don't mean you freighters, Mister, I mean these Pioche ombrays. If I was a stranger like yourself, I'd be first to go see it, too, but after seein' a killin' most every day or two, seems like Piochers would finally get used to it." Father says "ombray" is "man" in Mexican talk.

"Well, I hope you don't have many shootings like this one," Father said to him.

"Naw, not so many, leastways in the daytime," the store-keeper said, spitting same as before. "It's the night when they like to kill each other the most."

While Father and him were talking I climbed on top of the counter to look behind it. I wanted to see where he was spitting so much. I thought it was on the floor, but it wasn't. There was a little box filled with sawdust and chewed-up tobacco. Soon as I got off the counter I saw another box on the floor on our side which I hadn't seen before. This was for people coming to buy things to spit in. I hadn't noticed before. Now I stood by the counter and watched the men spit. If all that bunch was in our house spitting in the fireplace, they would soon put the fire out.

When he was through with the plug-cutter, the storekeeper put a couple of empty boxes on the end of the counter. "There you are, Mister. You can get at that egg bizness. Dick here will help you." Dick was the man with short whiskers. He helped father count the eggs. They had to dig them out with their fin-gers, one egg at a time, careful with every egg. Soon as the first layer of eggs was out they scooped the loose oats with both hands and put them into a half-bushel measure the man had put close by. Father could sell the oats same as the eggs. They started on the next layer, both working the same box.

"Now be careful, Dick," the storekeeper said. "Every egg you jab your finger into is on the house." Father smiled and said he

was sure an honest man. Busted eggs mess up the oats something awful, and nobody will buy messy oats. Father was selling
the clean oats easy enuff to that same store. Some of the eggs
were rotten, we could tell, and Father didn't want any of them
making the oats stinky.

He and the hired man had a pencil and slate where they
marked the dozens as they dug them out. Dick would holler
"Dozen!" as he put the eggs in the other box, and Father would
make a mark on the slate and holler "Dozen!" back at him. It's
queer how you measure differnt things in differnt ways. Eggs
and candles go by dozens, wheat and oats go by bushels, salt
and sugar go by pounds, molasses and wine by gallons, thread
by spools, carpet and cloth by yards, land by acres, and roads
by miles. You have to know how much of anything there is.

There wasn't any fun sticking around watching them fingering
eggs out of oats and marking a slate, and for sure I didn't want
to stand around watching the men who came into the store
take quick turns spitting into a sawdust box by the counter, so
I went out through the back door just to look around. A little
ways behind the house there was a big pile of empty cans, and I
went over to it. It was a whole heaped-up wagonload, all kinds
of cans. I picked one up to look at it. Smelled like something
had died in it. I dropped it and wiped my fingers on my pants.
Got a stick and wiggled another can out. Right straight I could
tell it had the sweetest smell I ever smelled. I put it close to
my nose. No smell in all of Summit was so good as the smell
coming out of that can. I can't see why God gives Gentile towns
such sweet-smelling things, but don't give Summit any of it. I
wondered if it would be all right to take one. They looked like
they had been throwed away. One was all I wanted, anyways,
to take home to Mother so she could smell that sweet smell.

I had to bring her something from Pioche. She could put the can on a box by her spinning wheel or on the edge of her loom so she could smell it whenever she had a mind to. Mebbee she would like two of them.

I poked around some more with my stick and pulled out another can with the same red stuff sticking to the insides. Rebecca might like one, too. Bees were buzzing around that pile. They are good at smelling out sweet things; they got good smellers. I used my stick to push the jaggy corners down to keep them from scratching me and help hold the sweet smell inside it. I took one more for Father. Then I hurried out to the wagon, squeezing through the narrow gap between the houses. Father had already brought some of his empty boxes from the store, and I hid my cans in one of them. He could see me out at the wagon, so he'd know I wasn't lost. I waved to him. Then I ran back behind the store and picked up some shavings there and put them in my box to keep the cans from rattling. I had a feeling Father oughtn't to know about my cans. I'd make them a suprise for him and Mother.

When I went back into the store the men were talking about robbers. "Yes, it's a fact," one man was saying. "Lately quite a few freighters has been robbed. There's a whole gang doin' it."

"Heard folks say Idaho Bill is leader of it," another man chimed in.

"'S right," a third man said. "You got to look out for him. I tell you, if we ever lay hands on him, we'll give him a neck-tie party he won't soon forgit. Bank on it."

The first man cleared his throat and spit into the box by the counter. "Don't know 'bout Idaho Bill bein' part of this gang. Usually he don't stick with any gang. I've heard Idaho likes to go it alone and pick them to rob as he wants."

Father finished his bizness and we went out to the wagon and both climbed up on the springseat at the same time, him on his side, me on mine. We were all done with Pioche and wild times, shooting, dead men, and talk of robbers. I couldn't wait to get away. This town was in a State, but it couldn't hold a candle to my town in our Territory. Father yanked off the brake and we were off for home. When you've been a long ways from home and a long time on the road, it feels so good to turn around and start back. Just like when I been weeding onions or carrots most all day and Father tells me I can quit and go play with Earl if I want to. And now I couldn't hardly wait to see him and Mother, my sisters, even Bill and Sam. And Rebecca.

GREENBACKS AND IDAHO BILL

Didn't take us long to be clear of Pioche, and soon we took a differnt road. Father said the men in the store told him, what with
robbers in the neighborhood, we had better go back through
Bullionville and Panaca. That way we might get in with other
wagons going home, same as we did at Iron Spring on the way
out. Mebbee we would join up again with Lucy and her father.
The storekeeper told Father hardly anybody went back alone
by the steep hill. It was too easy for a robber to catch a person
out there all by hisself. Father didn't talk much about anything,
and I didn't talk much either. He looked bothered. Two or three
times he said he wished we were already safe back home. Guess
that talk in the store made him worry. Father's not so very used
to robbers. "Who's Idaho Bill?" I asked.

"He's a robber been robbing freighters lately."

"Why do people want to give him a neck-tie party? What
kind of party is that?"

"Oh," Father said, "that's the kind where they hang a man.
The neck-tie is the rope around his neck."

"Geeminy! I wouldn't give that kind of party to anybody."

"We wouldn't, Buck, but it's the kind they like to give horse
thieves and highway robbers."

"Huh! I'd just like to see some robbers. Bet they look fierce. Guess their belts are full of pistols and knives, and they carry guns."

"They do, that's a fact. That's what they do their robbing with."

"Well, what does Idaho Bill look like? I think his name is funny, sounds like it's backwards."

"The storekeeper told me he has red hair, and the horse he likes to ride most is black with a white stripe down its face. The men in Pioche think it's got too hot for him around here, though, and he's left the country."

"Wish we'd of seen him first."

"Too late now. Guess we will have to see some other highway robber. But I'm not one whit eager to do it. Just thinking about those varmits gives me a chill."

Right then, more than anything, I wanted to see a robber. I already seen just about everything else. Didn't want to see him when he was robbing people, just see him, even if I knowed sometimes robbers kill folks they're robbing. If Lucy's father had of been with us with his big shotgun, we wouldn't have to worry. No robber would dast start in on robbing him.

We got to Bullionville well before sundown. The wagon rolled easily behind the horses now that it was mostly empty. Bullionville's got a kind of gristmill, Father said, for rocks which have gold and silver in them. There was some white dust coming out of the mill. Guess they were bizy grinding up rocks that day. I have to say it's not much of a town, either. It's got only one store. I wouldn't live in Bullionville if they give it to me. But I did see a boy or two. Father tied the horses to a post outside a store and said I'd be safe, as he would only be gone a minnit. He went in the store to buy some bread, on account of we didn't have a single crumb in our grub box from what Mother sent with us. He had to buy baker's bread, which was all the store had. Myself, I don't like the stuff. It has too much taste and a funny smell.

Soon as Father came out, we drove over the valley to Panaca, which we could see a little ways off. Panaca is a real town. It has trees and a stream of water, which Pioche don't have any of. It has kids, too, plenty of them. I could see a bunch up the street. We camped by the edge of town close to that stream. Grass was all around and a long ways from it on both sides, just the thing for our horses. Don't think our horses ever saw so much grass in one place in all their lives before. They tucked right into it. Father said it was a meadow, which is a big piece of level ground all covered with good grass which grows without anybody planting it but God. The stream waters the grass without anybody but God turning the water on. Folks don't need to bother their heads a bit about either the grass or the watering of it. All they have to do is come and get it. God levels the ground in the first place so the water will spread over it. I wish we lived in a place where God does all that for the people. God don't do much of anything for Summit. Nothing grows if we don't plant it. God don't turn the water on it, either. We got to do that. If we don't, then everything we plant dries up and dies. We have to take the rocks and sagebrush off the land ourselfs, too. God don't do it. There's lots of things God could do for Summit which haven't been done yet, Father says.

After Father hobbled the horses out to nibble that grass, he made a fire. Before we got to Bullionville we had picked up some pieces of wood along the road, mostly little stubs of dead trees and bits of boxes. First thing after taking care of the horses and making a fire, he most always makes our bed on the ground close to the wagon tongue. He never likes to make the bed after dark if he can help it, on account of in the dark he can't always tell what he's making the bed on. We were going to have our bed on that green grass and not worry about any critter crawling under the quilt. While he got bizy with making our bed, he told me that one time he was peddling down to Orderville and he spread the first quilt out, but before it hit the ground he could see a big scorpeen crawling right where the quilt would of landed. He slept in the wagon that night. It give me the jimjams to hear about it. I hate scorpeens. Just thinking about them makes my toes curl.

For supper Father fried some of our ham. We been eating off it for quite a while now, and getting close to the bone where it didn't taste so good on account of we had it so long. We had only baker's bread to eat with it. I can't hardly go it. Father said it would taste better if I soused it in the ham grease. Even so, it didn't taste like Mother's crusty brown loaves.

We might of been more than half done with supper when a shortish man and his little boy walked up to the fire. He nodded at Father and sat down on the other side of the fire, away from the smoke. The boy and me didn't say anything to each other, just looked. The man said he always likes to step around and chin a few minnits with folks who are going through town. He picked up one of our pieces of wood, about as long as his boot, took out his pocketknife, and started to whittle. "Seein' you had your tad along, I thought you might be lookin' for a new place to settle. Panakie, here, is a right good town, on'y we could use a few more settlers. You kin see we got lots of meadow, quite a bit of water, and wood in these hills." Father thanked him for the invite but told him he already had a good farm over in Summit, back in Utah. We'd only been to Pioche to sell our eggs and chickens and things.

"Kind of skittish bizness, ain't it, Mister, this travelin' all alone? Too many robbers infestin' the road." He shook his head like he thought we shouldn't be doing it and spit the other way from the fire. He wiped the whittle shavings off his pants and pitched them into the hot coals. He was a good whittler, all right. He made the thinnest whittles and the longest whittle curls I ever seen. "Idaho Bill his ownself went through town yesterday."

"What's that you say?" busted out Father. Good thing he hadn't been drinking his coffee when the man said that, or he would of choked. "Which way did he go?"

"Don't know much 'bout it, on'y that a man here in town seen him and jawed with him a little while." He stood up and brushed off his pants some more. "Well, my boy and me, we oughter be headin' back to the house. Take care, Mister. See you another time."

Not long after they left, I crawled into the bed. Father had now moved the bedding into the wagon box, him probly thinking rattlesnakes and robbers. He brought the horses in and put the fire out. I didn't hear him much, on account of when I pulled the covers up I closed my eyes quick and must of gone right to sleep. First thing I knowed Father was shaking me to be up and about. He had hot water waiting for me to have a wash. Said it was about time, on account of I was beginning to smell mighty ripe. I didn't mind a bit. It felt good to get rid of the dust and the Pioche stink. If I didn't smell like me, Mother probly wouldn't let me in the house. She's fussy about her house.

After breakfast, Father put the dishes and things back into the grub box and then folded up our bedding. The sun had come up, and it was time for us to start. We always leave early in the morning if we can.

One of our quilts looked kind of raggedy. It had little holes in it, quite a few. You could see the white wool showing through in some of them. It's getting wore out on one side, on account of it's the side Father spreads on the ground or in the wagon and then makes the bed on top of it. He flopped the whole quilt over so the bottom side was up and spread out. He took ahold of his whiskers with one hand, looked at that quilt, and pulled down on his whiskers. Seems pulling them helped him think of whatever he was thinking about better. He pulled down to the end of his whiskers two or three times, then must of quit thinking on account of he grabbed up the quilt and brought it to the wagon tongue where I was sitting. I took a look at that quilt myself, but I couldn't see what he was looking at.

He made straight for the grub box, never saying a word, just went around doing queer things and thinking all to hisself. I wanted to laff. First he put the grub box on the ground next to the quilt. Then he sat on the wagon tongue next to me, pulling the quilt over his knees. Soon one of the holes was right in front of his eyes. He fingered it, then reached over and felt around in the grub box and took out his needle and thread packet. Now I could guess what he was up to.

"Goin' to sew up the holes in that quilt? Thought you said you wanted to get away from here soon as we could."

"I'm in a hurry, all right, but first I'll just sew up a few of these holes." He took a piece of gold money out of his pocket, big around as a dollar, and pushed it into the hole, mixing it with the wool. Then he sewed the hole up. He moved the quilt to another hole, took another gold piece out of his pocket, wiggled it into the hole, and sewed the hole up same as before. I kept watching him as he sewed more gold pieces into other holes. Next, he sewed some little gold pieces into holes that were about the size of two-bit pieces. Sewing up the holes was making the quilt look some better, at any rate.

"Why are you sewing up money in the quilt? Got holes in your pocket? I could carry that money for you. I never carried money before."

"I'm sewing up money into this quilt so if we meet any robbers they can't find it"

"We goin' to meet robbers!" I almost yelled at Father. "Why didn't you tell me so I would of knowed!"

"Don't be afraid, Buck. I don't think there's any robbers on this road, but I'm doing this to play safe. It's always best to think of things before something happens. If we do, then we'll be prepared for anything." He put the needle and thread back into the box. "There, I guess that'll do the job for us." He doubled the quilt up, lifted it to put it into the wagon, then stopped with the quilt still held up above his head. Quick he put the quilt back on the wagon tongue, reached out his needle and thread once more, and started sewing up all the other holes same as the ones which already had gold pieces in them. I was getting scairter every minnit. "Why you doing that? You got no money in these holes."

"Well, I got to thinking, if robbers looked at this quilt and saw I had sewed up only a few holes, they'd know right off I had sewed money in them. But if I sew up all the holes, they won't pay any attention to it."

I could tell Father was scairt of robbers, too, same as me. Guess that storekeeper in Pioche got his wind up and that whittling man last night cinched it. "Why don't we wait here till Lucy's father comes back through? No robber would dast rob us if he was along."

"I'm doing this so we won't be uneasy every time we meet someone on the road." He sounded calm, but I knowed inside he wasn't. When the quilt and grub box were stowed in the wagon again I didn't feel so good, myself, thinking about robbers. Last night the man said the road was 'fested with them. Guess he meant robbers was hiding all along the road ready to grab folks when they came driving along. Geeminy, I was glad Father hadn't let me carry that money in my pockets. I was watching Father pour water on the fire. If only we lived in Panaca and not Summit, we would already be home.

Of a sudden Father quit pouring and stood still, holding the bucket in his hand. I could tell he was thinking again. He was pulling at his whiskers with his other hand. He turned his eyes to where I was at on the wagon tongue, and I didn't like that look one bit. It was a look meant something about me. "Glad you thought of this, Buck. I'm going to let you carry the greenbacks."

"What!" I had jumped up and almost yelled at him again. "Want to get me robbed and mebbee kilt?"

"No one will know a thing about it, Buck, but you and me. You simply carry the greenbacks where no one would think of looking, that's all." He came over to the wagon and put the bucket up. Out of another pocket he took the bundle of greenbacks he'd been paid in Pioche along with the gold. Greenbacks is green paper money. "See, I'll divide this into a couple of piles, like this, and fasten a pile on each of your shoulders under your shirt." Now I knowed for sure Father was scairt. He didn't know what words to use. I don't even have a shirt. It's my waist I was wearing. I always wear waists. Father knows that much his ownself. "No robber would think of searching a little boy for money."

I didn't say anything. Couldn't. Father's idea sounded terrible. All this talk about robbers, then sewing money in the quilt, and now me with piles of greenbacks on my shoulders. Course I was scairt, looking for robbers right here in Panaca, and we hadn't even set out on the road yet. I could be robbed easy as nothing, mebbee shot, else stabbed to death.

That started me thinking about a story in the Bible about Isaac and his father. The picture of them was in our Bible at home. Now I was going to be sacerfised, same as Isaac. He was a boy just bigger'n me. Sacerfised means to be kilt by your father or someone else God picks out to do it. Only there wouldn't be any ram in the sagebrush to be kilt 'stead of me. A ram is a buck sheep. In the Bible there were lots of them around, but we hadn't seen any sheep anywheres in this whole desert country.

I didn't say anything. I did what Isaac did, kept my mouth shut. Father went to the grub box again and took out a ball of twine. "Now just take off your shirt and I'll show you how we'll do it," same as Isaac's father said to him. I knowed how Isaac must of felt when his father told him to take off his waist, then get up on that pile of rocks so it would be handy for his father to kill him on them. I looked at that pitcher in our Bible oft times. This was going to be the same, only happening to me. There wouldn't be any ram. There wouldn't be any angel, either. Didn't Lucy's father say there wasn't any angels on this road? He oughter know.

Father put a good-size pile of greenbacks on my right shoulder and held them there with one hand. With the other he wrapped the twine over my shoulder and under my arm, making the money lay close to my skin. It felt kind of bunchy. He pulled the twine across the back of my neck to the other shoulder and wrapped another pile the same way. He used plenty of string. And there I was, tied up just like Isaac's father tied him. Then Father told me to put my shirt back on.

When I was all fixed up to be robbed and mebbee kilt, Father hitched the horses to the wagon, had me climb to the seat, and we started for home, only probly I would never see Summit again. We were heading out to the hills where robbers were 'fested and waiting to kill us—me anyways.

From Panaca the road goes through hollows and hills covered with cedars and pines. The trees are not tall, but grow right up against the road, so close you can almost touch them from the wagon. Good places for robbers to hide. The trees would of been pretty to me, only when you're going to be kilt, nothing looks good. The road was twisty, and around any turn a 'fested robber could easy jump out and grab me. I had the money, stands to reason I'd be the one getting kilt. But the wagon kept on going. I could see horseflies on the horses, but those flies couldn't of been so worrisome to them as the greenbacks on my shoulders were to me.

On towards noon we came to a sort of long clearing where there wasn't any trees, only brush. Straight as a beeline, the road went through it clear to the other end. You could see almost all the road from one end to the other. Right after we started from our end of the road, away down at the other end a man on horseback rode out of the trees into the road and started toward our wagon. Even that far off, he looked like a robber. I could feel my skin shivering under the greenbacks. Soon as he rode a little way we could see him plain. My feet quit flopping and turned cold. He was riding a black horse, and I couldn't hardly swallow, on account of that horse had a bald face.

"Idaho Bill!" hissed Father, grabbing for the brake handle. He pulled on the lines to stop the horses, but straight changed his mind. "No use for it, Buck. We're caught and we got to face it." Soon as Father said "Idaho Bill" I knowed I was a dead boy. Never see Mother anymore, never see Earl, or Rebecca neither. Then Father said more clearly, "Don't be afraid, Buck. I doubt he'll even stop us. Just don't let on anything."

Easy for him to be brave, he wasn't carrying the greenbacks. The robber would easy tell I had them on my shoulders under my waist. The man riding towards us was coming to kill me or cut my throat. Then of a sudden both our horses whinnied at the robber's horse. I jumped and almost fell off the springseat, Father, too. He had to grab ahold to keep from falling, and nearly let go the lines. The robber came right on towards us, his horse at a slow, steady walk. Our horses walked slow towards him. Father didn't say another word. I couldn't of talked if I wanted to, on account of I was kind of crying to myself.

When the man got close I could see his gun was strapped to his saddle. I could see pistols around his waist. When I looked at his head I could see red hair sticking out under his hat. I squeezed my eyes closed, too scairt even to cry. Now he was right against our horses. I unsquozed my eyes a bit. If he was going to kill me, I had to see it. His horse stopped. He raised his hand. Father yelled "Whoa!" and slammed the brake. I opened my eyes a bit more.

"How you like this hot sun, Mister?" Idaho Bill's voice didn't sound so much like a robber's.

"Mighty uncomfortable," Father said, kind of husky-like. "But guess we can't do much about it."

"Say, got any water on you?" Idaho looked at me and smiled. Smiled? He hadn't kilt me yet.

"Lots of it," Father said, reaching for our canteen which we always keep hanging on our endgate post inside the wagon. "Here, drink all you want."

"Where you been?" the robber asked between swallows that were more like gulps. He was thirsty, all right.

"Over to Pioche," Father told him.

"Well, young feller, how you like Pioche?" He looked at me and smiled again. I liked him more each smile.

"Don't like it at all," I said, feeling a little better. "Too much shooting. Too much noise all night. And it smells bad." I was getting over being scairt.

"Can't say I blame you, kid. Pioche is a helluva town at night, if'n I say so myself." He took a last swig from the canteen and handed it back to Father. "Thanks, Mister, I'm much obleeged. Goodbye, little boy." He waved his hand at me, touched his spurs to his horse, and went on up the road at an easy walk.

"Goodbye!" I called back to him and waved my hand, too. Father frowned and leaned into me with a gruff whisper, "That'll do, Buck. There's no call to be so friendly. We could of been goners. We're just lucky he didn't pounce on us and take all our money. He might have his pockets full already, but he could easy change his mind and come back for more."

After we had gone on a little bit, Father said, "Yup, that was Idaho Bill hisself, in the flesh, all right. I don't doubt you'll remember him for a while. He probly thought we were two scrawny chickens not worth the pluckin'." His voice sounded like he was still a little trembly. Mebbee men don't get over being scairt quick as boys do. When we got almost to the end of the straight road, Father put his hand on my knee kind of gentle-like. "I could tell what you been thinking. My little boy turned out to be the ram which saved us." Funny how we both thought of that same buck sheep out here in nowheres.

ENUFF DESERT

I felt too good to be scairt anymore. When you feel good, you feel brave, and when you feel brave, everything looks good to you— rocks, brush, hills, and sky. You don't care about the jolting of the wagon or the hot sun, or even dust from the wheels.

Not far from where Idaho Bill had rode into the clearing, the road turned to the right. Father said we were going that way straight for Desert Spring. Some sagebrush was on the right side, then some hills a ways off. On the left side were cedars, then some bigger hills. We plodded on for a while just glad not to be thinking I was going to be kilt any minnit. I noticed that being scairt had made me kind of tired and thought I would go lay under the cover, but couldn't, on account of it was too awful hot and even hotter under the cover. Funny how empty wagons get more hot than loaded ones do, but I guess when most of the stuff is out there's more room for hot air to be.

I could tell Father was feeling better, too. He had started to sing. I don't unerstand how you can feel so good after being scairt so bad. Father hadn't sung a song on the whole trip. When he wasn't talking he was thinking, and I guess there hadn't been anything good enuff to make him want to sing till

Idaho Bill didn't rob us. Father and me are alike about songs. We don't know so many very good. Course we know a lot of Sunday School songs and sing them sometimes when campers stop by, but not a lot of reggler songs, on account of there isn't much need of them.

This song was about a old man whose name was Grimes. He was a good old man, but he was dead. Folks won't ever see him anymore. The old man had a couple of boys; both were brothers. One of them was named Bye Ankshus, the other Joe Seefus. They only had one overcoat to wear, which they took turns with. Bye Ankshus wore it on Sunday, Joe Seefus all the rest of the week. Which I don't think was fair. That's all I know about it. But it's much longer than that. Father kept right on singing at it till it was time to stop for dinner, which wasn't so very long after Idaho Bill asked for a drink of water 'stead of our gold and greenbacks. Coming along the road, I joined in the singing quite a lot, only I had to sing a little behind Father so I would know the words he was saying. He felt so good he kept right on singing while he made a fire, and seemed he felt so good he couldn't be shut off the song till it was time to eat.

Just about then I saw something I hadn't seen before. A lake, almost straight ahead of us, only off to one side a little. Father saw the lake, too. "Where was that lake when we went to Pioche?" I asked.

"That's not a lake, Buck. That's why we didn't see it before. You only think it's a lake. It's called a mirage."

"I ought to know water when I see it," I said.

"Oh, it looks like water, all right," Father said, "but it's not. We only think it is. Lots of people have been fooled by things like that."

"But lookee, there's cows by it. I can see them move, else mebbee it's horses. And there's trees growing on the edge of it, too. See?"

"You aren't seeing any real cows or horses or trees or water. It's this hot air fools us. I can easy see how a thirsty man would think it was water and run out through the brush to get a drink. But he'd never come back. Someday his bones would be found out there among the bushes. You didn't see your lake or cows on the trip out because our wagon was behind the others, and they kicked up too much dust for us to see one."

No matter what Father said, I could tell it was a lake out there. I took a good swipe with my sleeve across my eyes and looked again. The lake was gone. "How could I see a lake which wasn't even anything?" I asked. Father kind of laffed. "When you're a man you will find the hardest tasks in life are to tell which things are mirages and which are really what they seem."

I didn't know 'zackly what he meant by this, but I kind of remembered anyways. We quit talking for quite a while. The horses went along without any driving, not in a hurry, with their heads down. It was going to take us a long time to get home. But then I thought that even if the horses did go slow, they still were walking faster than oxen.

The air was too still for even a little whirlwind. After we'd been traveling a while we saw four freighter wagons coming towards us. At first I thought they weren't real either, but they kept on coming, and soon Father pulled off the road to give the wagons the whole road. He said it was good manners for empty wagons to clear off the road so loaded ones could keep right on going. The wagons didn't stop. To each of them, as the teams went by, Father raised his hand said, "Howd'do." Each of the men on the wagons said the same back and nodded their heads when they said it. I could see they had pistols and even a couple of shotguns sticking up above the front endgates of all four wagons. Father thought this bunch might be from over on the Sevier, like the freighters we met at Desert Spring. "From the looks of things," he said, "those men don't intend to be robbed." Which I could tell, myself, they didn't. Idaho Bill wouldn't be bothering them with all those guns and pistols. Soon as all the wagons drove past, we pulled back on the road and went on our way.

I got tired sitting on the springseat and crawled again back in the wagon to lay down. One heat finally seemed about the same as the other, inside or out of the cover. I'd been laying there a while when Father suddenly shouted "Whoa!" and pulled on the brake. The wagon stopped with a jerk. Out I scrambled. Mebbee another robber had come along! But there wasn't a robber, or anything. Father had only turned off the road onto a level piece soon as he saw it. The sun was right on top of the little mountain behind us, so I knowed we were going to camp.

That night when we camped Father was messing around the fire getting supper ready. He was dodging around on differnt sides trying to keep out of the smoke and fry bacon both at once. He was kind of laffing as he did it. When we sat down to eat a little later he said, "By now, Buck, you know that men standing around a campfire always draw the smoke to where they are standing. If two or three men are standing around at differnt places, then the smoke spreads itself to every side where the men are at. Seems smoke doesn't like to miss anyone who's there. If it's only one man, then he has to keep bobbing about, just as I've been doing."

I know myself that is the way with smoke from all the times Father and me camped on this trip and other times. It smarts your eyes which already smart some from the dust of the road. Campfires are best when the brush has burned down to red-hot coals in the ashes. I like to push a stick around so that tiny sparks brighten up and flip out same as the sunshine flips off the mountaintop when the sun sets. After a while we didn't say any more, just sat there feeling glad we hadn't been kilt by Idaho Bill and that our money was still there, even if it was scratchy on my shoulders. Then we crawled into our quilts.

It was almost noon next day when we got to Desert Spring. No other wagons were at the watering place, so we didn't have to wait to fill our barrels. Tasker's wife came down the trail from the house to sell us water. She walked kind of slow, like mebbee she had sore feet from living out here on the desert all the time, or mebbee just to have us at the spring a bit longer to get water before we left. She must get awful lonesome out here all by herself so much. I would. Sure enuff, she said Tasker was gone someplace up in the hills looking for lost horses. He's gone like that most all the time. She helped us fill our barrels with that long hose and laffed and talked a lot. I had to watch her white smooth teeth and pink tongue when she did. She asked if I'd changed my mind any 'bout staying on there to be her little boy. I told her I had to hurry on to Summit so I could see my mother and brothers and sisters. She said in that case I oughter come again sometime with Father on account of she'd purely like to see me again.

Father had unhitched the horses from the wagon so they could drink better out of the long deep water trough. While they were sucking up all they could hold, he paid Tasker's Maggie what he owed. Then we hitched up again and went on.

Father wanted to make only one more night camp before we got home. We didn't have much of a load, only empty chicken coops and boxes mostly, and we could travel fast as we wanted to. Only we had to let the horses walk slow for a while after leaving the spring. Father said it wasn't good for horses to hurry so soon after they had filled theirselfs full of water. Which I know myself it's not what you do, if you take good care of your horses. It's best to drive your horses slow till the water they've drank gets scattered around through their insides and into their veins. When the water gets into their veins, horses can carry it better. Then, too, they can sweat it out. Sweating keeps the horses' skin wet. Earl's pa says both horses and men have to have wet skins when they travel through air hot as on the desert. If they don't, their bodies dry up, their skins gets stiff as buckskin, and next thing you know, they're dead. That's why we have the canteen. When it is empty we fill it again from the barrels.

Couldn't see a thing whichever way I looked over the desert, so I sat there thinking, same as Father. When we got home I'd have lots of things to tell Earl, even if we didn't see one more thing on the road. Earl's probly too smart to believe everything which I tell him, and I knowed already he won't believe half what I tell him about this trip which is true. He won't believe about the wild horses, or the shooting, or the smell cans, or the water and the mountains which go away right while you're looking at them. I won't get mad if he says I'm lying to him, on account of if he told me things like that I'd know he was lying.

We stopped kind of soon for noon. The horses were still full of the water they had drank. You could see it had gone into their veins and was coming out of their skins in white lather between their legs and the harness straps. The horses were wet all over, the way they should be, in the hot desert air. That's what Father said.

After dinner we trotted the horses where the road was good for a little. The wagon pulled easy. It just seemed to follow the horses all by itself. It wasn't long till we were passing the place where that white flag had been. It wasn't there anymore. Father said mebbee, after all, Mr. Hanks was right about it being a road agent's trick. "Just the same," he said, "it would take a burden off my mind if I was sure no one had died out there from sickness or lack of water."

Couldn't see any coyotes or rabbits, or anything else alive. Father said when it's too awful hot the desert animals don't move about—well, only hungry coyotes looking to scare up their next meal. Everything else is laying in the shade of bushes, if it can find some.

This was the longest day of our whole trip. If I would of knowed it was going to be like this I wouldn't of come. Nothing to look at, only hot wavy air and the blue line of mountains behind Cedar City and Summit slowly getting taller. We bounced on the springseat, sweating same as the horses just as Father said we would. Once the wagon wheels squashed a big black trantler spider trying to get across the road before we got to him. That was as close to something to remember that day as we come. Right at sundown he turned off the road and said we would stop early in order to give the horses a good rest so's they would be fresh in the morning for the long pull to Summit. He drawed water from the barrels to give them a good-size drink. We had only enuff water left for the next day, but he would let the horses freshen up from the stream at Johnson Fort. He said the heat had been tuff on us and on the horses, too, and a good night's rest would freshen him and me same as the horses, and we would get back to Summit just fine.

On the desert, the sky comes right down to the ground and shuts off your seeing. You can't see past the sky on account of there's nothing to see. There's not much fun camping when there's nothing to see, nothing to hear, nothing to talk about. We didn't have any rattlesnakes like we had on the steep hill, no whoop-ala-la shouting and gun-shooting like there was in Pioche, no friendly whittle-man like we had in Panaca, and no cussing and laffing like Mr. Hanks and the freighters, and no bloody stories. Only stillness.

Guess I was kind of homesick. Before, everything had been so bizy I didn't have a minnit to be homesick, but now I felt I hadn't been home for a year. I wanted to see Mother. I wanted to see Earl. Seems like the more I'm gone the more I want to see Rebecca. I can talk to Earl and play with him. I can only see and look at Rebecca. But I'm going to get braver and talk to her. Honest, I am.

We had another night jammed into the wagon box 'stead of having our quilts spread over the desert sand on account of Father was still feeling jumpy about the rattlesnake in his ear. The moon was just coming up when we went to bed. I stood on the double tree a few minnits to watch it come up over the little mountain a ways off. The moon always looks more pretty coming up than going down, bigger and brighter. It was getting kind of cold when I climbed in beside Father in the old wagon. I'd almost ruther sleep in a cellar than in a covered wagon, 'cept cellars smell bad, and there's lots of toads and little spiders and long crawly santy-peeds. But out on the desert there's rattle-snakes and trantlers and scorpeens. Guess there's always something anywheres that gives you the jimjams.

It was sort of late when we drove off 'stead of early. One of our tires had come loose, and we musn't start away with a loose tire. If we bust a wheel out here on the desert you can't tell when we would get home. Somehow we would have to go after a blacksmith, and it would take him half a week to mend the broke spokes and busted fellows, and after that he would have to put the tire back on. We would never get the wagon home with only three wheels. We would have to pay the blacksmith a live hog, else a calf, or mebbee ten bushels of potatoes. If we didn't have them, then Jim and Bill would have to work a whole week on the blacksmith's farm. No, we better not get a busted wheel, not out here on the 'Scalanty desert. That would be awful.

Father made some wedges from an egg box and hammered them under the tire good and tight. It took a lot of wedges. In the hot sun tires come loose lots of times, but we been lucky on this trip. Father and me didn't want a single bad thing to happen now, we were so close to home. Father said we would get there sometime tonight. Guess I'll be pretty darn glad on account of I'm getting tired of this trip, tired of this desert. Summit is going to look pretty good to me.

On account of that wheel Father didn't trot the horses like he figgered he would. I stayed on the springseat keeping my eyes peeled for something to see. Seemed like the desert was just holding everything in now that we were leaving and didn't want to let anything out. I was hoping at least to see another bunch of wild horses. Father just laffed at me. "If we waited here till you had whiskers longer than mine, we wouldn't see another band of wild horses like that."

When we pulled up to Johnson's Fort it was almost dark. We could see freighters camped there, sitting around the fire and talking. We only stayed long enuff for the horses to eat their

oats and drink what water they needed from the stream running there. It was the last oats we had. Our meat was gone too,
since dinner, and so was most of our bread. We were coming
out even with things. No matter if it was getting late, Father
wanted to get home.

It's uphill after you leave Johnson Fort. We had to go slow.
We didn't talk much. I had learned to think, same as Father.
Grandmother had told me if I always think good thoughts I
would grow up to be a good man. That's the kind of thoughts
I'd been thinking, all right, ever since we started up the grade,
about Mother and Rebecca and Earl, which I know, myself, are
the best things to think about.

After a while we hit on the main road which goes from
Summit to Cedar City and then to St. George. It's the Dixie
road. The horses knowed just which way Summit was as soon
as we got to the forks of the road, all by theirselfs. They turned
the wagon north toward Summit. It wouldn't be long now.

We had gone a little ways all quiet and still, when of a sudden
Father must of thought of something which he had forgot to
think about before. Quicker'n scat he slammed on the brake
and yelled "Whoa!" I jumped almost off the springseat.

"Great Caesar, Buck!" he hollered at me. "I forgot about
those greenbacks. Holy Smoke! Hope you haven't lost them!"

But I had forgot the greenbacks, same as Father, even forgot
there was a bunchy place on my shoulders. I knowed I had a
string around my neck on account of oncet or twice when I
wiped sweat off, my finger sort of slipped the string. But I had
forgot what it was for. Probly on account of I sleep with my
waist and pants on. All I take off when I go to bed is my old
raggedy straw hat. This trip had made it even more raggedy. If

I didn't keep my pants and waist on I'd be plum nekked. Who wants to sleep nekked when santy-peeds or scorpeens or even trantlers are crawling around the bed or even on it?

"Quick, take off your shirt," Father said. He was in such a hurry he couldn't wait for me to take it off myself, he had to help unbutton the buttons. But our fingers got tangled. Now that it was dark we had to do it all by feeling, and we kept getting ahold of each other's fingers. Next we couldn't untie the string which was around my shoulders and neck, couldn't find the end of the string to begin untying. "Confound that string!" Father grumped. He got out his big pocketknife and held it up in the moonlight to see where to put his thumbnail on the blade to open it. That knife didn't look so good to me. He put the cold blade against my neck to get under the string and snip! I started to breathe again.

Now Father had his greenbacks, which he counted slowly one by one, and they were all there same as back in Panaca. "Imagine that, Buck, I been out of my head to forget our money." He stowed them in his pant pockets. "We been lucky, and I was foolish to leave Hanks and the other men to go it alone. Won't do that another time." I put my waist back on, shivering a little. Father yanked off the brake, shook the lines at the horses, and we started straight for Summit.

When you're in a hurry horses walk slow as oxen, only now it didn't much matter; we didn't have far to go. The night air along the road wasn't so cold as on the desert. Father had his greenbacks, I had my smell cans. Good gosh! I dived back under the wagon cover. I had forgot the only things I was bringing home to Mother and Father. The moon shined a bit through the front cover, and I could find my box which I had put there where it would be handy. I didn't stay back there long enuff to take even one smell on account of I didn't want Father to know what I'd gone back to do.

Back on the seat, I could tell Father was feeling better. He had started to sing a song, same as after Idaho Bill didn't rob or kill us. This time it was a differnt song. Didn't know Father could sing so many. This was about an old man name of Uncle Ned. He lived a long time ago. He had long fingers but didn't have any teeth. Where there should of been hair on his head there wasn't any. 'Sides being poor, he was blind. He was in a bad fix all right. When he died they laid his shovel and hoe down. They hung up his fiddle bow, too. I'm going to learn that song so Earl and me can sing it and feel sad.

Father and me were still singing when we drove past Ray Linn's ranch. The dogs came running out to the wagon barking and barking. Father said he wasn't sure if the dogs were barking at the wagon like dogs mostly do, or if our singing had sent them wild. But what did we care what those old dogs thought! Just ahead was Summit's darker shadow on the ridge. I could see the shape of the cottonwood tree at the corner of our yard by the road. A light winked where the door would be. Mother and the others must be looking for us. I couldn't wait to jump off the wagon and run in the door. I was busting with things to tell.

PART THREE

HARD LESSONS

A HECKUVA TOWN

Soon as the wagon drew close, old Herk must of knowed right off it was us, on account of he came running to the street, barking loud and fast, to meet us. His bark is differnt from Ray Linn's dogs. I can always tell if it's Herk. His is a glad bark. "Hello, Buck! Gosh! I'm glad you got home. I been lonesome ever since you been gone." We drove inside the yard and stopped the wagon.

Herk tried to climb up the wheel he was so happy to see us, specially me. Then Jim or Bill was hollering from the shed, "Hello, there! Is that you? Father! Buck!" They had their bed on the shed, and it took a minnit or two for them to pull on shoes and jump down. Guess Herk's barking and the wagon jolting had waked them up. "It's us, all right!" I hollered back. They came hurrying to take care of the horses. They knowed Father and me would be plum tuckered. Only now I didn't feel tired a bit. Father climbed off the seat before Jim and Bill got to the wagon.

Quick as I could I scrambled back under the cover to grab my smell-can box. I wasn't going to let anybody find out about my suprises just yet. While Father and the boys were bizy I took the box out past the chicken coop and close to the end of the mud wall, where the brush growed tall. Nobody would see it way out there. Herk went with me, else I wouldn't dast gone so far. The big moon made scary shadows wherever I looked. Even if I was at home I was scairt to go out in tall brush after night. You can't tell when the slithery shadows might try to grab you. I put the box by a big bush where I could easy find it in the morning. Then I hurried back, keeping a good hold on Herk's hair so he would not run back to the wagon and leave me alone.

Then I saw Mother talking to Father by the wagon, looking around. "Where's Buck gone to? I haven't had a hello from him yet." "Here I am!" I yelled and ran to get her hug and hugs from all the rest of the family.

Next morning it felt so fine to be home. Everything looked good to me. Summit was the nicest town what ever was. After breakfast I went out to our front gate and looked up towards Earl's house, then over where Rebecca's house is, only I couldn't see hers on account of houses and sheds and lots between it and our house. But I knowed it was there. Everything felt just right. Then I turned and looked out past where the Injuns camp close to the mountains and out from there to where Ray Linn's ranch is, where it is mostly stunty brush and rock and cedar trees. I looked up the mountain. Near its top I could see the Lone Tree, a big pine tree standing all by itself which makes a lot of shade. Sometimes big boys and girls climb clear up to that tree, mostly on Sundays or May Day, taking their picnics. Sam says they go up there to spark.

One Sunday afternoon Earl and me climbed up to that Lone Tree. It took us a long time, on account of we were barefoot. We couldn't hardly make it, but we did. Some bigger boys and girls were already there which was a good thing on account of the mountain was too steep for Earl and me to come down it barefooted. So girls took ahold of our hands and helped us get down almost to the Injun camp. We had to go slow it was so steep, but they laffed and didn't mind us being poky. If they hadn't of helped, we might of fell and rolled down the mountain like that chunk of cedar on the steep hill.

While I was looking around, I was doing a lot of thinking, and one thing I thought about was that it does you good to ride behind horses or oxen on account of it teaches you how to think. I knowed myself this is true. Father did a lot of thinking on our trip, sitting behind the team, and he is a good thinker. I can do it now, too.

I had not told the folks anything about my long trip yet, everyone being so bizy, but soon Mother came to the door and yoo-hooed for me to come in and talk with her. She had not seen me for such a long time it seemed to her like I'd been gone a whole year. She asked me to pick threads and tell her of my trip. She kept me talking all the time we worked at the loom and asked lots of questions, which I knowed she would. She had been ankshus ever since Father and me left. At night she wondered if Father had fixed a good bed for me. In the daytime she wondered if Father made that place for me to lay down on under the cover. She wondered if I wore my hat like she said to do and if I got homesick. Mother sure likes me, and I like her, too, more than anyone else in the whole world. She said every time she looked at me this morning, she did not know if she would laff or cry. If I was some other little boy she would laff. Since it was her own boy she figgered she ought to cry. "What you want to do that for?" I asked.

"You used to be a little bit sunburnt all the time. But now you are like a piece of cooked meat. Anyone who hasn't seen you before would think you were an Indian papoose."

"So would you be sunburnt if you had to sit all day on the springseat and wipe sweat," I told her.

"Anyway, till that sunburn wears off, don't you get close to any of Old Wibe's band. They would think your father had stolen one of their papooses. Can't tell what they might do if they thought that." The twitch in her mouth showed she was only joshing.

I told her about Lucy and Mr. Hanks and his guns and the wild horses and about Desert Spring and the steep hill and how glad we were to get through with Pioche in a hurry, and about Idaho Bill. I guess I started telling her that first. You ought to of seen her eyes bung out when I told her. "Just think of it!" she said. "A boy like you looking right in the face of a highway robber, a real robber!"

"Yes, and he had a pistol all ready to shoot and a gun, too." She shook her head at that. When I got to the part about the rattlesnake which wanted to get into bed with us, she just about fell off her stool. She thought that was worse than seeing Idaho Bill. When we were through picking threads she said I could go play. She knowed I had so much to tell it would take more than one day.

Felt like I had been away so long I didn't know if things would be the same as they were before. I would have to go in town and see, but mebbe I better see our own yard first. First thing, some of our old hens were scratching close by the fence. Our big black rooster cocked his head sideways and looked at me. He was not sure if it was Buck standing by him. He started scratching and stopped sudden and cocked his other eye at me. Guess he figgered I was not a papoose, anyways. He quit looking and went on scratching like heck. I watched him. Pretty soon he found something and gave a loud rooster cackle, calling the hens to come and get it, which they did on the run. The first hen to the rooster got the bug or worm or whatever it was he scratched up. Then he started scratching for another.

All our oxen were out in the corral. Bally and Red and Blue were laying down chewing their cuds. Buck was off to one side chewing his cud same as the others. I could tell he was thinking, mebbee wondering when I would get home. I went along the fence closer to him and climbed up and over. Right off, Buck came walking over where I was at, wiggled his nose holes at me, and flipped his ears and nodded his head at me. Buck was telling me how glad he was to see me home once more. He had been awful lonesome. Outside of my own family, Buck is the only relashun I got in Summit.

Doggone it, Earl should of been down to see me long before this. He could easy tell our wagon had got home. There it is in plain sight with the cover on. Might be he is sick or something. I went over to his house. But his mother told me Earl had gone to Parowan with his pa yesterday afternoon and probly wouldn't be back today. I'll bet if Earl knowed I was home from Pioche he wouldn't wait for his pa and come home on foot.

Then I went looking around Rebecca's place. She might be out in the yard somewhere, but she wasn't. I stuck around a long time hiding behind the fence in differnt places, but didn't see a thing of her. She could of gone to Parowan, too. She has got relashuns over there, same as Earl. Doggone relashuns, anyways!

What a heckuva town Summit is! It's deader than nits, that's what. The desert is more livelier than Summit is. Nobody was anywheres that I could see. I was lonesome same as on the desert, and beginning to feel like a lost coyote. If I could of seen

Rebecca for just one look half a block away it would of made everything fine again.

After dinner I poked around town the rest of the afternoon. It was the lonesomest place in the world. I met Earl's Uncle Lorenzo and another man. They both know me, but they walked right past as if I wasn't on the sidewalk. They didn't say, "Hello, Buck! Glad to see you home again. Did you see any robbers or wild horses?" They didn't even Pass the Time of Day. I saw Rebecca's brother and a youngish woman coming along the sidewalk. They kind of looked at me a second, but only a second, and went right on talking to each other. They didn't say, "Well, well! If that ain't Buck! How you feelin' after your long hot trip? Did you see any men get shot or see some Gentiles in Pioche?" No, they never said a word like that. I was not more than a chicken on the sidewalk.

Sister Harris was inside her fence pulling weeds out of her squash vines. She straightened up to see who was passing by and pushed her long hair away from her face and out of her eyes. She looked at me. She knows me, same she knows her own kids. She didn't say, "Stars! If that ain't Buck! Did you see any whirlwinds on the desert, or lakes of water which ain't lakes?" She was just like the others, did not even tell me I was sunburnt. She only stooped and went back to pulling weeds. Her hair flopped down in front same as before.

Gosh! What a town! What a heckuva town! Nobody cares if I been on a long, long trip to Pioche and just got home. I wished I was on the desert hunting flowers with Lucy. Next time I will stop with Tasker's wife for a while at Desert Springs. The freighters all know how to say hello, and she likes talking to me.

Supper was ready when I got home. I felt so bad I couldn't hardly walk back to the house and homesick for something, even

if I was in my home. I used to think Summit the best town in
the whole world, but it ain't. Summit is dead, dead as nits. All
the people are dum, too, dum as pigs. I wouldn't have the town.
No wonder God don't do things for Summit. I wouldn't either if
I was him. All I would give Summit is gofers and weeds, prairie
dogs and pisants. And I think God already has.

Next morning I had to tell Sam the things I had seen. He
had scolded me because I passed him up yesterday. Sam thought
the wild horses, Idaho Bill, and the way coyotes catch rabbits
were the best things on the trip. He wanted to of seen them
his ownself. Then I picked threads with Mother again, and we
talked some more about my trip. Mother says she is proud of
me. Course, she's got more sense than all Summit put together.

All of a sudden after dinner I remembered my smell cans.
Out to the end of the mud wall I ran. Geeminy Whiz! I had
been bad as Father forgetting his greenbacks. Seems like him
and me can think the same, then we forget the same. I had not
thought a thing about the cans since I hid them under that
bush. Right now I thought to bring Mother's can to her. She
will be suprised when she sees what a sweet-smelling present I
brought her from Pioche. Next I will take Earl's can up to him.
He ought to be home by tomorrow.

When I got to the bush, oh m'gosh! A million ants had
found where I hid the cans and were all over the box, all over
the ground by the box, coming from everywhere, going away
to everywhere else. I ran to the woodpile and picked up a club.
Soon as I got back I slammed that box hard as I could. Away it
went, rolling on the ground. Out tumbled my sweet-smelling
cans, covered with ants. I grabbed them and ran for the creek.
Quick I washed the ants off the outside, then got a stick and
poked inside. Ants were all over so I washed them out in a hurry

and looked inside again. The insides were as clean and shiny as the outsides. Everything was gone but the pitchers. Even they were mostly peeling off. Guess the water done that. Just then I started feeling really bad. I tried to smell the cans. That sweet smell was all gone. They were only just cans and did not smell any better than old milk pans. All on account of them danged pisants! I know it is wicked to say dang, but pisants are wicked, too. Dang 'em!

Now I would not have a thing to give Mother or Earl or Rebecca, or Father. I had saved the cans so long and so careful. My whole trip was spoiled. I didn't have a thing to show I been to Pioche. I throwed my good-for-nothing cans into the ditch. Down the stream they bobbled till they ducked out of sight. I sat on the ground and cried, holding my face in my hands, thinking of all the things I been thinking when I stood by that pile of cans in Pioche. Now there would be nothing. No one would have my sweet suprise. After another long time I got up and walked toward the house. My face was looking down. My arms only hung loose from my shoulders. Guess I looked sick, which I felt bad enuff to be. Guess I would just go tell Mother about the smell cans, anyways. Then she would know at least I been thinking of her.

THE THUNDERSTORM

I told Mother all about my smell cans which I didn't have anymore. She said she was glad I had remembered her with such
a nice thing, but for me not to feel bad about what happened
to them, since knowing I had thought of her was the nicest
part. It was not so much the gift, she said, as the spirit inside of
me which made me want to bring her something special from
Pioche. That made me feel a lot better, and I knowed Earl would
feel the same way. I'll have to think about something else for
Rebecca sometime, but not another go with a valentine. After
a while she said I did not have to pick any more threads if I
wanted to go into town. She thought I ought to go tell Aunt
Mary about my long trip.

Aunt Mary's house and Rebecca's house are not so far apart.
If I could see Rebecca only once it would help a lot. Summit
would feel better to me than what it does now. When I got up
to the street and looked around hopefully, I did not see a sign
of her. I went on to Aunt Mary's, walking kind of slow and
keeping a look backwards.

I have not been up to Aunt Mary's for a long time. Now I
want to see her. She is not dum like some women in Summit.
She has got sense, same as Mother, and she will bung her eyes

out when I tell her the things I seen since I been gone. Don't think she has ever seen so many Gentiles in one place like I have.

Almost before I knowed it, I had come to Brother Gray's pigpen, right against the sidewalk. Earl's grandpa has a pigpen against the sidewalk, same as this one is, and a sheep pen, too. So has the Bishop. The pigpens are so close to the sidewalk that the sidewalk fence is part of the pen. I could easy tell Brother Gray had only this morning spaded all the messy stuff out of his pigpen. He had throwed it out on the inside of the fence. Then he had put nice clean straw in the pen, most of it back under the roof. The back part of pigpens always has a roof made of straw and dirt. That is so the rain cannot soak through and so there will be shade for the pigs. That is the way everybody has it. Back under the roof is the pigs' sleeping place, night and day.

Two good-size hogs were in the pen. They came grunting over to the front soon as they saw me looking at them. They did not squeal but acted like all they wanted was to see the boy what was gawping at them. They have seen me lots of times before, but they could not tell who I was today on account I was so sunburnt. Earl and me have looked in the pen lots of times and talked to the pigs, but they didn't know what we said. Pigs are dum that way. Not like oxen or Herk. But sometimes we can tell what the hogs are saying to us when they grunt a differnt grunting from a reggler one. A reggler one don't have much talk-meaning to it. Talking grunts are kind of short, low ones which come from back in their throats quite a ways.

When I went through Aunt Mary's gate she was out by the walk fixing her flowers. She turned and looked at me kind of queer, bending her head to one side and looking same as that rooster had and then bending it the other way and looking some more. She said afterwards she could not figger out who that boy was coming to her house. Soon as I got close I hollered out, "Hello, Aunt Mary!" Then she busted out laffing. She said if I had come with a gang of papooses she wouldn't of knowed which one was Buck. Eliza had gone to play with Jessie Black. Laura was over to Harris's visiting their good-size girl named Zina. Sarah Ann was not home, either, don't know where. Women in Summit gad around quite a bit. Today Aunt Mary had me to dinner just by ourselfs. She said she was glad it was that way. She thought I was a wonderful boy to see so many things on just one trip and asked how I liked Summit after being gone so long. I told her I didn't like it a bit. It was dum and dead as nits. She laffed and said I must have had a wonderful time on that trip to make me feel that way about our Summit.

Aunt Mary is Hinglish, and so's most everybody else in town but my family. Some talk Hinglish that is differnt even from Aunt Mary's. Theirs would sound like "Hi can heat with the girls every day, but Hi don't 'ave a chance to heat with Buck very hoffen. Hi'll fry a hegg for you and one for me." Aunt Mary drinks tea. Everyone in Hingland drinks it. She knows I'm too little for it and it would stunt me.

She had made a sweet cake only yesterday. Most of it was left, and she gave me a big piece. Sweet cake is made with molasses and some more differnt things that smell mighty good. She told me to bring Earl over sometime and she would bake a pie for us. She knows we like pie better than any eating thing there is. Earl and me have been to her house lots of times. We have been to Earl's grandpa's other wife's house, too. She's Hinglish same as Aunt Mary. We been to everybody's house in Summit, it seems. They all know us, but Earl's ma says she thinks the hogs and dogs know us better than our own folks do.

After we had dinner I went out and got on top of the shed where she keeps her pigpen. The boys had made the roof clean and tight. She said I could sit there long as I liked to look at Rebecca's lot, which I could see was not far from Aunt Mary's straw shed, but I couldn't see all of her lot. I could only see her house and a piece of the lot. So I kept sitting and looking, sitting and looking. Then all of a sudden, oh m'gosh! There was Rebecca, in plain sight. Now I felt good, oh, so good all inside me!

She had come out her kitchen door. Quick as scat, I dropped flat on the straw. There was a corn patch not far from her house, and I could only see the end of that patch. A little carrot patch was close to the corn. I had sneaked into it a couple of times to look for her. She went to the carrot patch and pulled a few and layed them on the ground. Then she pulled another one and wiped it with her hand. Mostly carrots come out of the ground clean enuff to eat. You don't have to wipe them hardly a bit. She stood there a minnit or two and ate that carrot. I am glad she likes carrots, same as me and Earl. I could see her plain as anything from where I was at. Even if she was quite a ways off, she looked sweet and pretty. She always looks that way. I could see a ribbon in her hair. She keeps her hair fixed nice. She wouldn't have it scraggly like a boy's. She couldn't see me 'cause I layed flat as I could on the straw. I stayed there till she went inside her house again. Wonder why I never thought before of getting on Aunt Mary's shed to look for Rebecca. I felt lots better about everything. Guess towns never seem so good to you till you feel good in your ownself. Now I'd seen Rebecca, I wanted to see Earl. Then I would know things are still the same as before.

Earl's ma had said he would be coming home sometime today. I guessed I would go out along the Parowan road to meet him and his pa and ride back with them. I felt so good I could walk all the way to Parowan and not feel tired. Earl and me can sit back in the wagon and talk. Mebbee his pa would like me to tell the things I seen. If he does, then all three of us can sit on the springseat. That might be best. I'll sit on the outside so I won't be turning my head sideways and back again looking at Earl and then at his pa. If I am on the outside I can look the same way and see both of them together.

I been so bizy looking at Rebecca and feeling good that I had not noticed how awful hot the sun was. But when I started out on the road I could feel the hot ground was almost burning my feet which are pretty tuff. A little past the edge of town I stopped for a while on the bridge where Summit creek goes under it. I let my feet dangle and swish around in the clear cool water. Water feels so good to your feet on hot sunny days. No wagons were going or coming along the road. Some clouds on the mountains toward Cedar City looked almost black. I was wishing they would sail over and give me some shade. Cloud shade is good, but not good as tree shade. I had left my straw hat at home. It was so shabby I did not want Rebecca to see me wearing it in case she saw me when I saw her.

After I had give my feet a good soaking I started again along the road. Earl and his pa would be coming most anytime now. I bet Earl will open his mouth plenty wide when he sees me coming down the road towards his wagon. He don't know I am sunburnt, so mebbee he won't know who I am, either. He might take me for a lost papoose from Old Wibe's tribe, too.

I had gone quite a ways, but I didn't dast go any further. I had got to thinking mebbee Injuns might come along the road before I met Earl, and I did not want to be stole. So I stopped where there was a tree not far off the road which had some shade. I went over to sit under it. If Injuns came along I would crawl around to the other side and lay flat. It was a good place to sit and wait. No rocks, no ants, just shade and soft dirt. The shade felt good to me. I had walked far enuff to make my skin plenty hot. Soon as I sat down and got settled I started thinking of Rebecca. I shut my eyes to see her plain as if she was dancing with me. Probly I must of shut them too tight, on account of next thing I knowed I was asleep, only I didn't knowed I was asleep.

I waked up sudden. I knowed I been asleep, on account of a long, loud, roaring noise had waked me, coming from everywhere. Sounded like thunder. But it could not be thunder 'cause the sun was still shining all around me. But it sounded so much like thunder that I got scairt while I was listening. Boooom-mm-mm! Crackety Bang! That was thunder all right! Felt like it shook the ground I was sitting on. I jumped up and looked around, but only for a second. Coming fast over the mountains from Cedar City rolled a black cloud about a mile wide and aiming toward Summit and me, with thundering and lightning something awful. Looked like rain might be pouring down under it.

In a jiffy I left that tree and began running up the Parowan road toward Summit. I would be kilt if I did not get home ahead of that cloud. I ran the fastest I ever could, tightened my fists, gritted my teeth. Folks do not know how fast a boy can run till he is almost scairt to death. But that big cloud of lightning and thunder was coming fast, too, faster than wild horses. Almost before one thunder had quit, another one started bigger and louder than the one before. The lightning flashes were getting closer to me. Soon it would be close enuff to hit me and kill me dead as nits. I crossed the Summit bridge fast as a rabbit chased by dogs, but even that was not fast enuff. The storm was already close to our house. I knowed I couldn't make it. But I kept on running. I wanted to cry but didn't dast. Couldn't use the breath.

Thunder was busting right over my head. Lightning was striking close to my face. Once I almost strangled trying to swallow pieces of it which had slipped between my gritted teeth. My mouth had a terrible sour taste. Brother Gray's pigpen was coming up close. Booomm-mm-m! Crackety Bang! Over his fence I jumped and crawled under the roof. Rain poured down in a stream, a reggler cloudburst. But I was safe, plum out of breath and tired. I had run a long ways, at least a mile, could of been more. I never stopped once to breathe. Now I couldn't hardly get my breath back.

The roof was too low for me to stand up. I had to stoop over. Brother Gray's hogs were laying on the clean straw close together. It was a tight fit, but I snuggled in between them to get away from that terrible thunder and lightning and pouring rain. As I wiggled down to rest better and get my breath back, each of the hogs grunted some short little grunts which said, "It's all right, Buck, but don't wiggle so much." I knowed pretty much what their short grunts mean. The warm feeling of the hogs and the good feeling on account of not being dead made me sleepy. Right there, safe from the storm, I went to sleep and plum forgot I was in with the hogs.

I waked up kind of sudden, like I did under the tree. Must of been the stillness which woke me. The storm had gone. I could hear it somewhere far off in a tired rumble. Everything was quiet in Summit. I scrambled from between the hogs and crawled away. They grunted at me in a friendly way to say goodbye. Then they went to sleep again.

Careful, I peeked out over the pigpen. No one was in sight as I climbed over the fence and quick got back on the sidewalk which was all puddles from the rain. I walked kind of slow, as if I hadn't been anyplace else. Water was everywhere, streams of it pouring down the street. The ditch by Rebecca's house was full of muddy water. Everything was stink and smelled like a flood had been. The mud and water felt cold to my feet, specially since they had just been so hot before.

Guess I was the only live person in town to get out on the street so soon. I straightened up and walked slow past Rebecca's house, wishing she would look through her window and see me and think I was brave to get out so soon after that awful storm. Not even a man was out yet. Not a horse or a cow, dog, or chicken anywhere. Clouds were all over the sky, and I was shivering. Everything was so still I could only hear water running wherever there was a ditch for it to run, and some of it spilled over onto the ground.

Mother was at the door when I got home. "Where in the world have you been in this terrible storm!" I said I had been to Aunt Mary's, just as she told me to do. She couldn't see why I came home so quick before the water was off the street. I told her I was still feeling kind of homesick and couldn't wait. Father made a fire in the fireplace, and I backed up to it to get warm. I still felt shivery, but pretty quick my pants and waist got to steaming a bit. Mother sniffed the air, just two or three sniffs. "If smell goes for anything, I would say you just got out of Aunt Mary's hog pen." She twisted her nose a little. I shook my head. "Honest, I haven't." Which was the truth, sort of.

I went outside soon as I could. I didn't want any more of that pig-smell floating around the house. Mother might be asking more questions, like if I wasn't in Aunt Mary's hog pen, then whose hog pen was I in. I went out to the ditch and washed the rings off my legs just above the ankles. I had them standing in the pig-water in the hog pen while I looked over the top to see if anybody was close. The rain had put a lot of water in the pen, but it was awful piggy, anyways. Yet that rain just kind of shined up Summit, and I felt good to be home in it.

SHOES

The freighter-man with a great big wagon and two spans of horses unloaded some boxes at the co-op store in Parowan just when Earl and me and his pa had come with Father on an errand. They went inside. Earl and me were waiting on the street when the freighter came driving into town, and when we saw him stop at the store we went over to watch him unload his stuff. The way he went about it showed he was in a hurry to get done and be on his way. Father says he hauls goods for the stores all along the road from Salt Lake City to St. George.

He had let his endgate down and was taking boxes off when we got there. He carried boxes in his ownself. The last one was a big box. His other driver had to help. They tipped it end over end, almost too big to get through the door. Don't know what was in it. Coming out of the store, the freighter-man was putting money into his big buckskin purse, which the store man must of paid him for hauling the goods. Right straight he fastened up his endgate, and him and his partner climbed onto the high springseat. He yanked off the brake, shook the lines hard at his horses, yelling at them, "Git up! Go on!" Just like that, he was off toward Cedar City.

While he was doing all this he did not say a word to anybody, not out by the wagon, not in the store. He did not even look at a single one of us standing by. Fact, in his hurry he almost knocked Earl over. Soon as he was on his way, old Brother Throstle, Earl's grandpa who was standing and watching with us, said he figgered the man was always in a hurry like that on account of roads is ruff, and he has a long ways to go each day. He moved fast so he could get to all the stores waiting for him to bring things to. Probly he did not have time to waste talking to anybody just watching him work.

"Just the same," another man said, "seems to me he could of at least Passed the Time of Day. I got my opinion of anybody who won't do that. He wouldn't of needed to stop his work to say that much."

"Well, of course I must admit," Brother Throstle hurried to say, "it is the first time I ever saw a man who wouldn't."

Passing the Time of Day is what people say to each other when they meet on the sidewalk or on horseback, or in wagons, or when they're just sticking around a store like Earl and me and these neighbor men. It is words folks say like, "Well, how are ya t'day?" else, "Good mornin'! Fine day, ain't it?" Mebbee they say, "Good afternoon! How ya doin' these days?" Or, "Well, well! Glad to t'see ya. How's your folks?" If it's a plum stranger they meet, and he's in kind of a hurry, they mostly just say, "Howd'do!" Sometimes besides what they say, they raise their hand and nod their head or put their fingers to their hat brim to the person they're Passing the Time of Day with. It just stands to reason everybody says something when they meet somebody else.

If you don't, people think you're sick or half asleep, else mad or too stuck up to speak to them. That time when Father and me met the freighters we didn't know on the other side of Desert Spring and turned off the road to let them pass, he raised his hand and said, "Howd'do!" to each of the wagons, and the drivers raised their hands and said, "Howd'do!" back at Father. And when the Injuns were coming down the canyon when we were on our way to Pangwitch, Father raised his hand and said "How!" to them, and they raised theirs as they passed us by and said "How!" to him. Father always uses good manners with Injuns. It's common curtsey. Earl's pa piped up and said that if Idaho Bill would of gone right by us without Passing the Time of Day, when he could of easy robbed us or kilt us but didn't, he would of been worse than a robber, he would of showed he wasn't no gent, so Idaho Bill must of been a robber-gent. All the men standing around had a good laff with that.

In one of the boxes the freighter left at the co-op store were shoes for everybody. Earl's pa bought a pair for Earl. Father bought me a pair, too. Haven't had many of these, leastwise not new. Earl and me looked at each other. Now the shoes are bought, we would have to wear them. Both our fathers said that. We hate like sixty to do it. But Father says it is high time we get used to wearing them, specially as Earl and me will be in school in the winter again. When we got back home, Sam laffed and said that is what comes of being part of the Rising Generation. Sometimes he gets under my skin. Folks think him and his friends are downright harum-scarums. He does not even go to church reggler and probly knows even less than me about the Rising Generation.

Boys' shoes are stiff and heavy. Don't see how we can ever drag our feet around with us when they are tied up fast in such things. But I bet the shoes will come in handy when we have another dance. Earl and me will jump around and stomp the floor and make noise like other boys do. Best of all, I won't be afraid to dive through the gang when I go for Rebecca. Those shoes will give me a chance to get even with some of them which been pushing me around. Some might be only barefoot theirselfs. Mother has knitted me another pair of socks from yarn she has unwound from the tops of Father's worn-out ones. With socks on, the shoes felt good at the beginning.

First thing to try them out, Earl and me went hunting cottontails out around Snake Hill. With shoes on we didn't have to care about rocks or bushes or stickery cactus. We just scuffed along. On account of us not knowing how to run fast with stiff new shoes, the cottontails got away from us easy. After we had run and fell over a lot, we caught a couple, one for Earl, one for me. That was all we needed. Good thing, too. Our shoes were feeling tighter all the time. We already had made little boxes to hold our cottontails on account of we knowed we would be catching them one day or another. Soon as I got home I put my bunny in his box which was close to the chicken coop and went to the house to take my shoes off, limping now and not feeling too frisky.

I did not know how bad my feet were till I went to take my shoes off. That running around among the rocks and bushes had made my feet feel queer inside the shoes. Quick as I got in the house I flopped on the floor and loosened the string of buckskin that tied the shoes and tried to pull a shoe off. Ouch! Ouch! Jeeminy Criminentals! Ouch! I couldn't hardly start to do it. The first pull made me yell out loud. One more pull, and I dropped the foot quick and yelled even louder. Mother hurried in to see what was killing me. "It's my shoes! My shoes! They won't come off!"

Mother got down on the floor and took the strings out of the shoes and pulled and wiggled them. I hollered she was killing me! Off came that shoe. I wished I was dead. Soon as the first shoe came off, Mother grabbed the other one and pulled and wiggled and twisted same as before. Soon as I knew I was dead again, that other shoe came off. My whole body felt like it had been inside a shoe. I cried plenty. I could see Mother had tears, too, on account of she had to hurt me so much. If the shoes had not come right off, she would of had to cut them off. My socks were bloody. Mother went for her scissors and split my bran new socks from the top clear down to the toes. Then, very careful-like, she took them off by spreading the edges both ways from the split place. She said in all her life she hoped never again to have to take socks off that way. My feet looked like a coyote been chewing on each one, my heels so skinned they looked like raw pig meat. Blood came from my toes same as my heels. My whole foot was skinned. And right there inside my split sock I could see a little bit of my own skin sticking to it. I felt kind of sick. Mother washed my feet, careful not to touch them very much, and put some salve on all the skinned places, which stung like blazes, and tied some clean white cloth on them. That felt good.

Earl had skinned his feet same as me. He told me his pa took a shoe off and nearly kilt him doing it, and shouted at his mother, "Just look at that! I call that criminal! Tarnation! What's wrong with the blamed shoemaker? Can't he make a shoe what'll not skin a boy's foot like that first time he wears it?" Earl said his pa was awful mad and yanked the other shoe off with a big twist and a pull. Earl said he didn't dast look where his feet had used to be, on account of he knowed his pa had yanked them off with the shoes. Now we both have to go barefoot till the sores are scabbed over so they can get well. I know all about how they get better and how long it takes.

Earl's rabbit got away in less'n a week. Mine got away first time I went to his box to see how he was doing. Out he jumped, right between my legs and hopped away fast as he could, ducking between the poles of the fence, and went for the tall brush and weeds without slowing down. Because my feet had got so hurt from shoe-wearing the day before, I couldn't run hardly at all trying to catch him. Easy as nothing, he got away and never stopped till he got to Snake Hill, where rabbits head for when they run away from us. But if there is anything Summit has lots of, it is rabbits, so we knowed we would find ourselfs two other cottontails some other day, barefoot, you can bet.

Earl and me have found something else our shoes are good for besides stomping the floor at the dances and chasing after cottontails. Already we been figgering on it. Earl has got a plan for us to take care of that Abner, the bully boy always after us. Don't know why. Probly on account of we're smaller than him. He bosses us off the sidewalk and pushes us around after school. He tells us he will cut our ears off if we don't do what he says. Every time we meet him he picks on us just because he can, like he did at the Panner-rammer. We don't want our ears cut off. Just thinking about it gives us the jimjams. In town, wherever he is, if we see him first, we dasn't go there. But now that we got heavy shoes, Earl has a plan. We have spit and shook hands on it already.

We got ourselfs a good flattish rock, about the size of our hand, with an edge on one side and hid it. One day soon Earl and me will take that stone out of its hiding place and walk around the town with an eye out for Abner. He will see us acting smart and give chase. But we will duck around a corner, and when he comes we will jump on him. Suprise! First off will come a few kicks with our hard shoes on his shins. That will make him yelp. I am good at dodging fists, so I will fight him in front. Earl is good at grabbing legs and jerking boys over, and he will dart around behind and grab his hind legs. Kerplunk! Abner will fall down on his behind, and Earl and me will jump on him and roll him on his belly, then pull his arms up behind him. While I sit on his back and hold his arms, Earl will pull that rock out of his pocket and rub the sharp edge of it behind Abner's ears, kind of hard-like, doing as if he was really cutting the bully's ears off. He might even scratch Abner enuff to make a little bleed. We can scarcely wait. But first our feet which look like they been chewed on have got to get over their scabs and sore places. I think, myself, it might take a while.

THE SLIPPERY SLOPE

Earl and me been watching blackbirds chase a big crow thief out of town. It was getting to noon and dinner, and Earl had to be home pretty soon else the pigs would be squealing for their weeds. We did not walk fast as we should of, stopping too many times to look at things along the way, but that is just what Earl's pa says our eyesight is for, looking at things. He scolded Earl one day for not seeing their spotted cow had got out of the corral. "No use having eyesight," he said to Earl, "if you go along not looking at things happening around you." Not long after we started walking home, we saw a snake swallowing a long-tailed mouse. We could see it was a water snake, which don't hurt anybody. The mouse's hind parts, his legs and tail, were sticking out and wiggling a little. Snakes always swallow things head first. It takes them a long time to swallow, on account of the things they swallow are sometimes bigger than they are. I don't see how a snake no bigger round than my big toe can swallow a thing big as my whole foot. But one time Earl and me seen a thin snake swallowing a fat gofer. We each got a stick and pounded this snake on his back till he let go that gofer, but the snake had cut off the gofer's air too long, and it just kicked a few kicks and was dead.

While we were walking past the lower side of Brother Lamb's orchard, we kind of hurried. We knew we had already stopped to look at things too long and could tell by the sun it was noon already. We did not dast stop anymore and began walking faster. Earl said he bet the pigs were already squealing. We were hungry, too. Just then Earl turned his head right where he shouldn't of. Quick he grabbed my waist and yanked me back a foot or two. "Hold on a minnit, Buck. Just look at what I can see!" I whirled around and looked where he was pointing. Oh, m'gosh! Big red ripe peaches hanging on Brother Lamb's tree. Never seen such pretty ones, and what is more, it seemed like the peaches were looking at us same as we were looking at them. When you are hungry, ripe peaches look the best of anything. "Don't you wish we had a couple or two?"

Through the high poles of the fence we could see the tree plain, straight up a few feet from where we were at. There were other trees, but only one tree with big red peaches. The longer we looked, the redder they got, and the more we wished we had one to eat.

"Gosh, Buck, I'm so hungry I don't think I can walk home from here."

"Me, too," I said. "I'm plum empty inside."

"I ain't tasted a peach all summer," Earl said. "If I had one of them in my hands I wouldn't take time to peel it."

"Me either," I said. "I'd eat it skin and all. Then I'd suck the seed till I wore it out."

We forgot all about Earl's pigs waiting for their weeds and our mothers waiting with dinner. Ripe red peaches hanging on the tree right before your eyes make everything else go right out of your head. We climbed up the fence a pole or two and looked around. The orchard was still and empty, only just some birds twittering in the leaves. We could hear bees humming among the weeds in the orchard. We could not see a person anywheres.

"Wonder if it would hurt if we took just a couple," I said to Earl. "Looks to me that the limbs are almost busting with all of those peaches."

"Yup. A couple of peaches might take the weight off so the limbs wouldn't break," Earl said. "If the limbs broke, he would feel awful bad. Pa got mad one time when a limb busted on our apple tree. He said some of us should of seen what might happen and taken the weight off with a board."

"Guess Brother Lamb would feel same as your pa. If he knowed we were so close and didn't help him when we could, he would say we do not have good sense," I chimed in.

"Course he would," Earl said. "Brother Lamb is almost too old to do it his ownself, and he would feel good if he knowed a couple boys had took the weight off for him."

Brother Lamb has got two wives. The name of one is Goodenough. The other is Kindness. I know Sister Kindness, and she knows me, too. Sometimes she makes a Relief Society visit to Mother at our house. Last summer she gave me a whole double-handful of ripe pottywatomy plums. Sister Goodenough is kind of old and stays mostly in the house. Kindness is more younger. She has a chair in the shade of tall trees at the upper end of the orchard. From the fence Earl and me could easy see the chair, straight in line with the peach tree. Mostly she sits in the chair when she isn't doing something else.

We crawled down from the fence. There was a kind of little low place just under the bottom pole where we could just squeeze through one at a time. There was not a single person to see us.

It would be easy. In just a minnit or two we would hurry home and pull weeds for our mothers. Quiet as a couple of cottontails we crawled along a weedy furrow. About halfway to the tree we stopped to listen and peek around. Right then Brother Lamb's big yellow dog came up and stopped by Kindness's chair and looked down toward the peach tree. He started barking and barking. We layed still, flat on our bellies. At last the dog seemed to think nobody was apt to take his peaches, and he walked away toward the corral and straw sheds. Now we crawled fast as we could. Close to the tree we stopped once more. Doggone it! Sister Kindness had just come out of the house and went straight for her chair. She looked comfy and glad to be out in the air. She sat and sat and sat. We didn't think anybody could sit so still and so long. She wasn't doing a thing but looking straight down towards that tree. Once in a while she would take a quick look over at the house. All the time she was in that chair we did not dast even to whisper or wiggle the weeds, only lay still as rabbits under a bush.

After a long time she walked back to the house. We started to crawl again, this time on our bellies, which is hard work for elbows. We were almost to the tree when Jeeminy! She was coming out of the house again. We layed flatter than flat. She had a little bucket on her arm and was going straight toward the peach tree! When she got there she reached up and pulled down on a limb loaded with big red peaches. She was humming a song I knew, the Babble On song. The bucket slipped off her arm and rolled against some tall weeds. Earl was behind those weeds. I was behind some others just like them. I put my cheek on the ground so I could peek out of one eye. She picked a peach from the limb, rubbed the fuzz off with her hand. She wiped the fuzz off her hand onto her apron. She peeled the peach kind of slow with her teeth and fingers and bit off a chunk. Juice squirted all over her cheeks and fingers. She made a slushy noise eating that peach. It sounded so good. We were awful hungry for a peach that would make a lot of juice in our mouths. She licked her fingers, then wiped her hands and cheeks with her apron. She picked some more peaches slow and careful, looking at every one. At last she picked up her bucket and started humming that same song again and went back to the house.

Soon as she got in the house, we stood up by the tree, looking at it for a minnit to see if she had left any peaches for us. We thought there wasn't anybody around, but we did not figger on the Lamb boys, two of them almost big as men. They must of come up close to Kindness's house while she was picking. They couldn't help seeing us when we stood up and walked around the tree. The limbs were too high for us to reach any of them. I got on my hands and knees. Earl stood on my back. Kind of shaky, he was reaching for a limb when all of a sudden they came on us, cussing and calling us names, awful names. "Hey there! You dang little thiefs!" I tried to jump up. Earl fell on my back. Both of us went sprawling. We scrambled to our feet and made for that high pole fence faster than coyotes. We did not try to go through the hole—wasn't time enuff. Over the top we went like cats chased by barking dogs.

On the other side of the fence was a field of corn, now grown high and over our heads. Into that tall corn we went and right straight lost track of each other. The Lamb boys quit chasing us soon as they came to the fence, but I didn't know they had quit chasing and kept running fast as I could. Thought I would sure enuff see Earl at the other end of the field, but he wasn't there. I did not dast wait long for him. Mebbee the boys had grabbed him in the cornfield. Quick I ran crossways toward a deep gully. I could not see it, but I knowed it was there. It is the gully Sam says was made by high water from Summit creek when it used to run into the Little Salt Lake. The gully has been there before Summit was where it is.

In a little while the gully got so deep I could not climb out, but I was glad. No one could see me now. I kept on running. By and by was a place where the gully flattened out a little, and I walked right out onto level ground. I looked around me. Now I felt more ankshus. Summit was back behind me. I could only see the tops of the trees. I was way beyond Summit. Bears or wolves could easy eat me and nobody would ever know it. Or Injuns come along and steal me.

Home is on the west side of town, same as Brother Lamb's orchard. I musn't go back that way. I did not dast be seen on the street. Mebbee folks would already know all about it. I made a kind of circle around the north side of town, the Parowan side, keeping in the high sagebrush where I could. It seemed a long time before I crossed the Parowan road and went on toward the canyon, on account of the brush wasn't high enuff close to the road. I waded the creek, which wasn't so deep, and went along the side of Snake Hill, where it was rocky and I had to go slow. I was so tired I was staggery, but I didn't stub my toes any. Then soon as I got to the Injun camp place I made straight for home.

Only I couldn't run anymore. I was so hungry I was starved. And I felt bad, awful bad. I did not want to go home, but I had to. I was wishing it was Aunt Mary's week for Father, on account of then he would not be home to scold or whip me. But it wasn't. I wouldn't be lucky.

By the time I walked through the door, seemed like everybody in town knowed all about it. A couple of women had been to our house and blabbed it all to Mother and Father. Folks in Summit find things out quick, specially when boys size of Earl and me gone "stealing peaches." That is the way they told it. Guess the Lamb boys had come straight uptown and told everybody they saw.

Mother said that right off Father got a birch switch and told Grandmother Cragun, who was visiting from St. George, that he was going to give me a larruping I wouldn't forget. Grandmother took the switch from him and broke it into pieces. She told Father a larruping would not be necessary. All this she did before I even got home, but she told me about it later. It is mighty nice for a boy to have a grandmother in the house when his father goes on the rampage. That is what Grandmother told me, herself. Why are fathers like that? It wasn't easy for me that night, but it could of been a lot worse.

Next time I saw Earl was more than a week. He said he had not got home till after sundown. He did not dast come out of the cornfield till he knowed the Lamb boys had quit looking for us. And when he walked into his house there sat three women, two of them his relashuns, talking to his ma in loud, high voices. They did not see him standing by the edge of the door listening.

One said, "What's the Young and Rising Generation coming to! My, oh my!" She shook her head.

Another said, "And would you believe it! Boys in the Sunday School class a-stealin' peaches. Think of it! Such a sample to set for the little ones." The last one said, "And what do you think? Sister McCarty got real huffy 'cause we warned her about her little Buck going bad, just like Sam."

Earl said his ma was wiping her eyes with her apron. Guess she had been crying. While Earl was standing there his pa snuck up and grabbed him. He took Earl to the back of the house and give him a licking, then sent him off to bed without a bite to eat, and here poor Earl was starving same as me. After a while, though, his ma brought him his supper.

"Too bad you did not have a grandmother in the house," I told him.

"Wouldn't of done no good," he said, shaking his head kind of sad. "Pa says he's a man of his word. When he says he's goin' to give me a lickin', I get the lickin'."

Earl says if he was big as his pa and his pa little as him, he wouldn't whip or cuss him if three women had come to his house and called his little pa a peach thief. He'd box their ears and kick them out of the house. Which I know, myself, that is egzackly what he would do, all right. I was sorry for the fuss and scolding, sorry to make Mother and Father unhappy. Earl and me knowed we probly were as bad as those women said, but even so, we still wished the Lamb boys had come out to the orchard just a minnit or two after we got to the peaches. My mouth could almost taste them, and that hurt me the most.

ANOTHER DAVID

Mother did not scold me so much about Brother Lamb's peaches. She said she felt more like scolding the women for bringing their tattle into her house the way they did, specially now when her hands are full taking care of Ellie, who is feeling sicker all the time. That was why Grandmother had come up to Summit to stay a while and help out. I'm glad Mother felt to stand up to them. Mostly Mother does not jump on me quick as Father does.

In her everyday voice she said stealing things always made people unhappy, and she was sure that was the way I was feeling right now. Stealing things always brings trouble to them that steal. Sister Kindness would of give us a peach or two, mebbee even a whole hatfull, if we had but asked. She knows Sister Kindness likes little boys, which I know, myself, she does.

"But we didn't mean to steal, to really steal," I said. "The limbs were bended down so low they might break any minnit. If we took a peach or two off, the limbs wouldn't break so soon." Then Mother laffed, not a reggler laff, more a smile mixed with giggles.

"But you did not have the right to go inside the orchard or even touch a peach, no matter how you felt about not stealing." Course I knowed, myself, it had to of been stealing, else I wouldn't be feeling so bad.

Emily had already let me know how Mother told those Sisters that she didn't need any help raising her children. When she needed that, she would ask. She told them to look after their own children a little more and quit worrying about other people's children. They jumped like being stuck with a pin and did not say another word, but tried to slam the door when they went out. Mother has a little piece of old carpet close to the door for people to wipe their feet on when it is wet outside, and it got in the way of the door.

Father was lots madder. He thought a whupping was in order. Grandmother came in and soothed him down, and took me out on the front porch. She sat in the big rocking chair Uncle Jim had made. I stood close by with my back against the house and my hands behind me. I was looking down at my feet, but I wasn't thinking about what I had done to make Mother sad and me sorry. I was looking at my feet and put them side-to-side to see which had the biggest big toe. Each was just the same. The skin on both my feet looked good, too. I did not have a scab or a stubbed toe. All of them were straight and even. None of them was on top of some other toe, like on Father's feet. Even if my feet aren't so big, they can run fast enuff to catch grasshoppers, butterflies, gofers, and cottontail babies. And didn't they catch that old hen by the steep hill?

I had forgot that Grandmother was talking to me. She likes to talk about How Things Were when she came to Zion a long time ago, when Mother was just a little girl. Sometimes I don't unerstand all she is talking about. Just now it seemed to be about someone being in prison till the Judgement Day. All at once she reached over and pulled me closer to her, and then lifted me up on her lap. Oh m'gosh! If Idaho Bill would come riding his black horse along the street and see me sittin' on a woman's lap, even my grandmother's, next time he will rob us for sure. But quick I thought how good Grandmother has been to me. And she kept me from getting a whipping. Guess I could sit on her lap for that. She gave me a squeeze, twitched her legs for me to slide off, and told me to go run and play. But wagging her finger at me, she said I should never do such a wicked thing again. Not never. Then she went into the house.

Wish I knowed what Grandmother said when I was looking at my feet. Then I did remember, sort of, and it made me scairt. I think it was about Johnston's army and wicked people who stole things going to prison. I think she said that Johnston's army would take boys who stole peaches off to prison, too, and they would not come out till Judgement Day. There I was, standing with my back against the logs of the house, same as before, my hands behind me, my face pointed down. Only I wasn't looking at my feet, or even thinking about toes or peaches. I was thinking about Johnston's army and being caught by soljers. I knowed Judgement Day is a long ways off, clear to the end of the world. All that time Earl and me would be in prison. When we get out we will be just a couple of old men with aches in our legs and backs, mebbee have a cough and stick our tongues out a lot. I was feeling sick down in my stummick. Wish we hadn't of seen those danged peaches. Now everything was going bad, bad as can be.

But sudden-like I felt better. I just remembered a pitcher in our Bible. It is of a fight with David and Goliath. I have looked at that pitcher lots of times. David, who is not very much bigger than me, is slinging a stone into that old giant Goliath's fork-head. The Giant is falling over. On the next leaf, the Giant is on his back, plum dead, and David is ready to cut off his head with a big sword. The Giant's army is running away, plenty scairt.

I got a sling my ownself, and I am a good slinger, too. This summer I knocked a chimpunk off the corner of our mud wall, and he was deader than nits. Sometimes I am almost sorry to be such a good slinger. One day our big red rooster chased all the little roosters out of our corral and hopped up on the fence to crow about it. It made me mad. He was a coward to pick on little roosters like that, so I took my sling and knocked him off that fence.

After that rooster had flopped around a while in the corral, he layed still. When Father got home from the field and saw his dead rooster, right off he blamed Herk and grabbed him by the neck and dragged him over to make Herk look at it, shoving his nose down on it. "See what you've done!" he scolded. "You long-haired, low-down mongrel! I ought to kick the living daylights out of you." Then he gave poor Herk a hard kick in the ribs so that Herk ran yelping towards the house. He went around on the shady side and layed down all by hisself. He knowed he hadn't kilt that rooster. When Father had gone into the stable with the oxen I went over to Herk and told him I was sorry, awful sorry Father had kicked him so hard. He tried to lick my face. I told him I might of got a licking, which would of hurt me worse than just one kick. That is what I think, that is what I hope. He did not know how sorry I felt when he licked me like a kiss when I didn't earn it.

I had a sudden big thought. With my sling and lots of little smooth rocks I could keep off a whole army, just like David did. But I had to get ready in a hurry. Johnston's soljers might be coming to Summit any day. I was feeling like a fighter. I needed a new sling. My old one might not stand up to a real fight. We make slings out of the leather from women's shoes. I knowed where there used to be one old shoe over to the Bishop's corral. Before dark I went after it, which was not stealing on account of that shoe was on the trash heap. Sam made the sling for me. He is good at it. I had him put a couple of good buckskin strings on it. "What you want such a big sling for? You already got a good enuff sling for a kid your size." I let on like I didn't hear him. Sam likes me a lot, even if he does smart off at me sometimes. He didn't ask any more.

Next morning after breakfast I went out in the brush toward the Injun camp and gathered up a good-size pile of small stones and brought them in and piled them up by the corner of the chicken coop. I had to make several trips to bring them all. I made three piles, one by the corner of the coop. I planned to fight as long as the stones lasted. From the chicken coop to the house I could easy kill a soljer. Another pile I put at the end of the mud wall, where I already kilt a chimpunk, close to the chicken coop. Not so far out in the brush is a gully where I put another pile of stones. If I had to run from the mud wall, I would fight from the edge of the gully. Old Johnston's army could be bigger than I figgered, so if my stones on the edge of the gully were all gone before the soljers were, I would drop over the bank and crawl into a long hole I dug one time when I was playing I was a badger. I did not know what I would do with the hole after I got into it.

Watching for that army to come was a big job. I stood or sat on top of that chicken coop a lot of days. Father told me I looked like the watchman on the tower. I didn't dast get off hardly long enuff to eat dinner or supper. I sweated a lot. I tried to get Herk up there so he could watch while I had my meals. But he could not climb up his ownself, and I couldn't lift him. Father had not asked me to pull weeds. He must of knowed I was up to something 'portant. At night Jim and Bill slept out on the shed same as usual, Sam too, and also me. We had our beds of straw, and I got some old gunnysacks and a bit of straw to make a bed for Herk by the corner of the house closest to the gate. I took him to it and told him to sleep there and keep watch in the night. If he saw any soljers coming down the street he was to bark like sixty.

"What you sitting up there on the chicken coop so much for, Homer? You have been there every day for a week," Mother said to me one morning. "I am beginning to worry about you. Every time I come out of the house I see you squatting up there like an old setting hen." She would be suprised when Johnston's army showed up.

"I sit up here 'cause it's nice and sunny. I can see anyone coming to the house," I told her. But she did not hear me. She had already gone into the coop for eggs. When she came out, she said, "I believe you are making the hens nervous. I only got three eggs this time." I didn't say anything.

Next morning when I got up on the roof I had a new feeling which didn't feel so bad. I been thinking about things before I went to sleep last night. It didn't look like the soljers wanted to come for me at all. None of the folks in town seemed sorry or felt good or bad 'cause I might be took to prison for stealing peaches. None of them was talking about Judgement Day. Not one of them had said a thing about Johnston's army. I bet Grandmother never told me about soljers taking Earl and me off to prison. Now I know I made it all up my ownself on account of I felt so bad. The hurt feeling inside me for trying to steal Brother

Lamb's peaches had gone away. I felt just like I used to when I was good all my life. Right straight I climbed off that chicken coop. Being on top of it so many days had kept me from lots of fun and play, and my legs felt stiff.

Mother said I could go see Earl. I been wondering why he hadn't come down to my house to see me all this time. When I got to his house he was out in his lot pulling weeds for the pigs. His pa had give him a licking he wouldn't soon forget. That is why he hadn't come. He told me about that licking and about the blabbing women who had also come to see his ma. She has even more ginger and Irish in her than mine and sent them on their way. Then he asked what I been doing all this time we hadn't seen a thing of each other since we dodged into the cornfield.

"I been watching for Johnston's army to come."

"It's coming here? They still around? I thought they moved on out years and years ago. That's what Pa says," he spoke up quick.

"That's what I finally been figgerin', too." I did not feel to tell him about me being on our coop for a week. "You know about Johnston's army?" I asked.

"Sure I do. Everybody does. But I ain't scairt of 'em," Earl said. "I heard Pa tell a man once that Brigham Young licked the stuffing out of Johnston's army a long time ago, all by his ownself, too. And he didn't have to fire a gun to do it. He just had all the folks in Salt Lake City move out, and old General Johnston marched his army into a empty town. So he just turned around and marched back." I felt kind of shamed for being so scairt of a army Brigham Young could lick so easy as that. I wouldn't of needed half as many stones as I had piled around if they'd of showed up.

"What you been doing all this time besides pulling weeds?" I wanted to quit talking about that army till I could think about it some more.

"Oh, Pa made me stay home and pull weeds every day for the pigs and cows. He said it would keep me from stealin' peaches for a week, anyways."

"Can't see why our fathers want to come down on us so much," I said. "We didn't hardly do anything."

"Once when my Uncle Gideon was the size of my big brother, he stole a little calf he saw wandering by its ownself. He's the one got the bumblebee sting under his nose.

"Stealing a calf?" I shouted. "That's lots worse than stealing peaches, if we had of stole them."

"Right in our house Ma told me he stole it. He said the little thing didn't have a brand on it, and how could a poor little calf know which way its home was at if it did not have a brand to tell it which way to go, so he guessed he would give it a home. She said she wished another bumblebee had of come along just then and stung him till the calf got away."

"Well, I don't think it is so good to be stealing calves or peaches or anything," I said, feeling clean inside and out, "on account of it makes us feel bad, and we catch scoldings, and you get whipped, and everything."

"I been thinkin' the same all week," Earl said. "Let's make a bargain we won't try to steal anything anymore, never again forever and ever." Which we did, and we are done with stealing till Judgement Day, whenever.

DOCKING THE DEVIL

In Summit we have babetizing days in summer when the water is not so cold in the creek which comes from the canyon and runs through town in the ditch. Up by where the water first comes down, a wide hole is dug in the ditch where the water runs slow, and a dam is made across the lower end of the hole so that the water backs itself up till it is deep enuff to reach the children's shoulders. An Elder takes ahold of the boy or girl by the arm, the one to be babetized holds his nose with his other hand, and the Elder dunks him straight under the water and then up. Mostly it is boys and girls which are eight years old who get babetized, on account of bigger ones already been dunked. When you are eight years old, you are s'posed to know the differnce between right and wrong. I been learning about that and still have a ways to go. Even if the ditch has a dam in it, the water keeps running around the dam in a little ditch the men have made for the water in the hole. That way the water is always clean for the children. Earl and me will have our birthdays in the winter and will be babetized together next summer.

We had a babetizing day soon after Father and me got home from Pioche. Earl and me went to it on account of Earl heard a woman telling his ma that angels come to look on whenever there is a babetizing. They may come to Summit then, but I know they do not keep a lookout on the Pioche road. Right straight, Mr. Hanks told us and the other freighters that it is no place for angels. That is why we never looked for them on the desert. Earl and me sat on the bank and watched the babetizm, but mostly we were watching for angels. We didn't see any.

Day after was Sunday. Earl and me went to Sunday School like we mostly do. Teacher told us angels could of been watching there at the babetizm even if we did not see them. He told us all boys and girls which have been babetized got rid of their sins and someday would go to heaven if they lived good lives. All them which do not get babetized would someday have to go to hell. Earl wanted to ask teacher what kind of place hell is, but I whispered that he didn't need to. He could just come to our house after Sunday School. "We got hell down there. I'll show it to you," I whispered.

Earl and me ain't babetized yet on account of we are still only seven. And anyways, we figger we do not have enuff sins for doing it. We have talked about it a lot. All we can put our hands on is one sin and a half. The one sin was when we learnt to swear that time among the sunflowers by Dan Harris's wheat stack. The half sin is when we were going to take the weight off Brother Lamb's peach tree, and probly would of if the Lamb boys had not chased us off. But they did, so we figger that was only half a sin. We do not think folks get stuck with a sin just by thinking of it. And besides, anyways, I got a scolding that nearly took my hide off and Earl got a licking that did. "If lickings don't help pay for sins, why do they lick us?" Earl asked me.

We think the same. We do not care what folks in town say, we will not agree to more than one sin and a half. Even that sin was only a little one. It did not hurt anybody. Well, it did make Mother feel sad. None of Earl's folks said a word to him about it afterwards, only the licking. I bet Earl's pa, right now, don't know Earl can swear 'bout as good as he can. Anyways, that was last year when we were only boys which had not been to Sunday School enuff to know any better. We think God does not blame little boys like he does men. My folks would not even of found out about our cussing, either, if I hadn't of stubbed my toe on that piece of curled-up carpet warp by the door. We don't think one sin and a half is enuff to have a reggler babetizing. Course we don't want any more sins, but Earl and me have made a bargain we will not do any more. Our mothers felt sad, but our fathers snorted and faunched around as if a cow had dropped dead in Earl's corral and Old Buck had died on account of it. When our turn comes, Earl thinks if we tell the Elder that we got only one sin and a half, which ain't enuff for a reggler babetizing, he will only put us down in the water a little ways and jerk us out quick. That way we will not get so wet, or strangle for breath like some of the children do. Which I think, myself, he will on account of he is one of Earl's relashuns, too.

Soon as Sunday School was out, Earl and me went straight for my house. When we got there, Mother had just made dinner ready for everybody. So we had to eat before we could look at hell. When Earl eats at our house, Mother puts his plate next to mine, sometimes at my box on the floor. Then him and me can sit together. So does his ma when I eat at Earl's house. I have to say his ma makes really good biskits, same as mine. Both of them say it is as hard to fill us up with hot biskits as it is to fill a couple of shoats with bran and slop. A couple of shoats are two little pigs which are growing up to be reggler hogs. Not Earl and me. We are growing up to be men like Father and Earl's pa, only not so angry. We do not want to farm. On a farm you have to work too hard. Mebbee, after you work hard, a famine comes anyways. We want to ride horses with saddles on. We want pistols in our belts, a couple each, and a gun strapped to our saddles like Idaho Bill. But we do not want to be robbers. They get neck-tie parties. We want to be something else, only we don't know for sure what it would be.

Mother had her fly switch handy by the table. Flies are bad in summertime and fall. When we eat, we have long leafy switches to wave over the table to keep the flies off our food. It ain't healthy to eat a fly. Later, when it is colder the flies gather on the ceiling, and Mother sweeps them down with a broom. She gets plenty. Then we put straw in the fireplace and onto it she sweeps the flies. Then she puts more straw on top of them and touches the straw with a lighted match. In less than a minnit we don't have any flies. Next morning she has to sweep again. That goes on pretty much till snow time.

After dinner I took our Bible off the little table in the big room, and Earl and me went out by the apple tree, where there was a bit of grass and some shade under it. Earl's folks do not have a big Bible same as ours, which has red and yellow pitchers in it. Some are big. They take up a whole side of the leaf. My folks got the Bible quite a bit before I was borned down in Santa Clara from people who were going to Californy to bring home a wagonload of gold. The Bible was one thing too much in their wagon. And anyways, they said, they didn't have a need for it. Father got it for nothing.

I knowed right where to find hell. I had looked lots of times. Soon as we sat down and I opened the Bible, there it was. Hell was a red and yellow pitcher which covered the whole leaf. We both looked without saying a word. Finally Earl breathed a big breath and said, "So that's hell, is it?" He was still looking hard at the people and things in the pitcher. I could see that mostly it was a dark place.

"Yup," I said. "Ain't you glad we don't have to go there? It would be an awful place to stay in all your life."

"You bet," Earl said. "It don't look so good, does it? Lots of people there in hell, but not so many as Pa thinks there be. Looks to me hell is plum full of people, but he says lots more oughter be there who ain't."

"Well, just wait till Pioche gets there. It will be as full as the Panner-rammer was that night."

"How you know Pioche people go to hell?" Earl asked.

"They be Gentiles, don't they? 'Sides, didn't Idaho Bill say Pioche is a helluva town? And he ought to know."

Then we looked at the pitcher some more. That big crowd of nekked folks was standing around a little way off from a big fire hole in the ground. Everybody looked like they did not know where they were at and didn't like wherever it was. They looked tired of the place already. Now they wanted to go home. Some children were pulling on their mothers' hands. The devil was standing on the edge of that big hole, and in his hand he had a pitchfork with three tines that looked like sharp arrows. He was looking over at that big crowd of nekked people and laffing. There were flames in the hole, and quite a lot of people were in it already, burning up.

I scrunched up my face to see more. "Geeminy, Earl, I would hate to be throwed into that hole."

"Wonder if the nekked ones are waitin' their turn to jump in."

"Must be," I said. "I bet that is why they left their clothes home. No use burning good clothes, is there? Oh see, Earl, there's even little babies size of Horace and your little sister."

"It's the hellest place I ever see. Hope none of our folks go there," he said.

"Gosh, I would hate to stand there plum nekked in front of all them men and women and boys and girls."

"Count on it, I wouldn't do it. If Ma was there she wouldn't let me. She would tell the devil right to his face her boy was not to stand there all nekked in a crowd like that. She wouldn't take off her clothes, either."

"Neither would Mother or Father. And Bill would tell the old devil to go straight to hell, so would Sam. But it must be awful warm there on account of the devil is nekked, too.

"Couldn't help but be. I'll bet that fire hole is goin' all the time."

"And the devil is standing right on the edge of it, too. Don't see how he can do it. I would think his feet would burn. I know all about burning feet," I said, remembering the salt ponds at Little Salt Lake.

"Look, Buck, he's got feet like Pa's black bull. Couldn't blister feet like those. He's a ugly cuss, ain't he?"

We kept looking at the pitcher and thinking. We didn't talk for quite a long time. Him and me have learnt to think almost as good as Father. Only we don't have to sit on the springseat like Father does. After a while, Earl said, "Know what I would do soon as I got to hell? When the devil was sleepin' sound and dreamin' what he will do with all them people, I would sneak up on him slow and quiet, like a cat sneaking up on a bird. I would have Pa's sharp hatchet in my hand.

"What would you want the hatchet for?"

"I'd raise my arm and whack! Off would come his tail!"

"Oh ouch!" I hollered. "Quick as scat he would pitch you into that hole of fire."

"No he wouldn't. I'd whack it off so fast he wouldn't know it till he waked up, and then I would be gone in the dark with his tail. I'd be plum away before he waked up and looked at his tail which wasn't there anymore."

"That gives me the shivers. Don't you think you ought to leave a piece of his tail, a sort of stub like? His wife could put some salve on it and wrap a white rag around it."

"I could do that, all right. Mebbee I should."

"But what would you want his tail for? It wouldn't be no good to you."

"I been thinkin' about that while I was thinkin'. I would get Pa to straighten it out for me on his workbench. Then we would nail it on the side of our house in the sun. Soon as it got dry enuff and stiff, I would have a good spear to fight the old devil with."

"You know what I been thinkin'? Only I thought it just now," I said. "When you would sneak up on that old devil, I would sneak by your side. Soon as you whacked off his tail, I would grab his pitchfork, and away we run, faster than fast. You would have his tail, and I would have his pitchfork."

Earl laffed. "A bob-tail devil without any pitchfork! Wouldn't nobody have him for a devil anymore."

"Specially they wouldn't when they saw all he had for a tail was a white rag on the stub of it." We both laffed so hard we nearly fell on the Bible.

"What you boys laffing at?" Father asked us. He was passing the tree on his way to the house. "Just laffing at the devil," I said. He didn't hear me.

"I bet when he would wake up and find his tail off and his pitchfork gone, he would yell and roar loud enuff you could hear him for a mile," I said to Earl.

"Mebbee he would get so mad he would pitch all them people into that hell fire," he said.

"But we wouldn't let him, would we? You would have his sharp tail, and I would have his pitchfork."

"No siree! You bet we wouldn't let him do a thing like that," Earl said. "We'd wait till we got him standin' on the edge of that hole. Then both of us would take a runnin' start."

"I would gouge him in the neck with his pitchfork!"

"I'd stab him in the belly with his tail!"

"And then we'd push him over into the fire."

"And that would be the end of the devil. And after we'd burned him up, we would quick put out the fire. And after that, there wouldn't be any hell to go to." We looked at each other and laffed again.

But then I had another think. "What is going to happen to all the people which are in hell already and ain't had a chance to burn up yet?"

"Easy," Earl said. "They will go home and put their clothes back on. Next time they will go to heaven."

"They will have to go to heaven," I said. "There won't be any other place to go."

"Then we don't have to worry anymore, either," Earl said.

SORROW

Ellie is sick. She has been poorly ever since last winter, just hasn't felt better any of the time, only slowly feeling worser. Mother looks terrible worried. We all feel bad. It has been more than a week since I was up to Earl's house, and he has only been down here a few times, and then we have to go out of our lot to play so our noise won't give Ellie a headache. Not much use for him to come down, on account of I feel too bad to play, only walk around the corral and yard. When I get tired I sit on the ground by the fence or the chicken coop. Herk follows me everywhere I go and pushes his nose against my hand to tell me he feels bad, too. When I sit down he wants to lick my face. He can tell something is wrong at our house and this is his way of trying to kiss it all better, like Mother can. But she can't kiss Ellie enuff to make her better. The more I hurt inside my stummick, the more Herk wants to lick my face.

Seems all the mothers in town want to do something to help. Even Ray Linn's wife has come up from the ranch several times to help out however she can. Earl's ma comes over and helps Mother with bathing and poultices and then shakes her head as she gives Mother a hug. She told Earl she had never seen anything like it. Aunt Mary says she just can't tell what kind of a sickness it is. She never heard of one which started in the feet and legs that way. Don't know what we would do without the Bishop's wife and Sister Persis, who are at our house a few times each week, often as they can come. Even if Sister Persis can easy bring babies to our house, she cannot figger out what is making Ellie so sick. She asked if a bee had stung her, or if a spider had bit her. Ellie shook her head the best she could. She did not think so.

A pain started in her foot last spring, a while after the measles, not a big pain at first. It only made her kind of slow the time we had the rabbit drive. But it got bigger and bigger. She could not go to the Wonderful Thing, and finally she could not go to school or help Mother in the house. It had started all at once. She woke up with it one morning, and it never went away. Mother tries everything she can to help Ellie, but nothing does. Sister Persis has brought poultices and salves they use, and she has made herb teas to clean out her body. She and Mother have wrapped strips of clean cloth around Ellie's feet and legs to help the swelling. But it has got so bad Ellie can't walk anymore. She has had to sit in a chair, and now she is in bed all the time, looking white and tired. Both feet and legs are hurting something awful, and she is kind of swoll up and sick all over. At first Sister Persis told Mother there might be something in Ellie's foot which had festered deep inside, like a stone bruise. That is why she brought the poultices, to draw it out. But all the poultices have not helped. Now she and Mother think the pain and swelling will keep on till they get to her heart.

Father brought the Elders of the church in quite a few times to ask the Lord to make her well. Father is an Elder, too, and prays for her every night. They told Father she would get well. I heard them say so. But the Lord must not of heard their prayers. She is not better and only keeps getting sicker.

Everybody in town likes Ellie, it seems. She has been so sweet to everyone all her life, folks tell Mother, they couldn't help liking her. I know, myself, how sweet and kind she is. That is the way she has always been to me. She has been Mother's special helper. These days when Mother is working about the house she stops now and then to cry a minnit, but never says a word. She just wipes her eyes and face with her apron and keeps on with her work. Mother tells me I am not to let Ellie see me crying. None of us dast cry where she can see us. We must not let her know she might not get well.

But one time I went close to her bed. I knowed she could tell I wanted to cry. She reached for my hand and pulled me over close and told me I must not feel bad for her. She would soon be all right, same as she used to be. She could only whisper, and even that was hard for her. She held my hand. "When I'm well you and me will hunt flowers again, won't we, Homer?" She always called me Buck before. I nodded my head. I would bust into tears if I talked. "We'll go out to the Injun camp and get red bells and bluebells." I stood by her bed with my hand in hers for quite a while. I didn't talk any. I didn't know how. "Oh, yes! And I will make you another valentine, nicer than the one this year. You can count on it. I been saving a piece of paper just for it. Rebecca is sure to like it, I know." Then Mother came in the room, and I tiptoed away.

Ellie never talked to me anymore. Sometime next day she got so bad she could not talk to anybody. The Elders came again that day and prayed once more for Ellie to get well. Brother Throstle gave the prayer. His old voice shivered with his feelings. After that they all took Father's hand and patted Mother's shoulder and went away. I looked in where Ellie's bed was. Mother was by her pillow. I didn't go in. I ran off so I could cry.

Mother and Father been talking with Sister Persis and the Bishop's wife. They think Ellie should see Dr. Higgins, who lives down in St. George. Mebbee he could tell us something to do for her. Father said he had been thinking that way his ownself, specially since the sickness has got all over Ellie's body. He thinks we should do something fast if it was going to help. He and Mother will take her to St. George, even if it is more'n sixty miles of hard going with a wagon.

Quick that same afternoon Father mended the harness and greased a few of the straps. There was not time to grease the whole harness. Jim and Bill greased the wagon wheels and put the wagon bows on. They spread the cover over the wagon bows, then fastened it down tight. Sam filled a tick with nice fresh straw, plenty thick and put it in the wagon box to make a comfortable bed for Ellie. Mother and Sam brought some blankets and quilts from the house, all clean and soft. These were blankets Father had got from Orderville the time he took Laura. They had never been used. Everything was fixed and ready so we could leave before sun-up in the morning. There would be me and Martha and little Horace to go along. Mother couldn't go without us, as she thought we were too small to leave behind. Emily wanted to come, too, but there just would not be room on account of Ellie's bed took up most of the wagon box. Mother said she would be proud of her if she would stay home to help Sarah Ann and Eliza keep house for Jim and Bill and Sam. Aunt Mary would look out for everyone, too. Emily sniffed up her tears and said she would. Sister Persis, Earl's ma, and Ray Linn's wife, who had walked up from the ranch, came to help Mother fix Ellie a bed of quilts in the wagon so she could stand the ruff, long trip. Mother told them it was a terrible road to take a sick child over to see a doctor, but she and Father would do anything to help their little girl. They comforted Mother, saying they would do the same if it was one of theirs. Earl came down that evening to say goodbye to me.

Next morning Earl's pa was at our house before daylight. He and Father carried Ellie out to the wagon, and it was not long till we had everything ready we would take. It was just coming daylight when Father drove the wagon out on the street. We turned and started the horses down the road toward Ray Linn's ranch and St. George. I sat on the springseat with Father. He didn't talk any. Mother was in the wagon with Ellie and Martha and Horace. She didn't talk either. We were all thinking of Ellie.

All those days Mother stayed mostly back under the cover with Ellie. She had Horace back there, too. Father and me were glad it was not so hot as it had been on the desert. Martha came up and sat with me on the springseat with Father. I was on the outside on account of I knowed how to hang on to the springseat and not get shook off. Martha held on to me. We slept in people's houses along the road, mostly but not always. Once, Father and Martha and me slept on the ground, Martha between Father and me. That kept her warm. It took a long time for us to get there, and we had to go over the Black Ridge to do it. I was glad my shoes were broke in and not killing my feet. Father eased the wagon down that broken-up hill like it was glass so as not to hurt his sick little girl. He sent word with a traveler on horseback to Grandfather Cragun that we were on the way. When we finally rolled into St. George it was past noon that day, but Grandmother and Grandfather Cragun and Uncle Jim were waiting for us at their house.

Father and Uncle Jim carried Ellie on her bed into the house. Two other men were there to help. Grandmother had fixed a nice place for her in a cool room. Till winter comes it is mostly hot in St. George. Right straight Uncle Jim went to find Dr. Higgins. Grandfather went to bring the Elders over. They got to the house first and put their hands on Ellie's head and prayed for her same as our Elders done in Summit. Father joined with them same as he had in Summit. They told Ellie she would get well, which we hoped she would but were awful worried that she would not.

After they been gone quite a while, Dr. Higgins got to the house. He was a long time by Ellie's bed. Father and Mother and Grandfather and Grandmother sat in the room long as the doctor was there. I stood close to the door and looked in. Right while he was there he fixed some medicine for Ellie to drink. Then they all went out on the porch, and the doctor talked with Mother and Father a long time. Even if Ellie did go barefoot much of the time, he didn't think it was a spider which had bit her foot. He thought it was a sickness that children and young folks get sometimes, specially after measles or sore throats. If it was, then no doctor would know how to cure it. He shook his head while he talked. That made me feel even sadder.

We were in St. George for only about a couple of weeks when I got up one morning and saw everyone crying. Tears were running into Father's whiskers, and he was holding Mother. Grandmother was the first to see me. She came over and gave me a big hug. While she hugged me she said that in the night God had sent his angels to take Ellie up to heaven where she would never be sick anymore. Oh, how I wished that had been a lie.

FALL WORK

Father has gone back to Summit. Mother did not want to go back home so soon. She said she could not go back on that same hard road over which she had brought her poor sick girl such a short time before. If she went home now she would feel she was running away, leaving Ellie all alone in a far country, in that little grave all by itself in the red sand with no trees and not a flower near. It looked so lonesome, she told Father. If she left right away, she would never forgive herself long as she lived. She needed to stay close to her little girl for a while. She did not even know if she would ever get back to St. George anymore. Mother said it seemed like if she stayed on a bit with Grandmother it would be company for Ellie and for herself, too. While she was here she would go out to the grave every day if she could, and that would be a big help to her sadness.

Father figgered the last of summer was going pretty fast. He needed to get home to start the early fall plowing. He needed to clear the brush off a new piece so he could seed it to wheat before the winter set in. If he could do that, we would have an early threshing in case we ran out of flour. By the time he got that land cleared of brush and seeded, he said, it would be almost time to dig potatoes and get them in the potato cellar. Then, too, the fences around the corral had to be mended for winter. The corn had to be shucked and dried in the open air. After it dried Father would shell it. We got a corn sheller, you bet. Soon as it is shelled and sacked, Father takes it to the grist-mill in Parowan. I know, myself, on account of we are reggler cornbread eaters. It is best with lots of molasses, which we don't have much of, not like here in St. George. Father has so much work waiting for him he cannot stay another day, whether he likes to or not. He said he would come for Mother and us when she was ready.

Besides all the things Father talked about to Mother, I know about the work he and the boys have to do in the fall. Almost the last thing before winter we pull our onions and get them in the chaff bin. They need to be covered with chaff, lots of it, so they won't freeze. A little after the onions are dug we have to dig the cabbages out of the ground, which we do by their roots. Father digs a long little ditch trench and puts the cabbage heads right back in that trench and then covers them deep with dirt. Now the heads are in the ground where the roots used to be, and the roots are standing in the air where the heads used to be. If the cabbages freeze in the ground in winter, they will thaw out in the ground in the spring and be same as if they never got froze.

Besides all that, Jim and Bill have to haul our winter's wood from the hills which have plenty of dead pine and cedar trees. They take a wagon into the mountains and find wood laying on the ground ready for them to load. We got to have wood else we would freeze in winter. By the time snow comes to Summit, everybody in town has ricks of wood stacked in their yards. Sometimes pieces of dried mud we call chinking mud falls out from between the logs of the house. Then even if no wind is blowing outside, cold air comes in the house like sixty. It takes lots of wood to keep the house warm if there are holes in the chinking. If it drops out in wintertime, which it mostly does, we have to mend it in a hurry. We mix fresh mud in the house with warm water. Mostly we mix it in a big pan or bucket and have to be careful not to mess up the floor. Mother won't stand for that. We got a trowel which Jim is good with. He slams the mud into the cracks good and tight and squeezes the mud down hard and smooth with the trowel. He says he is thinking mebbee he will learn how to build 'dobe houses for people. Father says we got to plaster the whole inside of the house next summer, else build a new one which will be of 'dobe.

It will be only just a few weeks when nights in Summit will be getting cold. Flocks of ducks and geese will go flying past by days and by nights, the geese crying out their "Ha-onk! Ha-onk!" Don't know if they are talking to each other or singing, same as Father and me do on the road. I think it is kind of a sad song, like they hate to leave their home and find a new one somewhere else. They fly slow in bunches that spraddle out in two long lines which come together at the front end and look like a big wishbone. Ducks don't make any noise when they fly, their wings whizzing so fast their talk would be snatched right out of their bills and probly no other duck would hear it. Genny ducks and geese fly smooth, not wobbling around like blackbirds and crows and magpies. Earl says his pa always likes it when the nights get cold and the geese go flying over the mountain on account of then it is hog-killing time, which I know, myself, it is. His pa don't need to tell us.

We got a couple of fat hogs to butcher this fall. One is up in Aunt Mary's pen, the other in ours. After they are kilt we salt them down in barrels where they soak a long time in the salt which turns to water. Then we put the pieces in our smoke cellar for a while. When we take them out they are home-cured ham and home-cured bacon, some of the best eating what is. Grandmother Cragun and the other folks in St. George do not have meat often as we do. The weather is too hot for that. When summer gets to Summit you can't eat fresh meat. It spoils in a hurry. That is when smoked ham and bacon make good eating. Father says it would be mighty nice to store some of the winter's snow for keeping meat. We should look for an ice cave in the mountains.

Mother told Father he could get all those things done with the boys. For herself, she was going to stay for a while in St. George. Father always seems to know when to give up with Mother. So her and me and Martha and Horace stayed on with Grandmother and Grandfather Cragun. Martha and Horace are so little they do not care what they do or where. But I want to spend more time with Uncle Jim. He teaches me a lot even if he is mostly grumpy. I think him and Bill are a lot alike.

Father took a load of dried peaches and fresh grapes back home with him, and two good-size barrels of molasses. He said he knows for sure where he could sell both of them in Parowan. Every bit of bizness he can do helps out just that much. I wish we could stash both barrels of molasses out in our shed and have all we can eat of it.

Every morning before breakfast, here in Grandfather's house, we have prayers same as in Summit. Then, too, we have prayers and food blessing before supper. The people in Paragonah, where Father and me had dinner that time we went peddling, don't call it "asking the blessing." They call it "saying grace." Grandfather always asks who he wants to pray. When we get seated on our chairs he asks someone to say the blessing on the food. I already learnt how back home. One morning he asked me to say the blessing, which I did. I can speak right up and say it loud so everybody can easy hear what I am saying. When I got through I peeked out of my eyes and saw Mother and Grandfather smiling a grin at each other. Uncle Jim was shaking his head discusted-like. Aunt Tish was laffing inside her mouth. She is my real aunt. I got lots of them here in St. George. They are all Mother's sisters. After breakfast Grandmother told me that I say the blessing real good for a boy my size, but I should try saying it a deal slower. "Why, you just rattle it off lickety split and don't think what you are sayin'." I said I would try to think more and let the words out slower.

Father and me don't have any relashuns together. He never had any brothers or sisters. He didn't have any mother, either, only for a little while, then she died and his father left him at the house of some of his mother's cousins and went off to marry again. After that he died. That makes it so Father and me only have relashuns with Mother's folks. I like all the ones I met.

After a while Uncle Jim and me walked downtown together, which now we do lots of times. I was walking kind of close behind him. He kinked his head around and looked at me with his eyes sparkling. "You don't know how to ask the blessin' at all, Buck. All you do is speak a piece as if you was in school."

That stung my Irish. I told him right back he didn't ask the blessing, either. "All you do is mumble and mumble so nobody can hear anything you say, and it's so long the potatoes and gravy get cold."

He was still walking. I was only talking to his back, but he stopped quick and turned around, his eyes spitting anger at me. Guess he has Irish, too. "Say-y-y, young feller! If you was my boy I'd spank your bare behind so hard you couldn't set down for a week. I ought to spank you anyways just for sassin' me back like that." We both stood still, him looking down at me, me looking up at him.

"Ah, c'mon! Let's just go where we're goin'," I said, kicking the sand with my toes. I started to go, walked past him a little, then stopped and looked back. He hadn't moved and his eyes were still glaring at me. "Beats all how children get raised these days," he huffed, shaking his head. "No wonder the country's fillin' up with horse thieves and robbers. Whatever has happened to the Risin' Generation!" He started walking and got ahead of me in about two steps. I walked behind him best I could, careful not to say anything. We went on downtown.

UNCLE JIM

Since Mother and me and my little sister and brother been staying on in St. George, I do not spend all my time in Grandmother's house. Mostly every day I go around town with Uncle Jim. Him and me are together wherever we go.

He has got a town lot all his own, two or three blocks from Grandmother's house, where he goes most of the time mostly just to fuss around. I go to have fun. Seems like there is plenty on the lot for him to fuss with, and there are things for me to have fun with. Some day he is going to build a house on that lot. When he does, he will have a house all to his own. All he has on the lot now are peach trees, apple trees, and grapevines. Everybody in St. George has them, too. He has quite a lot of garden stuff growing there, besides. What he is the proudest of is the cellar he has dug to put his house on someday when he gets around to building it. It is a kind of deep cellar with straight up-and-down sides. The house will go right on top of that cellar hole. Right now it is just only a dark hole.

Uncle Jim is a batchler. Grandmother says she wishes he would get married soon as he can. It is not safe to be a batchler too long. She wishes, really wishes, he would put on some steam and get that house built, then mebbee if he is lucky some woman will marry him right off. I do not know about that. Seems to me he is too grumpy for anyone to want to marry him.

Earl has got a uncle who is a batchler same as Uncle Jim. He was the one got stung by the bumblebee. Earl's pa says batchlers cannot get into heaven or even peek over the wall on account of they don't have one wife at least. God won't have them sticking around in heaven doing nothing. Which I don't blame him for it. I wouldn't either, if I was him. Earl says if it was him doing it, he would let the batchlers into heaven long enuff for them to weed the onions and carrots and pull weeds for the pigs and cows. But at night he would make them go outside and sleep by the wall. Grandmother probly already knows Uncle Jim cannot get inside heaven, and that is why she tells him it is not safe to be a batchler too long. And he likes that St. George wine.

Uncle Jim is a housebuilder his ownself. He has got saws and hammers and things like that. When he gets the stuff all ready to make the house with, he will use his own hands, and he says it will be a house fit to live in. Right now he is helping to build the St. George temple. Uncle Jim won't take me down to see it building. He says it is too full of things a boy my size should not be around. I could easy get hurt. But I been there anyways. Aunt Martha Cox took me over in her wagon and held my hand tight as we walked around, and I saw the great big stones and the 'traptions the men use to lift them. Don't look like much now, but Aunt Martha says I should just wait and see. She is one of my aunts, and I specially like her.

When I was with Uncle Jim one day to his lot, I went down in his cellar hole by climbing down a ladder which leaned out from the bottom of the edge of the hole. He was bizy doing something with his grapevines, so I was all alone and wanting to know about things. When I got down to the bottom I got scairt most to death. It was pretty near dark, and I was barefoot clear up to my knees and standing in a soft sandy floor full of toads! The icky, glummy kind of toads you can't hardly bear to touch. I did not see them till I was right in their middle and quite a ways from the ladder. They wiggled theirselfs backward into that soft sandy dirt. Lots of them had got so far down only their eyes and faces stuck out. I had not seen any of them when I was looking in from the top. But now the floor was full of buggy toad eyes staring at me. Toad eyes give me the fantods.

My toes felt like they were standing on something soft and wiggly. Before I could move my foot, something slipped out from under it with a squashy feel, and something cold and glummy rubbed against my ankul. "WHOOPS!" I hollered. Back to that ladder I jumped in one big jump and scooted up the rounds fast as I could go. At the top I flopped over and layed there puffing. Felt like I had lost all my breath. My whole skin shivered when I thought of all those toads digging in the dirt down in the dark and rubbing theirselfs against my ankuls. I would not go into that cellar again, no siree. Not for anything at all. If I was Uncle Jim's wife I would not live in any house made on top of a toad cellar. He would have to build another house where you could not even see this lot, else I would make him shovel that cellar full of dirt and pound it down hard so there could not be any toad peeking his eyes out anywheres. Uncle Jim says he doesn't care at all having toads in his cellar, as he is not using it for hisself yet and doesn't mind having a few noisy squatters down in the dirt till he gets around to building.

I like going all over the whole town with him, even if he is a grump. He says I am a reggler newsants, but I don't take the hint. He tells me right out he wishes I would not tag around with him so much. He says folks might think I was something he had found in the hills and didn't have the sense to leave it where he found it. He wants to know when I am going home. He says he bets the folks up in Summit miss me a lot. That is what he said one morning before we started down to the lot.

"When I go, I bet you will miss me, too," I said back at him. "A bunch."

"Course I'll miss you," he said. "I'll miss you like I would a sore on my toe."

"Yes, and I'll miss you like I would a stone bruise on my heel! A stone bruise is worse than a sore toe is."

After a while when he got really ready to go to his lot he hollered at me, "Well, come on, newsants, if you want to go with me today, hop on it." In a little while I was walking behind him like always.

He likes me anyways, I can tell he does. He will be lonesome when I go. But one day I heard him talking with a couple of men. He said, "Buck's a nice youngster, all right. We all like him. Only he ain't been raised like he should of been. He sasses too much. What he needs is a good spanking every time he opens his mouth." I sneaked away from the other side of the grapevine he was standing by. I didn't want him to know I had heard what he said. He might get madder at me.

Right soon after that, when him and me were finishing off some grapes, he said, "Why don't you stay home and help your mother sometime, stead of trottin' around with me?"

I answered right back, "Why don't you help yours? She's older than mine and has got gray hairs besides." Right straight he quit eating grapes with me and went grumbling over to another vine, saying how he wished I was his boy only for a week. Soon as he got to that vine he started eating grapes and not tossing any to me.

When we go places I walk close to him only once in a while. Mostly I tag along behind looking at things I like to stop and look at. Earl and me do this all the time. Uncle Jim keeps right on walking. I run to catch up. Pretty soon I see something else and stop to look. Then I run and catch up again. That is the way we keep doing till we get to where we are going. He could easy walk away and lose me if I didn't look out for myself. Once I got so far behind I had to run like sixty. When I caught up I did not have hardly any breath left in me. He hadn't missed me.

"If you are going with me, why don't you keep up?" he said kind of sour-like. He talks that way a lot.

"I am up with you now, ain't I?" I was still puffing.

"If you whinnyed once in a while folks would think I was an old mare and you my colt tagging behind."

"If you was a old mare I wouldn't be your colt. You'd have to find a donkey if you wanted a colt."

"Hmmph. I'd ruther have a donkey for a colt anytime than you." Seems like Uncle Jim don't care for kids my size very much. He is lots crankier than our batchlers in Summit and awful hard to please. Grandmother says if he had two or three children of his own, it might sweeten him up a bit. Which I think, myself, it would, specially if one of them was a sweet little girl like Rebecca, which it could be on account of his hair is almost the same color as Rebecca's, only he don't keep it combed so nice. Folks say they can tell I am my father's boy 'cause I got black hair like him.

When he's working on his orchard and garden he pushes a big wheelbarrow with all his tools rattling in it. He has a bit smaller wheelbarrow, too, which looks like he hasn't used it for a long time. I been pushing it and putting things in it that I find when I go with him to the lot. I like to use it even when we just go around town. It is fun to make a wheelbarrow move without tipping on its one big wheel, only hard to do. He can easy get far ahead of me, even two or three blocks, but I just keep pushing that wheelbarrow till I find him somewhere. He has ditched it once or twice and said he will spank me out in public if I don't quit following him about with it. But the other day he made a dandy little wagon just for me so I wouldn't be tagging him all over town with that "dam'd wheelbarrow."

One day when we were having our little parade he pointed out a long-looking house up on the hill, not so far from the fence. "Know who lives in that house?" He was turning part around and bending his thumb at the house I was looking at. He kept right on going.

"Course I don't. I don't know who lives in anybody's house in St. George, only Grandfather's and Aunt Martha's."

"That's Brigham Young's house," he said, not missing a beat with his walking.

"Geeminy Whiz! Wait a minnit! Really Brigham Young's house?"

"Sure! That's where he keeps one of his wives, when he comes down here for the winter, which ain't so far off. But you better step along if you're coming with me." I stopped for a minnit or two anyways and looked at that house. Then I had to run fast to catch up.

We only just went to Uncle Jim's toad cellar. I could just as well of stayed back there and looked at Brigham's house. Mebbee I might of seen him, his very own self. When we got to the cellar, I layed on the ground by the edge and peeked over the rim. I could see a few toads. Once in a while one would walk a little. Toads have a ugly walk, all slow and spraddled out. They hold their bellies quite a ways off the ground. I could see some toad eyes peeking out of the dirt. I was glad not to be down there with them.

A busted grape had dropped into the cellar. A good-size toad squatted close to it. He was catching flies which stopped to drink the juice of the grape. Toads catch flies with their tongues, which is a little reddish or brownish thing. It's thin and limber, too. When it stretches out it is almost long as two of my fingers. When a fly stopped on the grape, quicker than scat that tongue shot out at the fly and jerked it off the grape and inside the toad. The toad give a little jerk of a swallow, and batted his eyes once or twice like he was saying "Thank you." I would hate to be a fly and be et by a toad. Makes me pull faces and my insides shiver just to think about it.

S'posing a toad was big as a horse. It could easy hide behind a tree waiting for a boy like me to come walking past on the sidewalk. Soon as I got even with that tree, out would shoot that tongue. It would be huge. Next, where would I be? Inside the fat glummy belly of that toad, that's where. I could hardly stand to even think about it, so I jumped up and ran back to Grandmother's house, pulling my wagon lickety-cut.

BRIGHAM YOUNG

People mostly call him Brigham and not Brigham Young. Earl knows another man named Brigham. Folks call him Brig. Guess all Brighams could be nicked to Brig, but not Brigham Young. Well, Sam says the *Salt Lake Tribune* calls him that every chance it gets. Father says that Brig is the best of the names that newspaper calls him.

It wasn't long till I was back at Brigham Young's house by myself. I wanted to take a look at the Lion of the Lord, which folks call him, proudly, for myself. Grandfather Cragun told me he is called that by our people for taking on the job of leading the church after Joseph Smith was kilt, and moving all the folks from Nauvoo in Illinois to Zion in Utah, and for building Salt Lake City and settling the big empty Territory with little towns for folks to live in.

Uncle Jim says he really got that name when he stopped General Johnston's army that was sent by the president of the country to put down the Mormons oncet and for all. This was a long time before I was borned. Uncle Jim says he was just old enuff to remember all that trouble, and how Brigham Young had folks clear out of Salt Lake City so there wouldn't be anyone there when Johnston's army marched in. I wonder if he had a big loud voice that sounded like a roar and scairt people but got them to move and do.

Kind of stooping, I sneaked along the fence very easy and quiet and still. If he was sticking close around in his house I did not want him to see me. He might think I was sneaking up to steal something, like grapes or apples. Soon as I got to the gate I sat on the ground, I mean on the sand. They don't have much ground in St. George. Some wide bushes were growing outside the fence by the gate. I sat behind them and peeked at things. Looked like no one was home. But I could sit and wait. Sand is nice to sit on.

There was a big chair on the porch, a rocking chair, like the one Uncle Jim made for Mother. Wonder if he makes rocking chairs for everybody in St. George. Nothing was on the porch but that chair. I could not see anyone looking out of a window. The house was so quiet it seemed empty. Earl and me do not specially like quiet houses. Squirrels and owls and ghosts live in still houses where no people stay. I could not see any squirrels or owls. Ghosts come only in the night. I wanted to see Brigham Young, I heard so much about him. Then I thought mebbee I ought not to see him, on account of if he could lick Mister Johnston's army all by hisself he could probly knock me down with just a look from his eyes. I wished again for Earl. I wouldn't be so scairt with the two of us. I know Earl would like as much as me to see the man who took the stuffing out of old Mister Johnston's army.

And just then, oh, m'gosh! A old man with white whiskers and smallish beard came out of the house, so quiet I did not hear the door open or close. He rolled his eyes around to see whatever there was to see. I hoped it was not me. He had on a long black coat, a hat on his head, not black, not white, something in between, with a stiff rim, and he had a walking stick in one hand. He used it to walk to the middle of the porch. Then he stood up straight and looked in the sky a minnit or two, pushing his shoulders back, like he was taking deep breaths. That is the way Father takes deep breaths.

He walked straight for that chair, pulled his coat tails to one side, and sat down. He put the walking stick across his lap, rocked a few rocks, then stopped. I thought he was going to look straight at the gate. I was just to one side of it in the bush. He held his walking stick straight up in front of him with the lower end on the floor and rested his hands on the top of it, and looked at his feet as though he had not seen them for a while.

"So that is Brigham Young," I sort of said to myself. Yes, I thought, it is Brigham all right. I could tell soon as I saw him come out the door. Good thing he couldn't see me for the bushes if he had been looking my way. He has got whiskers, but not so many as Father, and his whiskers are only just in a kind of circle from his ears down the back of his cheeks and around the lower end of his chin, and are mostly gray or white. You can see his lips and face. His lips were clamped together, and he looked kind of frowny. So he is the man what sent old Johnston's army packing. I couldn't hardly believe my eyes. He did not look like he would be an awful fighter if he got mad. He just looked sort of tired and old. I guess being president of the church is a lot harder job, even sitting down, than I s'posed. His face did not look as though it was used to smiles. I don't know how he would look when he was angry. But still, it did not look much like a lion's, either. Wish I had been close by him when he was fighting that army. I would of been a lot of help with my sling. It must of been some fight. I could of easy knocked a soljer dead as nits with only one rock, just like David.

Now he was looking straight towards me, only over my head. His chin was on top of his hands, which were on top of his walking stick. He lowered his eyes again and looked at the ground between me and him. His face didn't move at all, like he was thinking things deep inside him. Next he took his chin off his hands and leaned back in his chair, put his walking stick across his lap, and looked at the sky again, just quiet and still. He rocked a few more rocks, then got up and stood for another minnit or two, then walked to the front edge of the porch, turned and walked back to the chair, but did not sit down. He leaned hard on his walking stick. Now I could only see his back. Seemed like he was thinking of something he had to think about a lot, and being president of the church took a lot out of him. I hadn't thought about that before. He seemed to me to do things easy, on account of he is the Prophet. He turned around so I could see him more clearly, like a wore-out old grandpa, mebbe sick besides.

A woman came walking on the sidewalk past the house. I did not see her till she was right on me on account of I was looking at him so close. You cannot hear folks walking on sand too well. They move along quiet as snakes. She saw me peeking through the fence. "Looking at President Young, my little man?" she asked in a nice voice and went right on. She seemed pleased I was doing that. It must be what good little boys are s'posed to do. Course I was looking at Brigham Young. She could easy see that. She kept looking backwards and walking frontwards. Mebbee she wanted to look at him much as I did. The way she was walking and looking she could easy of stubbed her toe and gone sprawling on the sand, but you can fall on sand and not get hurt. Red sand is everywhere in St. George, all over the streets, along the sidewalks, around the house, among the trees and grapevines. You don't go anywhere in St. George without you walk on sand. When you sit down you are sitting on sand and getting it between your toes. And all of it is red.

That is what I like about St. George. I like to walk on sand. It feels good to my feet, and it is warm, too. There are no rocks to stub your toes on. Grandmother Cragun says there is no snow in winter to freeze your ankuls or the calves of your legs. There is one bad thing, though. Sometimes stickery things are hiding in the sand. Folks call them sand burrs. Up in Summit we call them watchdogs, on account of they lay in the dirt just like a watchdog, waiting for your bare feet to come along and hit them. St. George sand burrs are bigger than Summit's watchdogs and stick in your feet and hurt like anything, same as prickly pears and greasewood. If it wasn't for Rebecca and Earl and the rest of the family, seems like I would ruther live down here in Dixie. My toes and heels would not be always hurting. And it is fun to walk on sand. Everybody here goes barefoot all the time. Wonder if heaven has got sand in it like St. George. Ellie would like that. All the pitchers in the Bible show angels with bare feet.

Just then Brigham Young had started walking. First he stepped a few paces one way, then come back to the same place. Then he walked it again, slow and looking at the floor of the porch. I bet he had lots of things to think about, and walked like they bothered him. I would of liked to go closer and talk to him 'bout Mister Johnston's army and lots of things I been thinking about. But I did not dast do it. It is funny with me. I can talk to all the girls but Rebecca, yet she is the one I want to talk to most of all. I can talk to all the men I see but not Brigham Young, and he is the one I would want to talk to most of all.

I was getting ankshus someone else might come along and see me peeking through the fence and say something out loud to me, same as the woman did. He might hear and stop walking and look where the talking was coming from. Next he would probly step off the porch to come see who was hiding by his gate. He might poke at me with his stick. He might cuss me for being there. So, soon as he turned and walked the other way, I ran back along the fence, stooping and looking over my shoulder. But he did not call out, so I guess he had been too bizy thinking to see me. When I got to the corner I made straight for Uncle Jim's toad cellar, flopped down on the edge of it, and took a few deep breaths of my own.

ST. GEORGE

Mother thinks Father will be coming in a few days to take us back to Summit. She would like to stay a while longer, but she has got to go home and take up her housework and sew a waist for Sam to wear to school and be with Emily. She misses her. And she needs to get things ready for the baby that will come to our house soon. The big boys will be going to school over in Parowan. Emily and me will go to school in Summit. It will be my second time. When Father gets here with the wagon we have to be ready to go. He will not want to stick around for visiting.

Time has gone faster than we thought. We have been in St. George a long time, nearly two whole months. I am like Mother. I could easy stay a little longer here with Grandmother and Uncle Jim, but I feel homesick for good old Summit. I want to play with Earl again, and see Rebecca. Last time I saw her she was walking with her mother on the other side of the street. Quick I jumped behind a tree so she did not see me and peeked careful around and watched till they turned the corner. Then I hurried up to the corner, but they were out of sight. They had gone someplace and already were there.

This time Father brought Emily. She was needed at home when we came down to bring Ellie, and we are all glad she has come now. Grandmother is making peach pie for her. We will have to leave in just a few days, but first I will take her around to show her all the places in St. George she needs to see. Only we will have to hurry doing it. We will go to Brigham Young's house first. Mebbee he will be sitting in that rocking chair and we can watch him rock a few rocks before he gets up to take deep breaths. Next I will take her to Uncle Jim's toad cellar, but I won't let Emily go down that ladder. We will just peek over the rim and watch a toad catch flies. Emily goes mostly barefoot, same as me, saving her shoes to wear to school. Here in St. George she will like how the soft warm sand feels on her bare feet. I really want to get home to tell Earl how good it is down here for boys like us. I bet his eyes will bung out. He won't hardly believe me.

Emily will want to see all the peaches and grapes there is to eat in St. George. But you do not go around eating grapes and peaches everywhere you see them hanging. That would be stealing. I only eat them on Grandfather's lot or down to Uncle Jim's or Aunt Martha's, which is only a block or two from Grandfather's place. You walk right up to the trees and vines no matter who is looking, and stand there picking and eating, not just at one tree like in Brother Lamb's orchard. You do not steal when you take things like that off your relashuns' trees. Relashuns just about always say you can. Too bad we can't take some grapes and peaches home with us, but they would spoil in all the heat and the long days of traveling.

Cox's lot is my Aunt Martha's lot. But it is only part hers. Brother Cox had a couple of wives or more to start with when he married my Aunt Martha. That is why it is only part her lot, the other parts belonging to the other wives. She does not give it much mind anyways on account of he is mostly away, and she is mostly teaching school somewhere off in the Muddy River country, which is even hotter than St. George. Father helped her become a teacher. The other wives help out with the children so she can earn money for food. Folks in St. George are same as those in Summit, always thinking 'bout something to eat. Father says people in Dixie have knowed what it is to be hungry and can easy get along without fine houses and nice clothes to wear, but not without something to eat. If you are hungry, just see what good are fine houses and nice clothes. I think, myself, Father is right.

When I am not tagging Uncle Jim, or when I am not somewhere else, then you can find me always over to Cox's lot playing with Cox boys. There are lots of them, every size; mine, too. They do not want to beat on me, which is differnt from most boys I know. They been brought up to be friendly. Course it helps that they are relashuns. Haven't had a bloody nose since I been down here.

Every time I go over to Cox's a few of the littler boys and me practice flying. We jump off the pigpen and flap our arms same as birds do their wings. Each time we jump and flap our arms it seems like we go a little farther. But we always go bump. The bigger boys say we only fool ourselfs and are dum little kids. We never fly a speck farther. They say we do not fly at all. One of the littler boys I fly with says folks in St. George will gawp their eyes wide open one of these days when they see us, one behind the other, circling around St. George in the sky like a flock of crows, flapping our arms like wings, going sixty, and our legs hanging only halfway downward, on account of we are flying so fast. But mostly I think the bigger boys are right, after all. We won't ever learn to fly like birds. We don't have the wings for it.

Besides all these good things in St. George to show Emily, there is molasses, lots and lots of it. You don't need to be careful and spread it on thin, like we do in Summit. Here we can load it on thick, thick as it can stay on your bread or biskit. With cold molasses you can almost heap it up. Biting into molasses is so good! Sometimes a bit of it squeezes out the corners of your mouth. But you can spare a little like that; there is plenty more.

They make molasses in St. George where they grow the sugarcane. Funny, here in St. George folks call molasses *sorghum*. Sometimes they say *trickle*. If you say *molasses*, they look at you like you don't know much. When you want molasses, you have to ask for sorghum, else for trickle. Father just smiled through his whiskers when I told him I wouldn't mind going hungry same as the family did in the hungry time in St. George if only I could have all the molasses I could pile on my bread, and get all the peaches and grapes I could eat. I could easy go without corn or carrots. Father says those would of been a feast for his family. And even with all the fruit and molasses, folks in St. George can be just as raggedy as Summit. Could be that where the weather is so warm mebbee they don't need better clothes than what they are wearing. Barefoot seems to be the way to go. But Grandmother says you got to have clothes to wear and have some money to buy things with. Peaches and grapes and molasses are soon et up, and are not filling for your body. You got to have bread and meat and potatoes. Those are things St. George does not have enuff of.

I wanted to see Santa Clara which I never seen 'cept when I was just borned and did not remember one thing about it. Santa Clara is a few long miles out in the hills and is a pretty little town now, so Grandmother says. Uncle Jim says five miles is too far to go just to see a town. He thinks there ain't any town worth that much traveling in the hot sun just to see it. In fact, he would not go that far to see Salt Lake City. And what is more, St. George is just as good, a lot better-looking town than Santa Clara any day. I can see it some other time. It will keep. Father grumbles he has to get us back to Summit. He has a feeling a storm is coming and does not wish to get caught on the way home, else he might of took me to see Santa Clara. Guess I will have to wait.

Day before we started home we all went out to see Ellie's grave one more time. Father took us in the wagon. Emily hadn't seen it yet. Mother wouldn't leave St. George, anyways, without going to the grave once more. I been out to see it with Mother quite a few times. It always makes her cry. When we drove up close we piled out and walked over, not far, just down the sandy slope a ways. Father carried Horace, Mother held Martha's hand, and Emily and me walked together bringing some flowers from Grandmother's place. The cemetery is just bare red sand, with nothing growing on it that you would call a flower, and no trees around to give shade, or anything you would call green.

Mother had kept the grave all smooth and clean. Father cleared the ground close around some more. Mother had brought flowers from Grandmother's place, too. Emily and me put our few with those. Ellie loved flowers. After Mother layed them on the grave nice and pretty, we all kneeled in the soft red sand, Mother and Horace and Emily on one side, Father and me and Martha on the other. We bowed our heads while Father prayed. Nobody said anything. We all stood up and walked back to the wagon slow and quiet.

Mother leaned her head on the wheel and cried, mostly just to herself. Emily and me cried, too, but not loud. After, we turned and looked back at Ellie's grave once more. It would be the last time we would see it before we went back to Summit. There it was, all alone, with just our little flowers to tell where it was, nobody and nothing around it anymore. Not till we went to heaven our ownselfs would we see Ellie anymore. Mother said we might not even see her grave another time. She leaned her head on the wheel again, sort of holding it so it wouldn't move, and cried to herself some more. Father patted her shoulder and took her arm to help her up into the wagon. She looked over at the little grave and said, "Goodbye, Ellie, sweetheart, loving daughter. Dear God, we leave her now with you."

PART FOUR

GOING TO THE DEVIL

BACK IN SUMMIT

It makes me feel good to be back in Summit again. Been here quite a while now, and everything looks like it used to, mostly, but feels so kind of empty, even with all of us in it. Ellie isn't here. We would of been home sooner, but Father was bizy with farming and did not have time to come all the way to St. George to pick us up. Mother thinks he came down when he did because he got to feeling lonesome for us and wanted us back home before we taken root in St. George.

Father knowed the weather would still be warm in St. George, where mostly it is either warm or hot. Up here in Summit it is differnt. Already winds blow down off the mountains which turn our night air cold. Every evening Father makes a fire in the fireplace. When you go to Dixie, right after you get down past Cedar City a ways, by the Black Ridge, you go downhill and downhill and downhill, so the horses trot and you have to brake the wagon. You keep on going downhill till you get clear past all the cold air that folks have in Cedar City and Summit. Soon you find St. George folks are sitting in the shade of their porches laffing and having a good time eating grapes or peaches while folks in Summit are standing by their fireplaces trying to keep warm and eating hot soup. That downhill bizness makes a lot of differnce.

When we drove in that afternoon, Earl was the first person to get to our house. He said he been watching the road every day and knowed we would be coming soon on account of his pa told him Father had gone to fetch us. More than once he watched a wagon come up the road from Ray Linn's ranch. Each time he thought for sure it was ours and kept his eyes on it till it got even with our house, but when it did not stop, he would walk back to his house feeling lonesomer than if he hadn't of watched the wagon at all.

The day we got home he said he been watching a covered wagon coming up the road, same as usual. He was hanging on the fence by the road keeping his eyes on its dust. The wagon seemed to look like one he had seen before. It takes a wagon a long time to come almost a mile, but he kept looking till it turned off the road and the horses headed for our gate. He ran like crazy back to his house and yelled at his ma, "Buck's come! They're just drivin' into his lot!" Then out through the gate he went and down to our house in a jiffy. He said if he had thought about it he would of brought a couple of carrots with him, but no matter, pretty soon we would be filling up on them same as always.

Under the edge of the wagon cover I'd been watching for Earl's house. While Jim was letting down the bars so we could drive inside the fence, I saw Earl running. But I could not get out till we had drove inside and Father had helped Mother and the children to step out. Then, kind of crowding Martha to hurry, I jumped down and there was Earl tearing toward our wagon. Gosh! I was glad to see him. We almost put our arms around each other, but boys don't do that. It is only girls which hug. But we each of us felt so good inside to see somebody we had been missing. Right soon after we got home some black clouds bullied their way across the sky and brought a thunderstorm.

For a while after we got home Mother cried a little every day. I would see her wipe her eyes with her apron. She did not talk as much, either, and I knowed she was feeling bad about Ellie. We all were feeling sad and lonesome. Without Ellie going round the house smiling and humming little tunes, it did not seem quite like home to me. Nothing felt anymore like it used to feel.

Sister Persis has come over every day or two. I want her to bring Rebecca with her but am scairt she might do it. I would not hardly know what to say to her. Sister Persis and Mother talk a lot, and she says things which make Mother smile. I know how much Mother likes her visits on account of I catch her looking up the sidewalk to see if Sister Persis is on the way. Seems like all the women in Summit have come to see Mother, one or two at a time. Some say they know just how Mother feels 'cause they have had a girl or boy called away same as Ellie. Everyone wants to be nice.

Ray Linn's wife has come to see Mother quite a few times, too, walking all the way from her ranch. She says it does her body good. When Ellie was sick, she came up as she could to help Mother, cooking our dinners and washing dishes and helping with washings. Sometimes she would let Mother sleep while she tended Ellie. Then before it was dark she would strike out again for the ranch. Jim took her in the wagon when she would let him. I do not see why Gentiles give some folks the fantods. Ray Linn's wife and Sister Persis worked together making poultices and wrapping Ellie's legs and feet with strips of clean cloth they had brought. Mother had to burn so many of her cloths she was getting short of them. Aunt Mary scouted up all she could from her rag box. After the cloths were used, they were washed and hung on the line. Nursing Ellie was more work than Mother could of done by herself. She says so long as she lives she will not forget how sweet and kind have been these women, which I know, myself, she won't. Mother says you can forgive and forget a hurt but you cannot ever forget a kindness.

While we were away, Aunt Mary had Sarah Ann stop at our house and cook for the family. She was company for Emily, and Laura and Eliza came by to play with Emily and give a hand. Sarah Ann is a big girl now, older than Ellie, and has got a bow. Mother says Sarah is the best worker she has ever seen. Seems the more she works, the more she likes to work. The house is cleaner than when we left it. Sarah scrubbed the floor and washed the windows and doors, cleaned the cupboard, washed the table and chairs, and blacked the stove. Besides all that, she washed every piece of cloth she could find in the house. Sam says Sarah will make a good wife someday for some good man, which is not just smart talk, I think.

Do not know why, but I don't feel the same way she does about work. I cannot see any fun in wanting to work so hard and doing it. I like to work, but not so much that I am working all the time. How would I have time to play? Stands to reason nobody weeds carrots or onions, or pulls weeds out of the furrows just on account of he likes doing it. I always get tired quick when I am weeding. It helps for me to think about things besides weeds while I am doing it, but my thinking is mostly about things like how nice it would be if Earl and me could be off in the sagebrush catching lizards. The sun doesn't feel so hot when you are playing. Work makes me more tired quicker than anything else there is to do. Earl says if he knows he has to weed the carrots or onions tomorrow, it makes him so tired today he would rather his pa did not tell him about that work so soon. Then he wouldn't get tired before he needed to.

Earl and me thought if we learned to work, the days would go faster, and we would have our birthdays that much sooner, but we found out that days go slower, lots more slower, when we work. Some work we may do more easily, like pulling weeds for cows and pigs, but most work is much harder and not any fun, like weeding carrots and onions in the hot summer sun. Mostly when we have finished the work our mother or father has told us to do, Earl comes to my house, and we might go down to our field where Father is working. We know he wants to be rid of gofers and mice and grasshoppers. That is just the kind of work I like to do. Earl and me can run all around doing it. Another kind is going with Father and the oxen to Parowan. That work is nearly all sitting.

One night when I was sleeping with Sam on our shed, hunkered down in our blankets, I was watching shooting stars shoot. Every time a star went whizzing through the sky I told him about it. He got kind of grouchy with me. "If you are gonna sleep out here with me, then shut up and go to sleep right now. I got work to do in the morning," he scolded. Gee whillikers! Sam is only just half a man. He won't be a whole man till he is big as Jim. But already he talks like he wants to work. "Sam," I said, "when I am a man, will I have to work?"

"You will have to work or starve to death, and I think you would rather starve." He turned over and went to sleep. I did not go to sleep, but I did not watch for shooting stars anymore. What Sam had told me made me feel kind of queer, and I began to do some thinking, same as Father and Brigham Young go about it. I do not want to work all my life. I do not want to starve to death. Next time Earl and me talk, we will talk about work some more.

'POSTATE

Earl and me are half past seven and quite a bit more. Father says we are coming up fast on eight. We are glad for that on account of then it will be our turn to get babetized. You have to be at least eight years old to know right from wrong and can probly take being dunked all the way in the water. We are already counting the days. We figger every day that goes by is one day we do not have to count anymore. If they come fast enuff, it will not take long. Our birthdays come in the winter, so we will not ackcherly get babetized soon as we are eight. We have to wait for summer. That's when they do the babetizing.

These days we go barefoot only after the shoes have skinned up our feet. We are careful not to get big blisters. That is the way we are learning to wear shoes. Soon as the sores get well, we put the shoes back on again and wear them till they rub our heels and toes and ankuls again. Then off go the shoes. They come off easier now than they did when they were bran new. We go barefoot till the sores scab over and get well. Earl's pa says doing it the way we do is tuff on the feet, but the shoes wear longer.

Soon school will start, and when it does we will be having too much fun to count days. Father says a week is almost nothing to a bizy person. In fact it seems like you hardly get home from

Sunday School and it is Saturday night again, and you have to get washed and cleaned up for Sunday School next morning. We both wish the folks who first made weeks had made them a whole month long.

But there is some good in the cleaning-up bizness. When I go to Sunday School next morning mebbee Rebecca sees me and sometimes says "Hello, Buck" to me, and right straight I say "Hello, Rebecca" back to her. By that time I cannot speak another word. Mostly I run away and get in the crowd where she won't see me but where I can peek at her. After that I do not hear much that is spoke by anybody else on account of I am thinking of her. All week after that I sometimes sit in front of our house against the fence and shut my eyes and see Rebecca smile and hear her say, "Hello, Buck." If I am standing when I shut my eyes, I have to hold on good to the fence, or I would soon not be able to tell if I was standing up straight or leaning over. If I lean over too far I could fall and bump my head, which I did once. Now I always take ahold of the fence before I shut my eyes.

Earl does not have a girl hisself. Guess that is why he thinks that scrubbing is not hardly worth going through every week. A month should be plenty quick enuff. If Mother and his ma were not women which like getting scrubbed their ownselfs, we think they would get tired of having all of us boys and girls go through with it every Saturday. His ma told Earl that if he did not get scrubbed up once a week he would draw flies worse than a rotten apple.

This winter in school we are going to learn words, real words which mean something more than just saying our ABCs. Emily thinks I will learn to read a whole line of words, just like her and

Rebecca can do easy as pie. Rebecca started school a couple of years before me, with Emily, so they are already good readers. Teacher told us last time that soon as we can do reggler reading we will start getting some sense, which is the same as being smart. I can't wait.

One day Earl said his pa told him that us two boys ought to plan on being mighty good all this winter if we wanted to be babetized in the summer. If we do, then when we are getting babetized, there may be angels watching. He said lots of things can happen between now and then, and sometimes things which happen are not so good, so we need to be specially careful. That made me think. Seems like things are happening already and have been happening since quite a while ago. I knowed they been happening right along but didn't think they were bad, least not enuff to feel really bad about them, not like Ellie getting sick and dying. Right now the bad things which are happening are on account of the Bishop's sheep.

Father does not like sheep, never did. Now he hates them. I heard him say so. I don't blame him. I do not like sheep, either. Since sheep have come to Summit they have eaten all the flowers growing up toward the canyon. They have been grazing out by the Injun campground and have eaten all the red bells and bluebells, and the larkspurs. Father says we will have to give the Injuns hay for their horses on account of the sheep have grazed down the grass around their camp.

Summit gets its water from that creek in ditches that go past the houses. Sometimes the Bishop's sheep feed in a fenced-in pasture just before our place, along the piece of the ditch which goes past our house. Ours is the last house, at the end of town. He keeps that pasture full of sheep and has a man to take care of them. This man does not seem to mind if the sheep get right in the water. We drink water out of the ditch, and now it has a taste you can't hardly miss.

One time at dinner Sam took a drink from his cup of water, looked around the table at all of us, smacked his lips, and said, "Mother, what is the use of you buying tea from the store? Seems we got a whole creek full of it. We got lots more than we can use, and we get it for nothing." That was not just some of Sam's smart talk. It was the pure truth, even though Father looked like he could give him a smack for forgetting his manners and talking about it at the table.

One day after Sam's bad manners, Jim brought a bucket of water from the ditch for us to drink. He put it on the bench in the kitchen where we always keep our drinking water. There is a long-handled dipper hanging close by the bucket. With it handy we do not need to look around for a cup every time we want a drink. Some campers had stopped at our house and were staying with us for the night. The woman went to the kitchen to get her a drink. "Well, well, Sister McCarty!" she called out to Mother. "I see you got a sheep berry floatin' around on this bucket of water." I came out with Mother to see about it, and she grabbed the bucket and throwed it all out on the ground at the back of the house. She rinsed the bucket out with boiling water from the teakettle, then went to the ditch herself and brought in a fresh bucket.

Soon as Mother had come out of the kitchen after bringing fresh water, the woman said to her, right in front of us all, "I don't like to drink water, myself, which tastes sheepy, but when my children at home get the measles I always give them sheep-berry tea, and make it sorta strong, to bring the measles out better than anything else I ever tried." I would hate to be her kid and have measles. I do not think Mother needed to throw that first bucket of water out on the ground just for that woman. Neither did Sam. But Mother did not want to be a part of the woman's sheep talk if she could help it. Sam says that camper woman ought to take a keg of our water home for her kids, just in case some of them ain't had measles yet.

The sheep turds and all that talk about the water made Father angrier than I ever seen. Right straight he went to see the man who takes care of the Bishop's sheep, though mostly it is that man's son does the herding, and he may not be too careful. Father told him to keep the sheep off the ditch. Father must of got kind of carried away on account of he told the man a lot of other things which would not sound so good in Sunday School. That is what Bill told me, who went with him. I just bet Father let loose, all right. He is that way when he gets mad and starts talking. Sam says when Father finishes with what he has to say, the other man is mostly mad enuff his ownself to eat nails. Then Father cools down. He has told me more than once that one drop of Irish in our blood is one drop too many, and I should mind my mouth. His talking did not keep the sheep out of the ditch, anyhow. The water stayed about the same. Sometimes it was sheepy, sometimes just plain water.

Then one Sunday morning when everyone went to Sunday School we found the church, which is also our reggler schoolhouse and special meetings place, jam full of sheep. From the smell it seemed the sheep had been there most of the night. Soon as they had been all drove out, Earl and me sneaked up close to the door and peeked in. The men would not let us go inside for fear we would step in the smelly leavings. We could easy see the sheep had slept on the platform which is where the Bishop and his helpers sit when Sunday meeting is going on. I bet the sheep had thought it the nicest place they ever slept in, where it was quiet, out of the rain, and nothing could come in to hurt them. Only sheep do not seem to have any manners when they sleep inside houses. These didn't.

We did not have Sunday School. It would take the men and women half a day to clean it out. They would have to sweep and scrub the floor and the benches and platform with soap and warm water. And then it would take a day or two for the room to sit out and dry and all the smell to go away. People were plenty mad, you can bet. When we got home and told Father what had been going on in the church house, he said he would not have believed it if his own children had not told him. Father felt bad enuff to feel sick. He said such a rascally trick was not smart or funny. And now, specially now, on account of him kicking up such a rumpus over the sheep fouling our water, folks would surely say it was him which had done it.

He was right. But it wasn't him. It was some big boys who just wanted to be smart-alecks. Don't know what their fathers did to them, or if they even found out. Probly didn't. And anyways, folks already thought it was Father's doing. After he mulled it around in his head a while he said, "I fail to see how it is any worse for sheep to sleep in the schoolhouse than it is for them to sleep on our creek. But no one gets worked up about that." Don't know if Father told any other people what he told us. But I think the same. Sheep do not have any more manners when they sleep on our creek than when they sleep in the schoolhouse. I seen both places, so I know.

After the sheep mess it seemed like other things happened which only made everything worse for Father. He likes to read

the *Salt Lake Tribune* when he has a chance, which is mostly at
the Parowan Co-op. He brought one home one day. Two Relief
Society sisters happened to of come to visit Mother and saw the
paper laying on the table. Right off, one came down on Mother
for having Satan's newspaper in the house with children. She told
her to get that filthy thing out before we all lost our testamo-
nies, and what is more, we were on the slippery slope to being
an infernal family. Mother was too suprised to say anything.
She just gawped at them. I knowed she does not like for Father
to bring the newspaper home with him, but she can take care
of her family's bizness without neighbors horning in. As soon
as her voice came back she steamed about it, but by that time
the sister had slammed out the door. Sam had heard everything
from the porch and slipped away to tell the boys in the corral.

A few days later, when Father was out in the field for the day,
and Mother was doing her own visiting with other sisters, Sam
and Bill thought it would be smart to paper our front room with
that newspaper. A neighbor sister stopped by to see if Mother
was at home, and her eyes bunged out at what she saw, and
she nearly jumped out of her shoes. "Wait till the Bishop hears
about this!" she cried out. "This house has gone to the devil!"
Just then Mother came through the door. Poor Mother.

She looked around the room and at the sister standing there
with her hands to her face and her cheeks all scrunched up
and red. Mother had a terrible frown growing on her forehead. "Well, I know some boys that will wish they could meet
the devil instead of their father when he gets home!" From the
sound of it, this was more awful than the sheep bizness. Myself,
I could not see what made the women so fired up. All I could
see was little pitchers of shoes and boots, sacks of grain, and
rows and rows of tiny printing. Sam read some of it, but not

the parts about Brigham Young. The stores in Salt Lake City
have just about everything for sale. You can buy candy by the
bushel and nice clothes like coats and shoes. You can buy axes
and plows and barrels, even wagons or carriges. What is so
devil-ish about that?

Then soon after that bad thing, Father told Mother he was
going to ask the Bishop to take his name off the records. First,
though, he would say a few words in the meeting about some
of the things that had gone on and were allowed to go on which
were a disgrace to Summit. All at once Mother looked suprised,
scairt, and sad, all at the same time. I do not think I will ever
forget her face. "Oh, Jim, think on this before your mouth hurts
you and all of us. Homer here is just ready for babetizm. We
still got Martha and Horace to do, and we got this new baby.
I won't stand for some of us in the family being in the cove-
nant and some not."

Father did not say anything. He took her arm and patted it,
but we could tell the anger had not left. Mother rubbed her eyes
with her hands to keep tears from showing. I never seen Mother
speak up to Father like this. "I got to tell you something my
father told me when we were married. He said you were a fine
man, but you did not have enuff of the blood of Abraham in
you to remain in the church. That has been a worry to me, but
you been through so many hard times giving your full lot to
the church, and now you are doing pretty well here in Summit.
Folks have been neighborly and nice. They gave a lot of help for
Ellie. I couldn't of got through that without them. This would
be a terrible, terrible thing for all of us."

I had a hole where my stummick used to be. Even Sam did
not have a word to say. But Father went right ahead and did it.

I was not at church that Sunday, neither mother nor the girls. Only Jim and Bill went with him. Sam could not go it either and sat out on the shed roof. And Father did tell the people what he thought. Stands to reason he was riled up, but only for the sheep and the paper flap. Don't know what else was stuck in his craw that he had to get out. Sam says mebbee the church was wanting him to take another wife. That would do it. Father always says he has more than a handful with two. The Bishop did what Father asked and took his name off the books. Now Father was cut off. I didn't think that was so bad. Nobody got hurt doing it. But seems everyone's name in the family was also took off. We were no longer in the church.

Next morning Father and me went to our field like we usually do, with the oxen, and stayed all day. I chased a few gofers and got a couple. Father did not feel to talk, so after a while I went to the wagon and took the quilt off the springseat board and made me a bed under the wagon. I slept till Father was ready to go home. When we were eating supper that night Father told us he was going to Parowan in the morning with a load of corn and wheat. We needed some more flour and cornmeal to eat. He said he would take me along if I wanted to go. Course I wanted to. I always go where Father goes if he lets me.

Seems some people in Summit do not like Father anymore these days. He says he can stand it on account of it is a little bit like him being a 'bolitionist in Kentucky all those years ago before he came out to Utah and joined the church. Those Kentucky folks not only did not like him, but said they would kill him if he stayed around. They did not agree about a man having slaves. Here in Summit, seems folks cannot like other folks which get cut off from the church on account of they think differnt. People do not like other people to be differnt from them.

These days Father takes his long whip with the handle made of hard slick wood. The boys call it a bullwhip. The handle slims down from the big end to the little end. The whip is fastened to the little end. The big end is awful heavy because it is filled with lead. The handle is a bit longer than my arm. The heavy end of the handle makes it easy to swing the long buckskin whip out to cover the backs of the oxen. Once Father told me that whip-handle made a good enuff club to knock down a bull. When you use it for a club you hold the little end of it in your hand and the whip length in your other hand.

On our trips to Parowan and back, Father likes to walk along by the side of the oxen. He says he does that to keep his legs limbered up. This time when we started from home I was sitting on the springseat board all by myself, Father walking by the side of the oxen. When we got more than a block from home we were passing in front of another house where three men were standing by the gate. One of the men raised his fist and shouted something at Father. It was the man who had the herding of the sheep to do. The other two were his relashuns. I knowed them all. Soon as the man hollered at us, Father said "Whoa!" to the oxen. The wagon stopped quick as oxen can stop.

The man seemed to be mad at Father for what he had said in the meetinghouse. All three men came out on the street in a hurry, looking mean. When they got a little ways from Father they stopped. One was swearing at Father and calling him awful names. The other men did not say anything; they did not have a chance, on account of that man was talking and swearing too fast. Seemed like they had only come out on the street to hear the man who was swearing and help him when he ran out of breath. Father talked right back to him but did not swear any. Guess that is on account of he does not know how to cuss properly. But he does not have to cuss to say things awful mean.

Bill told me Father never needs to carry a gun on account of his tongue can cut a man off at the knees and do a better job of it. It makes the other folks madder than if he had cussed them. Soon as the other man stopped a minnit, Father said something which made that man even madder than before. He was the closest to Father.

Quick the man doubled up both fists and came at Father, shouting he was going to beat the living daylights out of him. Father grabbed the little end of that bullwhip handle and raised the big end to hit the man. "Whoops! Look out everybody!" yelled one of the other men. They all jumped back. Father stepped a little closer swinging that whip-handle at them. Back they ran, but Father kept after them. This time the man ran for his gate where he had come from.

Father came back to the wagon and climbed back up on the springseat and spoke to the oxen: "Go on, Buck! Go on Blue!" But the oxen did not start quick. They never do. They did not know there was probly going to be a fight. I did not know before this minnit that they started so awful slow. I was in such a hurry to get away and get away fast, I pushed on the endgate with my feet. Seemed to me the front end of the wagon started quite a while after the hind end got going. The men could of easy come and jerked Father off the seat and beat him up like the man said he would, but they stayed away from the wagon and close to their gate. The man kept swearing and calling Father bad names. Now I knowed why

Earl could outswear me at Dan Harris's haystack. He lives close to that man.

Oxen cannot start quick, neither can they trot like horses. They just put one foot in front of the other, just one foot at a time. Then in a little while the next foot comes after and goes in ahead of the first foot. Oh, how I was wishing they knowed how to trot. They go so slow you cannot even count their steps on account of you forget the last count before the next foot comes along. The man knowed we couldn't get away very quick, so he just kept up his swearing by the gate. By and by we got far enuff away we could not make out any of his words and were glad we did not have to hear them.

When we got out along the road a ways and started downhill toward Parowan, Father said he was glad the men had jumped back like they did, because that whip-stock would of come down on that man's head and cracked his skull, all right. "Then I might be hanged for murder." My stummick jumped. I could not of stood for that. Father said there wasn't anybody going to knock the daylights out of him, not so long as he had that whip-stock handy. Which I could see, myself, none of them better even try. Guess that is what the three men must of thought their ownselfs.

Almost soon as we got into Parowan we found out folks there knowed all about Father being cut off. When we were in the gristmill, Father and the miller man talked a lot about it. "Well, Brother McCarty!" the gristmill man said. "You are a good man even if you be cut off. The church needs more good men like you. You should never been cut off." When we were about to leave for home they shook hands again. The miller-man had ahold of Father's hand with both of his. He said to him in a friendly voice, "God bless you, Brother McCarty. It will all be made right someday."

EVERYTHING'S BROKE

We did not get home from Parowan till way after dark. Father and the miller, along with a couple other men, talked too much. Seven miles is a long way to go with oxen and get back the same day. There is not time enuff between getting there and starting back to do much bizness, Father says. About all a person can do is to Pass the Time of Day with people you meet. We seem to of met a lot.

Next morning Father had to go to our field. He told Mother he guessed he would be taking me along, same as yesterday. We are good company for each other. When I am with him, we don't have to talk, we can just think. Then each of us does not bother the other. That day Jim and Bill had to go to the canyon for poles. They took Red and Bally, so Father and me took Buck and Blue, like we usually do. Seems Buck and me are good as relashuns to each other. We got the same name. Besides, Father thinks Buck is a good ox, and smart, too, just like me. I ain't a ox like him, but we are the same in everything else.

The poles which Jim and Bill bring from the canyon are long slim quaking aspen trees which don't have knots on. We will put the poles across the top of the new shed. The old one is too small. Then we will spread willows and birches on top of the poles. When we thresh our grain we will put straw on top of the willows and birches. That is the way everybody makes their sheds. We have some oats to thresh, but we don't put oat straw on the shed. No sir, you bet we don't. Oat straw makes good feed for cattle. Sometimes that is about all we have to feed them. We will put oat straw under the shed, dry and handy to feed the cattle with. That is where our new chaff bin will be.

I will sleep on the new one soon as we have our threshing. Us boys will sleep there till almost Chrismus time. Sam says it is not so bad out there in the fall. Only sometimes it is hard getting up in the morning, on account of the straw under the quilt is warm, but the air is cold. Long as the quilt feels warm, we will be on the shed. There I can watch the stars, the ones that shoot across the sky and ones that just stand still.

Father did not talk much that morning going out to the field. He was already thinking. He did not talk much all day. I could tell he was thinking hard about something. But he didn't look like he mostly looks when he's thinking. He looked dark and sad. Mebbee it was about being cut off last Sunday. I think, myself, that is what it was. He seemed to take it hard to be called a 'postate by those men. I guess that is a cuss word Earl and me had not heard before. When we started home at the end of the day he was still the same way, hardly talking at all, so I kept on thinking my ownself.

I was thinking of school, which will start in a month more. I like school. I like figgers, even. Ever since we studied on them that time in school, there's been figgers in my head. They keep going round and round, kind of in a scramble. Earl says figgers are too crazy for him. He would lots rather figger with a saw and hammer, the way his pa does it. I cannot figger anything with a saw and hammer. Give me figgers every time. I like them.

"Well, Buck! I guess you'll have to forget babetizm this coming summer that we been talking about so much." What had Father just said to me?

Quick I straightened up and the figgers flitted right out of my head. "What you say to me?" He had just busted out sudden and I had not heard him so good.

"I said you will have to forget babetizm for a while."

"Why I got to forget it?" In that minnit everything in me just quit. I could feel my heart going sick. I was sick below my heart. My buzzum started to breathe heavy.

"The Bishop won't babetize children of men who have been cut off."

"But Earl and me been waiting and waiting a long time to be eight years old. We are going to do it together, both ourselfs!" The world was falling down. Everything was going to pieces! I almost couldn't breathe.

"I know that, son, but you will just have to forget it now."

"How can I forget something I been waiting for such a long time? And it isn't till next summer. I just got to do it, Father, with Earl. I just got to." My eyes began to prickle.

"I know you feel bad, but I cannot help it. You will have to wait, till another time."

"But can't I? Oh, can't I, Father? Please, can't I?" I couldn't talk anymore and hot tears burned on my cheeks.

"No, Buck. Wish you could, but you can't." Father reached over and pulled me close to him. "You do not have to be babetized right now, anyway, mebbee never. It would not be the end of the world." His voice was sad. We didn't have the spring-seat, only the board with a quilt on it. Father pulled me closer, and I leaned into him and cried. Mostly I cried inside myself.

Father held me so I would not fall off. After quite a long time of no talking we got home.

I did not eat much supper. You cannot eat when you are feeling bad everywhere inside of you. You feel sick. Mother said to me, "Homer, you do not look good at all. Are you feeling sick?" Her face looked ankshus. Anyone could see I must be sick, else I would of been eating my meat and potatoes.

"Uh-uh, I ain't sick." But I was, sickest I been in my whole life. I went outside and walked around the yard a little. Nothing looked the same as it did yesterday. There wasn't anything looking good where I looked. It never does when you are feeling bad all over and all through you. The whole world was differnt. By the fence I sat and cried. No one could see me. No one would hear me. A long time I sat and cried, not loud, just soft and low, more tears than cry. You can feel so bad you cannot even cry like you do when you cut your finger or when you have stubbed your toe. You can get over that. No use even living anymore. But I did not dast die, either. I knowed what it meant if I did. I would be going to hell with the Gentiles. Mebbee I would be a Gentile, too.

It was almost dark when I went in the house again. I told Mother I guessed I would go to bed. She thought I ought to on account I looked so tired. I didn't let her see my face. If I had, she would of knowed I been crying and then be more ankshus about me. I layed on the quilt on the shed and cried some more, but not loud to wake up Sam, till I went to sleep. Did not look at the stars even once.

It was after dinner next day before I went anywheres, and then I walked slow, with my head bowed over, probly looking like a tired old man, which is how I felt. After a while I was walking along a sidewalk not far from Rebecca's house, just walking along with my eyes turned down, not looking at anything. I did not want to see anything or anybody, not even Rebecca. Guess I thought if I walked slow like I did, I would not have to think. Thinking made me sick. Wish I didn't know how to think. All I could think about was hell.

Before I knowed where I was at, that bully Abner was right in my face. It was him who jerked my waist and tried to push me out of my seat at the Panner-rammer. Right straight he began yammering at me. He was lots bigger'n me, and just then Earl was not along to help. He has not liked us a bit since the Wonderful Thing. But I was bigger'n I was a year ago at the Panner-rammer. "Yaah, so yer pa's been cut off, ain't he?" he said with a sneery laff.

"Guess I know it, don't I? And I am glad, too." I sounded like I meant it, but I didn't.

"Sure y'are. Glad to go to hell, both him and you?"

"Whatta you know about hell?" I was feeling so bad I did not even know how to talk back to him.

"Oh yes, I do, lots more'n you."

"You don't, either. I know more'n you do, and more'n even your pa knows," I fired back at him.

"Huh, my pa knows more in just his little finger 'bout hell than all your cut-off family put together."

"Your pa ain't so smart. He can't say who will go to hell and who won't!"

"Don't get sassy or I'll bust you on the nose. I ain't forgot yet 'bout you two pips."

"I don't care what you ain't forgot about. Your pa ain't so smart."

"My pa is, too."

"But he ain't smart as you think."

"My pa says yer pa's a poss-tate. He's a 'dulter, too."

"What's them names you're calling my father!" I hadn't heard any of those cuss words before. They sounded awful. That Irish in me which I am told to watch out for rose right up, and I was ready to fight him even if he was bigger than me, but he was barefoot and I had on my shoes getting them broke in for school. I could kick him on the shins and stomp his toes like Earl and me planned to do soon as we could. But Earl wasn't here with me just now, and I was on my way to hell and wouldn't have another chance at him. I would have to do what I could. My heart was pounding like a drum.

Abner sneered at me. "Pa says a poss-tate's a man what's cut off, and a 'dulter's a man what has more'n one wife and don't belong to the church. You got to belong to the church for that. Yer pa is both!"

"You take it back! I won't let you call my father names like that."

"No! Not today or never. I been waitin' to beat the whey outa you and Earl and guess I'll begin with you right now."

"Take it back now, this minnit!" I said, nudging up to him and doubling up my fists.

"You little feist! I can lick you with one hand tied behind . . ."

Bang! Before he was looking, I stretched and hit him hard as I could on the end of his nose. Hah! The blood squirted. Guess he couldn't see so good for a second or two. When he got his eye opened, blood had already run into his mouth, then over his chin. He looked like he might die. Soon as he saw all that blood, he began yelling and bawling and beat it for home. The fight was already over, and I did not have to plant a shoe on him. Just the same, I ran, too, kind of hog wild, didn't know where, didn't care. I just wanted to get away from where I was at before Abner dropped dead as nits.

I felt too bad to go home. Everything had been fine before Sunday. Now everything was differnt. There wasn't any use to live anymore, but it would be worser to die. I went over to the schoolhouse and sat against its log wall. No use going to school anymore. No use to learn figgers. Probly now all the boys know I am going to hell and won't play with me. Dropping my face in my arms between my knees I was so sorry for myself I had to blubber again.

Earl's house was just down the street from the school, but no use going there anymore. I wasn't feeling good enuff to play, not even with him. And likely Earl would not want to play with me, either. And even call Father terrible names. If he did, bargain or no bargain, I would have to bust him one and jump on him with my shoes. I had just stood up and started walking again when I heard him call out.

"Hello, Buck! What you doin' over there?" He came on the run. "Where you been? Ain't seen you since Sunday."

"Oh, I just been to the field with Father and over to Parowan. I ain't been feelin' so good. Want to sit down a while?"

"I got a better ideer. Let's go over to our corral. Pa has brought home a little black bull from the mountains. I been tryin' to ride him."

"Guess you know Father got cut off Sunday," I said soon as we got set down.

"Yup, I know. Pa cusses your father a lot. But we don't care, do we? They ain't us. We ain't them."

"That's why I haven't been feeling so good. I don't want to go to hell."

"Dam' hell, anyhow," Earl said loudly, trying out his own cussing.

All of a sudden something shot into my mind which made me feel better just to think it. "Earl, I am pretty sure we already kilt the devil and put out hellfire that time we docked the devil! Remember?"

"Course I do. We bargained we would, and I don't doubt we did it. You bet. We busted hell all up, me with Pa's hatchet to dock his tail, you with his tail for a spear and me with his pitchfork to push him into the fire. We had a good time and did a good job."

I was almost crying for gladness. "We did it, and everybody already there went home and put on their clothes again and went to heaven, didn't they?"

"Course they did! We taken care of him and hell proper. That's why I keep Pa's hatchet hid, for the next time we need it." Up he jumped and was reaching his hand to me. I grabbed it and jumped up. His hand felt so good. Oh, so good! I knowed Earl and me would always be friends, no matter what.

"You know what?" he said to me, with sparkles in his eyes. "Pa thinks that hatchet's been stole."

Just that minnit I felt the same like I always do. I felt good. I wasn't scairt of hell or the devil or anything or anybody, on account of there wasn't any devil or hell to be scairt of. Earl and me had put the fire out and the devil, too. Father and me wouldn't have to go there after all. "Come on, Earl!" I shouted at him. "Let's go ride that little bull."

He had already started running for the corral. I caught up with him quick. While we ran he said to me, "This will be some fun! We got to be careful, though. He's the buckinest little cuss Pa ever brought off the mountains. His pa must be same as the red bull calf's."

"Don't care how bucky he is. I feel so good I know I can ride him, even his pa, too, if he was here."

GOODBYE TO SUMMIT

I been eight now quite a while. We already have a good start with spring, and Summit looks green as it ever gets. Sister Persis has come one more time to bring a baby to Mother. His name is Norman Franklin. Won't be long before Earl and other boys and girls which are eight years old will be getting babetized. I will not be there even to watch. I won't know if angels come.

Father has been over to Monroe on the Sevier River and bought a home with a little farm there and has sold our place and farm in Summit. We are getting ready to move. It is more'n a hunnert miles around and through mountains to get there. First we have to go up to Paragonah and then through the mountains in a long winding valley we use when we go peddling south along the Sevier River to Pangwitch. But now we will turn north and follow the river through more canyons a long ways till we get to where Monroe is, which is called Sevier Valley. Father says Monroe sits under mountains bigger than any I seen before and has plenty of big trees and creeks.

He has sold all our oxen, on account of we won't have use for oxen in a town like Monroe. Besides, Buck and Blue and Red and Bally have lived so long in Summit they would be terrible lonesome so far away. They would not know the town, the people, or the other oxen. All the roads and fields would be strange to them. They have all growed up from calves right here in Summit. They do not go lots of places, like horses do. Father would never go far as Pioche or Pangwitch with oxen. Here they know all our towns and roads and people, the other oxen in town, and some of the horses. If we took them over to Monroe, Father is afraid they would pine away. I can easy see they would. Still, I will be missing them. Father hopes the man he sold them to will be good to them, same as he has been.

Before the man came to take the oxen away, I went out to our corral and said goodbye. I could tell by their eyes and the wiggle of their nose holes they were feeling bad on account of I would be going away where they would not see me never anymore.

Buck was standing off a ways from the others while I was saying goodbye to them. He was looking at me. I went over to him and patted his head and shoulder. He turned his head a bit to look at me more plainly. I could tell he was feeling bad same as me. We looked each other in the eyes. "Goodbye, old Buck." Tears just rolled out of mine. My windpipe felt tight. He flopped his ears backwards and frontwards at me and wiggled his nose holes a bit, telling me how bad he felt about him and me going away. When he winked his eyes at me I could see they were watery same as mine. "Goodbye, Buck," I said to him once more. Then I started back toward the corral bars. Didn't care who saw me.

When I crawled through the bars and looked back, Buck had walked close behind me and was standing there, looking at me. Same as friends, we looked at each other's eyes. I picked a bunch of green grasses and gave them to him. "Goodbye, old Buck," I said again, this time waving my hand. He flopped his ears backwards and frontwards, then straight up. We heard voices talking. I looked behind and saw Father coming with the man who would take the oxen away. Buck saw them, too, and turned around and walked slow and sad to where Blue and Red and Bally were standing.

I went over to the chicken coop where I could rub my eyes and no one would see. Herk came over and licked my face. I heard someone letting down the bars and I stood up to one side to see things better. Right straight, Red and Bally stepped out of the corral. They had their yoke on. Close behind came Buck and Blue with their yoke on, too. Next the man walked out behind them. He had Father's long whip rolled up in a circle like Father sometimes carries it. I stood by our front gate and watched the man and oxen walking slow up the street till they turned the corner. Buck was gone forever. More tears ran down my cheeks.

Herk licked my face some more. We are taking him. We could not leave him in Summit. The very first night he would run away from the place where he was at and catch up with us. And of course he will be a lot of help driving cattle. He gets to run around and bark at them. That is what he likes best of all.

Next day after the oxen were driven away, I went up to Aunt Mary's house to say goodbye to her and Sarah Ann and Laura and Eliza. Father is taking Mother's family over to the Sevier Valley first. Then when he gets settled in our new home, he will come for her and the girls. She will have her own house in Monroe, too. But while I was there, thinking of Rebecca, I climbed up onto Aunt Mary's shed roof to look for her one more time. I could see her house and lot plain as ever. But I didn't see her, didn't see anybody there at all, though I looked and looked, around and over her yard and lot. I wanted more than anything to see her just once before we went away. But I didn't, and she never found out I liked her so much. Nobody ever could tell her that on account of nobody knowed it but me, and I did not say it out loud.

Next day, which was the last day before we had to go, I was up to Earl's house almost all day, staying out from under Mother's packing and Father's stowing things in the wagons. Earl had a few red carrots left from last year. We dug some and went out under Earl's shed and had a real carrot feed, our last one together. We had weeded and picked a lot of them in our gardens, and now we only had to eat this bunch with each other this one more time. We laffed about it, only not very hard. We did not feel to laff much at anything. When Earl's ma had got dinner ready, we sat by each other at the table. She had made some pies and said since I was going away she would let Earl and me eat a whole pie if we could do it. "Now don't go at it like a couple of shoats," she said. "I'll cut you each a good piece to start with. Soon as you finish those I'll cut you some more." We laffed at that and tried not to eat like young hogs, but we finished that pie pretty quick just the same.

Father and the boys have packed our two wagons full of stuff. Every bit of room under the covers is plum full. We are too much loaded to take Mother's loom with us. So she is selling it to one of the sisters in Summit. Father has found a woman in Monroe who has a loom and will let us hire it for a while when Mother needs to until she can get another of her own to make cloth or carpets. She has stood at her loom nearly every day long as I can 'member, and I have helped her at it pretty reggler. That has been one of my jobs, one I like. We are taking the spinning wheel. Don't know what she would do for yarn to knit socks and stockings with if we didn't have one handy.

We have a good-size herd of cattle and horses, mostly cattle. The wagons will have to go slow. Cows and calves cannot travel fast and need to eat the grass and browse along the road, which is all they will have to eat till we get there. Herk will be a big help with them. Father will drive the head wagon with Mother and Martha and Horace and the baby. I will be riding with Jim in the hind wagon. I like being with him, on account of he is always nice to me even if he is about a grown man. He does not try to be smart like Sam or get mad at things so quick as Bill. Emily will mostly ride with us. Martha thinks she would like to ride with us sometimes, too. Of course Emily and me will walk alongside a lot of the time and look for things to pick up along the way and stretch our legs. I am glad Sam and Bill will be driving the cattle and horses. That way we won't be bothered with them bickering in the wagons. Mother wants to get to Monroe as soon as we can and get settled. If moving so far away is what we have to do, she wants to do it and be done with it.

Earl came down to our house to say goodbye. We took ahold of hands and looked at each other. We couldn't talk. It hurts to feel so sad. I can't hardly remember not having Earl to play with, can't think of playing without him. More than mebbee, we probly won't never see each other anymore at all. So we just stood there holding hands and looking at each other.

"Come on, Buck," Jim called. "Get up in the wagon. Father has started. It is our turn now." Soon as I was up on the seat, the wagon rumbled forward. I turned and looked around the cover. Earl was standing by our gate watching us leave. I waved my hand at him. "Goodbye, Earl!" I called out to him. There were tears in my voice. "Goodbye, Buck!" he called back to me, waving his hand. Then he hung his head and wiped his eyes with his fingers but did not start for home, just stood there looking at me. I kept leaning over and looking back at him. He waved his hand some more. I waved back at him. Right while our hands were waving, the wagon turned the corner, and Earl was out of sight. Seemed like something inside me died right then. Tears just came out of my eyes. Jim and Emily let me cry without laffing at me. Emily wiped some from her own eyes. She had friends she was leaving, too.

Now we were passing Rebecca's house. I looked and looked. No Rebecca. Probly she did not know we were going away from Summit. Mebbee her folks did not want her saying goodbye to folks which had been cut off. I looked backwards and backwards to see her and was still looking at her house when the wagon started going down the slope to Parowan. Then Summit was out of sight, and I would not see Earl or Rebecca ever again. I faced about on the springseat. No use looking anymore. Felt I was leaving my life back there. Never again would I know a boy good as Earl, or like as much. And I wouldn't ever, no never, see a girl I liked as much as Rebecca with her yellow hair and blue, blue eyes.

It took us eight days to get to Monroe. That last morning, we drove up a weedy road to our new place, and Mother set about making a late breakfast for us so the men could get started moving in. She said she had made eight breakfasts over a dirty campfire and this meal she was getting ready would be her last. She had to wipe her eyes and dodge about the fire to keep out of the smoke. She had a pan frying eggs for us, another pan with pork in it, and a big one with hot flapjacks. The coffeepot simmered on the hot embers. With a terrible frown where her smile ought to of been, she kept looking over to where our new house stood in its tangled yard.

She stepped out of the smoke to look at a long low log house with a weedy sod roof, made into two halves by a log partition in the middle with a door in it. A fireplace and chimney was in one end, a stovepipe hole in the other. A log in the middle of the roof stuck out at each end. Sam said you could hang a sheep or a pig on that log to skin or dress it. Mother shook her head hard. "Too many flies!" she said. "And it would stink." Worst of all, it had a dirt roof with stuff growing out of it.

Just then the coffeepot spluttered over and a big cloud of smoke boomed up, throwing ashes into the pan with the meat, splashing the eggs and flapjacks. Even the quilt with the plates on it waiting for us to come eat had ashes. It was a mess and not good for Mother. We made the best of it.

"I have a mind to jump into one of these wagons with the littles and drive clear out of here, 'less you all pitch in and build a decent house for us starting right now. What were you thinking of, a sod roof! That log thing over there won't be much better than a Pied wickyup."

Father tried to comfort her. "Now Mother, no need for upset. We're only just beginning. I will build you a 'dobe house soon as I can, and later a fine brick one, someday. For now, that roof will keep the rain and snow off."

"So will a dirt shed keep snow and rain off hogs," she snapped back. "If I'm to spend the rest of my days here, I'm going to spend them in a real house, so you better hurry." She gave a big sniff, but a smile twitched at the corners of her mouth.

We walked down to look it over. Good thing it did not have a dirt floor, or Mother would of gone packing for sure. As it is, she does not know how she will shoe-horn all of us into only two rooms, with a door to the outside and a window in each half. One room is for the kitchen where the chimney is for a stovepipe, the other for sleeping and working and everything else with a chimney for a fireplace. Don't know where she will have her loom or spinning wheel.

After we cleaned up the mess of our breakfast, we piled into the littler wagon and drove into town to look it over while Jim and Bill got the cattle into the new corral and the horses in the barn. Monroe looks lots bigger than Summit, but not as nice and clean. Father thinks there are at least fifty houses already. Everything is bigger here, I can see myself, but it is a heckuva town. Bill told us it is chock full of Presbeeterians, which have already built a school, and other Gentiles, also plenty Mormons. Good thing I'm not scairt of Gentiles, but I did not know we could all live together.

The wiggly streets are jam full of brush, growing right inside people's fences, and not many have fences, and everywhere greasewood, which isn't so good for bare feet. It has sharp stickers on it, and when a sliver stabs you in the foot, the hurt goes right up to your jaw and gives you a hurt and a ache at the same time, worse than prickly pears. I will have to be lots more careful of my bare feet here than in Summit. I myself won't ever like this town.

I could see a 'dobe house across the street from ours, a 'dobe house kitty-corner from us, and everywhere I looked, 'dobe houses and log houses everywhere, all sizes. The more I looked, the homesicker I felt, and I wished and wished I was back in Summit.

Jim tried cheering Mother up by saying it was a good thing the shed did not have a sod roof also, so us boys can sleep there as usual in warm weather, but he wasn't sure what we would do in winter. As they unloaded the wagon they kind of joked with Mother. Bill said that come to think of it, a dirt roof has lots of uses. We can throw our tools up on it, harnesses and broke wagon wheels, anything we can't find a reggler place for anywheres else. Sam chimed in that if Father misses the plow he should look for it first on the roof. Mother did not find Bill or Sam to be funny.

I heard Father say he will never move again. Five times he has grubbed up brush, built homes, made ditches and fences, and planted fields and tried to grow orchards. Right here, he says, he will live until us children grow up to be men and women. After us children have homes of our own, him and Mother and Aunt Mary will lay down their bones here in Monroe. I think he will have to work on Mother.

But just outside our house I could see high green mountains leaning close and reaching up in the sky, steep against the town. I can almost reach out and touch them with my finger. I bet the sun can't come up till almost noon. Anyhow, I like these mountains.

A little boy what lives across the street in a 'dobe house came over to say hello next day. He is my size, but more raggeder. He hasn't any galluses or even buttons on his waist and has to hold his pants up with one hand all the time, which gives him only one hand to do things with, which don't leave him with much he can do. He says his stepmother is going to make galluses for him pretty soon. She will sew buttons on after a while, too. A stepmother is your father's other wife when your own mother is dead. Seems a stepmother might not know how to do much for the little boys and girls she is step to. I am glad I got Mother, who does things for us all the time. Mebbee she can help him with his pants problem.

This boy looks to be friendly. He says his name is Dose. Him and me will probly play together, seeing he lives so near. Guess even if he can't be Earl, we can be friends. Dose went over to the 'dobe house kitty-corner from ours and brought another boy to see me, also about my size. Looks pretty much like I am going to have some fun in Monroe after all. Good thing, on account of since we been cut off I been feeling I was done with fun.

The boys and Father had lifted a lot of things out of our wagons. It had been more than two days since we drove in. Stuff was laying around on the ground. A big, scraggly yellow dog came into our lot to look things over. Right off, he started snooping around, smelling our differnt things. Herk growled a warning at him. The dog let on like he didn't hear and kept right on trotting about and putting his nose on our things. Herk growled at him once more, deep down in his throat.

Jim had lifted a sack of oats out of the wagon and leaned it against the front wheel. When yellow dog saw that sack he made for it, took one big smell, and started to heist a leg. Quicker than scat, Herk grabbed him right under the jaws and began shaking the daylights outta him. That suprised dog didn't have a chance. They danced up on their hind legs, with Herk chewing and shaking that dog like sixty. Down on the ground they flopped, rolling and tumbling, Herk still on top. They were making enuff noise to scare every dog in town. Jim and Father came running from the corral. Mother came hurrying out the door. Folks living in the houses kitty-corner and across the street pelted out of their doors. Everyone wanted to see the dogfight. Before Jim or Father got there, Herk let go, and yellow dog went yelping through the brush.

Herk came over and stood by me, licking his chops. He wasn't hurt at all and looked up, grinning a reggler coyote smile at me. He knowed he had done something really and truly smart, which I know myself he had. He was kind of faunching around Father's legs, hoping for him to say he was some dog. Father leaned an arm down to scratch Herk's ear and laffed out loud through his long black whiskers, looking right at Mother, and said it was a good sign. "Danged if we haven't just won the first fight in Monroe!" I had a sudden happy feeling. Now we can move into our new home and feel happy about it. Not the same happy we had in Summit, but a happy sight better than moping around.

Monroe, here I am.

AFTERWORD

THE STORY OF BUCK'S BOOK

by Coralie McCarty Beyers

1948. Bussing my way to the campus of the University of Utah
one summer day in Salt Lake City, I noticed an older man
striding purposefully up the sidewalk with a box under his
arm that looked as though it would hold two reams of paper
and bulged as if it did. Grandpa Homer! He was still wearing
the familiar brown tweed suit and felt hat squared on his head
that he wore on his few visits during my childhood in the far
reaches beyond the Wasatch Mountains. I had not seen him
since coming out to the university for my senior year in 1947.

We had maintained a friendly but not familiar relationship.
From time to time he had sent densely typed letters inquiring
in a genial manner about my interests and telling me about his
life with whimsy and humor. When he did come to see us, he
liked to tell stories in a stagey Irish brogue or something broadly
Swedish, brown eyes twinkling like a boy, sharing peppermint
drops from his jacket pocket.

I hopped off the bus and hailed him. After a moment's sur-
prise he recognized me with a smile. I asked where he was going

with that big bundle under his arm. "Well," he said, "I'm on my way to the university to attend a writing conference starting today." And he had a book he wanted them to read. It was my turn to be surprised. "I didn't know you were a writer. How long have you been at it?"

"Oh, a long time," he said. "A very long time."

"Well, what kind of a book is it?"

From under his hat's brim he gave a shy smile. "It's about me when I was a very young sprout growing up hardly tamed in a far-off place in Utah. I like to think it's kind of a western Huckleberry Finn."

I hoped my face did not betray amused skepticism. "I'm on my way to campus, too. If you like, I can show you where the conference is to be held." He said that would be a dandy thing for a granddaughter to do, so we caught the next bus and went together to the opening of the First Annual Writers Conference at the University of Utah.

Grandpa Homer sat straight and smiling, box on his knees, hat on his box, a conspicuous figure among the other, much younger participants. I noted that his black hair showed scarcely any trace of gray. He looked more youthful than his weighty age. Perhaps the zeal of scrutinizing childhood so closely had rubbed some essence of youth onto him. My undergraduate wisdom deemed his participation to be an old man's folly, and I hoped his disappointment would not be serious.

I did not remain for subsequent sessions but went on with my preparations for summer graduation. I was twenty-two.

1952. Grandpa Homer died at age eighty-four. I had not thought to ask about his book the few times I did see him. No one mentioned it. Judges must have indulged an old codger

even to read it, if they did. My father never saw the manuscript. His sisters, who had typed and typed, took good care of
it and him, and they were such zealous guardians that no one
was allowed to see it. The matter of Grandpa's cherished book
seemed forgotten.

During his last illness, he asked restlessly many times just
to "go home"—no one knew which home he meant. He had
lived in Salt Lake City since before World War I. Surely it was
home to him. I went with my family when they buried him in
the old cemetery in Monroe, Utah, near his parents and next
to his wife, grown son and daughter, and tiny stones marking
graves of two small sisters and a brother. Nearby was the grave-
stone of his father's second wife. It was the first time I had seen
anything of the Sevier country in central Utah where Grandpa
Homer lived in later childhood, and where my father was born
and spent his childhood with its winding river and canyons.
The mountains were big, bulking, and close, the valley green.
It was beautiful, and I wondered why I had not seen it before.
I had not yet learned of Summit, Utah, Grandpa's earlier childhood home.

1959. An exchange of letters between Professor Brewster
Ghiselin, director of the University of Utah's Writers Conference
Program, and Walter Van Tilburg Clark occasioned a flurry
of excitement, at least for my father, when Professor Ghiselin
forwarded them to him. Besides Clark, other distinguished
writers and critics, including Allen Tate, Caroline Gordon,
Mark Schorer, William Carlos Williams, Ray West, and Eric
Bentley, had participated in judging manuscripts submitted in
this First Writers Conference. Clark was inquiring about "an
elderly rancher [Homer actually spent most of his career as a

mineral surveyor] about whom the whole staff was curious," remembered for having attended practically every session in the center of the front row, smiling but never saying anything. His manuscript turned out to be "a huge and forbidding opus," over a thousand pages, or so Clark remembered, and was called *My Boyhood in Pioneer Utah*. For both of these reasons, Clark had put his conference with the old man last on his list. But when he came to read the manuscript he found it to be anything but forbidding. "It was actually his boyhood—not the stuff of papa's diary or grandpa's—for he was, almost incredibly (it was his first writing he said) well into his eighties, and it was delightfully written—a series of little, separate, for the most part chronologically arranged stories, vignettes, descriptive accounts of his actual boyhood—and all of them with a gently humorous ironic tone, yet with an astonishing variety of moods among them." More than ten years later, Clark still remembered several of these that he detailed in his letter. Clark stated it was definitely the find among all the manuscripts that he or the other judges read. Allen Tate and Mark Schorer, also acting as publisher's representatives, shared his interest and intended to see the writer after Clark had his conference with him. But apparently nothing came of that.

At his conference with Grandpa Homer, Clark suggested dividing the manuscript and changing the title, "but the old boy was reluctant to do so because he wanted to see it all out under one cover and before he died, and because he had another under way that was almost as long!" Clark did not remember the name of the old man but hoped Ghiselin would know what if anything had happened to him or to the book, or to the second book. He was inquiring because the president of

Wesleyan University had visited him recently, and Clark had told him about both the author and the books. He was interested in getting hold of either manuscript because the new Wesleyan Press had a particular interest in folk materials, and the president wanted to get in touch with the author. The letter finally reached my father, who was very much in favor of Clark's proposal and talked with his sister to release the manuscript. The prospect of publication at least should please them, he thought. But they had an adamancy worthy of Hawthorne and would have none of it. If the world had not been accepting of their father's book in 1948, when he was still alive, it was undeserving of it now that he was dead.

1980. I had edited and published *Man Meets Grizzly*, by Frank M. Young, my other grandfather, who had gathered bear stories over years spent researching the fur trade of the West and attending garrulous yarn-spinning sessions of the American Trails Society, where he was known as Grizzly Frank. Just before his death, in 1949, he asked me to complete the book for him. My eager promise took much longer to fulfill than originally planned, but I felt the published book carried out his ideas for it and he would be pleased. Made bold by my initial success, I asked my surviving paternal aunt whether she would entrust Grandpa Homer's book to me to edit also. In an instant I learned the meaning of the phrase "shuttered eyes" when hers seemed to disappear behind one. I could hear it snap closed.

1984. From Salt Lake City, Mother called to say that the last surviving aunt wanted me to know that she was burning her father's manuscripts and would I want to come down and watch. The Irish sprang to my cheeks and numbed my brain. Why would I want to watch Grandpa Homer's book go up in smoke, still unread by me or almost anyone else? I declined to go.

1985. Acting as executor of the aunt's estate, my sister discovered a large suitcase under the basement stairs packed to overflowing with manuscripts—many manuscripts. What had my aunt burned? Too late I realized her call had been a summons. When my sister had boxed everything, she gave it all to me with her no-nonsense mandate: "Now do it."

When I finally began looking, I felt just as Clark had when he opened Grandpa Homer's box: This is impossible. Everything was undated. I recognized early drafts by type fonts, but especially by the knowing, commenting adult voice and stilted formal mannerisms that fall on a person whose writing is intended for posterity. There were three drafts of the book, including, as far as I can determine, his offering to the Writers Conference. Soon after I began my work, a friend and colleague who had encouraged my work on the bear book took up the lumpy manuscript, manfully went through it, and declared it a "diamond in the rough." My editing would help smooth the rough so the diamond could shine.

After I read through the multiple drafts, it was clear that it took Grandpa Homer a while to relax and find the childhood voice of Buck, who could express remembrance in the natural and forthright voice of a curious and inventive boy of seven or eight years. I thought of him, caught up recalling a time in his life that was lean and narrow in most respects, even for the Utah Territory of the 1870s, but that was lived with enthusiasm in spite of anxiety, fear, and sorrow. Grandpa remembered Buck with twenty-twenty clarity, with true and great pleasure that surely revived the long-gone happiness of childhood. It was the

THE STORY OF BUCK'S BOOK 373

"memoir of a boy," which is not an oxymoron if childhood is intensely lived and looked back on with affection and understanding. Memories of youth flow like a freshet. Best of all, he had a friend—a true comrade, a partner, a buddy—to share in this most ordinary and obscure life made wonderful through Buck's eyes and remembered love. I know now what he meant by "home."

1994. Utah was preparing for its Centennial in 1996. One of the projects was an anthology of Utah writers. Editors Tom Lyon and Terry Tempest Williams requested one of Frank Young's bear stories, "Old Ephraim," and a portion of Grandpa Homer's book, "The Trip to Pioche" (*A Great and Peculiar Beauty: A Utah Reader*, 1995). Later, Terry Tempest Williams told me that "Pioche" was the anchor of the entire book.

2006. Buck's book took final shape after a long season of discovery that I am glad was mine. Though his past has slipped from personal recollection, his book captures a wonderful and rich sense of it. How simple Buck's world now may seem, when time was measured by seasons and occasions; when less was enough; when small was good; when interests and playthings of children were what their eyes could see, their hands reach out and take, their imaginations enlarge. It may strike us as strange, perhaps overblown, the importance he gives to bare feet, but not if you consider their role in his life. They were necessary for his freedom and sense of well-being.

Buck aspired to getting "good sense," which teachers and elders assured him he lacked. He came to realize it was a life's effort. He was game to work at it. Faithful Earl taught him true friendship, which he never forgot. When Buck left Summit, they never saw each other again, but when writing the book, he expressed a desire to dedicate it to him. So, in line with Grandpa Homer's wishes, this book is dedicated to Earl, his one true friend.

And, finally, at the age of twenty-two, Buck realized his childhood dream: he was baptized.